AM AND
MANTICISM

uslim Currents from
Goethe to Emerson

ISLAM AND ROMANTICISM

Muslim Currents from Goethe to Emerson

Jeffrey Einboden

Muslim and Islamic Contributions to Culture and Civilization

Series Editor:
Todd Lawson

ONEWORLD

A Oneworld book

The
as t
ir

ISBN 978–1–78074–566–4
eBook ISBN 978–1–78074–567–1

Typeset by Jayvee, Trivandrum, India
Printed and bound in Great Britain
by Page Bros Ltd, Norwich

Oneworld Publications
10 Bloomsbury Street
London WC1B 3SR, England

Stay up to date with the latest books,
special offers, and exclusive content from
Oneworld with our monthly newsletter

Sign up on our website
www.oneworld-publications.com

Contents

Acknowledgments

Charting intersections between Western literature and Muslim sources, *Islam and Romanticism* reaches back to my earliest scholarly efforts, and thus reflects a decade of intellectual debts. At the University of Cambridge, I thank Tamara Follini and Douglas Hedley, who first planted the seeds for such a study. Formative too was my participation in 2004 at a conference hosted by Uppsala University – an opportunity, like so many others, that I owe to Bernie Zelechow. I thank Annabella Dietz for graciously welcoming my 2007 visit to Schloss Hainfeld, Hammer-Purgstall's Austrian estate. The actual writing of *Islam and Romanticism* was first suggested by Todd Lawson, the editor of Oneworld's monograph series, Muslim and Islamic Contributions to Culture and Civilization. I am grateful for Todd's invitation to contribute to the series, and his generous encouragement of my scholarship more broadly. At the press, I also wish to thank Oneworld's excellent editors and readers, and most especially, Novin Doostdar and James Magniac, as well as all those who reviewed and commented on the book, entirely or in part, including Todd Lawson and James Vigus; any errors that remain are solely my own.

The book received essential aid from Northern Illinois University, including a 2012–2013 sabbatical, and years of previous support from the University's Graduate School. I have been favored with exceptional colleagues and friends at NIU, whose advice and advocacy have proved pivotal. I thank, in particular, Betty Birner, Lara Crowley, Tim Crowley, James R. Giles, Ryan Hibbett, William C. Johnson, Amy Levin, Jessica Reyman,

Luz Van Cromphout, and Mark Van Wienen. During the final months of writing *Islam and Romanticism*, my research received inspiration and assistance too from the Boston Athenaeum; I am especially grateful to the superlative curators, librarians, and staff who made my 2013 fellowship at the Athenaeum so memorable. I thank too the National Endowment for the Humanities for its support of projects that parallel the present book, funding my research into U.S. Arabic slave writings (2011–2012), as well as Islamic literacy in early America (2014).

I am grateful to the journals which first featured my research into Romantic receptions of Muslim sources, and which now informs the present book. In particular, I acknowledge *Literature and Theology*, which published my "The Genesis of *Weltliteratur*: Goethe's *West-östlicher Divan* and Kerygmatic Pluralism" in 2005 (selections from which appear, or are expanded upon, in Chapters 1, 5, and 6); and the *Journal of Qur'anic Studies*, which published my "The Early American Qur'an: Islamic Scripture and US Canon" in 2009 (selections from which appear, or are expanded upon, in Chapters 14, 15, and 16).

My writing of *Islam and Romanticism* received vital encouragement from my family, most especially Becky, Steve, Avery, Josh, and Rachel; Shelley and Mike; Syd and Lily; as well as from life-long friends, Andrew, Brad, James, Matthew, and Richard. As all my endeavors, this book would have been inconceivable without the inspiration of my parents – Pam and Ed – and the love and laughter of my wife and son – Hillary and Ezra. With a gratitude that remains inexpressible, this book is dedicated to them.

Introduction

Weimar, 2000: Memorializing Goethe's Ḥāfiẓ

On July 12, 2000, the President of Germany and the President of Iran met in Weimar, convening over two chairs. Neither an international summit, nor a bilateral conference, this encounter between President Johannes Rau and President Muhammad Khatami was instead occasioned by the two chairs themselves. Erected at the heart of Germany's capital of culture, these simple seats merited such global attention as they form the *Goethe-Hafis Denkmal* – the Goethe-Hafiz Memorial – a UNESCO site commemorating the pivotal exchange between the national poets of Germany and Iran: Johann Wolfgang Goethe and Muḥammad Shamsuddīn Ḥāfiẓ (Figures 1 and 2, below).[1]

A concrete reminder of Islamic contributions to Western art and expression, the *Goethe-Hafis Denkmal* seems, on first view, a rather stark and imposing "reminder", its grey vertical chairs rising up in unadorned stone. It is the chairs' horizontal base, however, that hints at a more rich and nuanced relationship, inscribed with scattered quotations in Persian and German, voicing a lyric dialogue between these writers of world renown. Featured in this floor space between the chairs is a Persian *ghazal* excerpted from Ḥāfiẓ's beloved *Divan* – his celebrated "poetry collection" – a masterpiece of mystical artistry which was posthumously assembled, surfacing in the years that followed Ḥāfiẓ's death (c. 1390 CE). The flowing script of this Persian poem is

Figure 1 *Goethe-Hafiz Memorial*, Beethovenplatz, Weimar, Germany. Author's photo.

Figure 2 *Goethe-Hafiz Memorial*, base inscribed with Goethe's poetry. Author's photo.

surrounded by more angular lines of German, reproducing verses authored by the aged Goethe, exemplifying a late period in his career when he was deeply impressed by Ḥāfiẓ – a period that would culminate in Goethe's own *Divan*, his 1819 *West-östlicher Divan* (*West-Eastern Poetry Collection*).

A meeting of dual "*divan*s" – not only two chairs ("*divans*"), but also two poetry collections ("*Divans*") – Weimar's memorial is built solidly upon diverse languages and distinct literatures, rising from ground that is culturally double, equally German and Persian.[2] It is not a dichotomy of culture, however, but a dichotomy of country and continent that seems most urgently implied in these confronting chairs. Situated in opposition, these vacant seats suggest a physical separation between "West" and "East", even as they face each other in mutuality; recalling the very title of Goethe's *West-Eastern* poetry collection, the Weimar memorial embodies not only geographic distance between Occident and Orient, but also their inescapable encounter. Complementing this spatial distance is the temporal divide which seems more subtly suggested in these chairs, the gap between the two seats mimicking the historical gap that intervenes between Ḥāfiẓ in the fourteenth century and Goethe in the nineteenth century, both connecting and contrasting the medieval and the modern.

An encounter dramatized across distinct spans – linguistic, geographical, historical – it is the polarities of language, space, and time implied in the *Goethe-Hafis Denkmal* that also embody the tensions and the traditions which are bridged in the present study, hinting at the confrontations and continuities between "Islam" and "Romanticism". Erected in the midst of Weimar streets and squares, this "memorial" furnishes *Islam and Romanticism* with a solid and stable symbol, offering a concrete and public place to begin our dissection of the dichotomies between the Eastern religious and Western artistry. However, in opening with a monument to these specific poets – Ḥāfiẓ and Goethe – the clear polarity between "Islam" and "Romanticism" is also compromised from the very outset of our study. Slippery representatives of their respective traditions,

these two writers elude easy labels and simple boundaries. Ḥāfiz
is, for example, a dubious delegate for normative "Islam", a Sufi
poet who is most often associated with the unorthodox, notorious, and mischievous in his religious writings.[3] Goethe, too, is a
questionable, even controversial, envoy for "Romanticism" – an
artistic movement which is frequently aligned with Goethe, but
also often opposed, due to his own "anti-Romantic polemics".[4]
This difficulty of definition is itself anticipated by the very work
that inspires Weimar's Memorial: Goethe's own *West-östlicher
Divan*. In a frequently cited couplet from his collection, Goethe
reflects on the term "Islam" itself:

> *Wenn Islam Gott ergeben heisst,*
> *Im Islam leben und sterben wir alle.*

> [If "Islam" signifies "submitting to God"
> In Islam, we all live and die][5]

At the crux of Goethe's startling confession – asserting that "we
all live and die" in "Islam" – is the problem and process of definition. Interrogating the very meaning of "Islam", Goethe posits
the religion's "significance" through condition and qualification:
if "Islam" implies "submitting to God" – *if* this term is understood etymologically – then its reach is universal, embracing each
and every one, spanning the entire spectrum of human existence,
not only "all" our "living", but all our "dying" too.[6] A literary confession, rather than a literal conversion, Goethe's surprising statement itself expresses the flexible definitions involved in
Romantic readings of Islamic traditions, as well as in our own
readings of "Islam" *and* "Romanticism". Rather than prescriptive
classifications, it is conditional questions that seem to befit such
an inquiry at its outset. What do "Romanticism" and "Islam"
signify as they confront each other, occupying seats of opposition
and influence? What is the "Islam" to which "Romantic" writers
appeal?

The *Goethe-Hafis Denkmal* subtly suggests the complex
dualities that motivate our present study; however, this "memo-

rial", and its 2000 inauguration, also helps to map the critical foregrounds to *Islam and Romanticism* as well. Celebrating a shared legacy of culture and nationhood, it is two presidents who attended the unveiling of the Weimar chairs – an attendance which recalls the political implications of "West-East" encounters in the nineteenth century, as well as their commemoration at the millennium. Exemplified by Edward Said's iconic study, first published in 1978 – *Orientalism* – Western literary engagement with Islam has been exhaustively portrayed in terms of coercive power, complicit in strategies of European colonialism and Middle Eastern exploitation. However, grounds for such critical recrimination are difficult to detect in the *Goethe-Hafis Denkmal* itself, the memorial's vacant and level seats denying easy placeholders for ethnic, cultural, and religious hierarchy. Similarly, while our own study is conscious of the historical contexts that shape its literary contents, *Islam and Romanticism* is interested primarily in cultural conversation, rather than political power, accenting models of imaginative reception, rather than material dominion. Consistent with the series to which it belongs – Muslim and Islamic Contributions to Culture and Civilization – the present book sketches a select genealogy of literary influence, mapping diverse Western debts to Islamic precedents incurred during a crucial century of authorship, reaching from Goethe's youth in the 1770s, to Emerson's maturity in the 1860s. Such a focus does not, of course, seek to invalidate a Saidean critique of Western "essentialism", which rightfully rejects reductive caricatures of Middle Eastern texts and identities, so often evident in Romantic writings. Indeed, it is undeniable that primary authors treated in *Islam and Romanticism* – German, British, and American – frequently express religious bias and racial bigotry that contemporary readers would find problematic. Yet, while Romantic participation in the dark legacies of Western colonialism has received significant notice, less attention has been given to the catalyzing effect which Muslim sources have exercised on Western creativity. Seated in distinct places, yet posed in dialogue, the Weimar chairs enact a tableau of mutuality that serves as a touchstone for my own exploration into the *generative* relationship between

figures such as Goethe and Ḥāfiẓ, as well as the broader traditions they elusively embody.[7]

Distinguished from a host of previous studies in privileging
intercultural exchange, rather than political exploitation, *Islam
and Romanticism* is distinct also in tracing a transnational arc
of Western dependence on Muslim sources, stretching from
Europe's earliest Romantic intimations, through the classic
products of British Romantics, to the exhaustion of American
Romanticism in the wake of the U.S. Civil War. Scholarly exploration of Romanticism and Islam is, of course, not a new enterprise, and the current book benefits from a wealth of prior efforts,
reaching back to the beginnings of the twentieth century, and
up to most recent years.[8] Unlike the narrower range of nation
and history addressed by preceding studies, however, the present
book adopts a more expansive approach. Reaching across distinct eras and areas, the book tracks an evolving Romantic tradition of Islamic appeal, positing a narrative that unfolds not only
between Romanticism and Islam, but also *within* Romanticism
itself, moving westward from Continental origins to New World
futures. Conventionally associated with "organicism", "imagination", "symbol", and "nature" – as noted by Thomas McFarland
– Romanticism is nevertheless notoriously "amorphous and multifarious", continually inviting redefinition; recalling Goethe's
own interrogation of "Islam" and its possible "significance", the
term "Romanticism" is fluid in semantic outline, resisting conclusive boundaries.[9] Rather than define Romanticism through
charting its internal coherencies, the present book finds a fresh
Romantic coherency emerging in an external index: namely a
shared appeal to Islamic precedents, spanning the periods, places,
and personalities which are most often associated with the movement. While significant change necessarily attends Romanticism's
progress from Europe in the 1770s to America in the 1860s, the
present study finds a consistency emerging in an enduring indebtedness to Muslim sources.

Of course, with such an ample span and scope, *Islam and
Romanticism* does not seek to supply comprehensive treatments
of individual authors, nor does it comprehensively embrace all

authors of interest, leaving aside fascinating candidates, from Karoline von Günderrode, to William Blake, to Thomas Moore, to Herman Melville.[10] The book instead offers mere glimpses of the most intriguing cross-religious and multilingual encounters, sustaining its broad historical horizons with specific detail. Shifting attention away from Western fascination with tired tropes such as "the harem", the book explores deeper encounters with Muslim prophecy and the Muslim Prophet, uncovering Romantic responses that surpass mere "Orientalism", forming the beginnings of an authentic, global literary culture with surprising roots in traditional Islamic sources. Attentive to Romanticism as a *literary* canon, my primary focus is the fine mechanics of textual influence; however, even while highlighting Islam's role as a creative catalyst, the book also suggests Islam's role as a spiritual resource, infusing the literary publications, but also the private lives, of Romantic writers. Accenting Islamic echoes that surface in personal letters and private diaries, the book avoids an abstract critique of Western exploitation, preferring instead to recount the most practical and personal moments of Romantic engagement, framing these discrete encounters with Islam into a progressive narrative. It is my hope that these elements and approaches of *Islam and Romanticism* may also act as encouragements for additional study, inciting interest in authentic exchanges between these traditions which have yet to be excavated, and which seem silently embodied in the two stark chairs planted in the millennial streets of Weimar.

1

Weimar, 1800: Dramatizing Goethe's "Mahomet"

I

Two centuries before the unveiling of Weimar's *Goethe-Hafis Denkmal*, the city would raise the curtain on another ceremony, dramatizing again an encounter between Western artistry and the Muslim world. Unfolding on stage, rather than encased in stone, this theatrical event in 1800 would also anticipate the tense polarities – spiritual, artistic, political – that receive concrete expression two hundred years later in the *Goethe-Hafis Denkmal*. At the end of January 1800, a new play was debuted for the Weimar theater, simply entitled *Mahomet: Trauerspiel in fünf Aufzügen* – i.e. *Mahomet: A Tragedy in Five Acts*. Interpreting Islamic origins for its German audience, and offering a dramatic portrait of the Muslim Prophet, this play would be the responsibility of none other than Weimar's most acclaimed author: Johann Wolfgang Goethe.

It may seem surprising to find Muslim prophecy forming the subject of a German play at the turn of the nineteenth century. Staged in the first days of 1800, Goethe's *Tragedy* stands on the brink of a new century, marking a turbulent time of industrial progress and political upheaval. It is not the forward momentum of Goethe's *Mahomet*, however, but rather this play's backward gaze that seems most obvious, recalling not only an Arabian antiquity, but also a longstanding European tendency to stage the Muslim Prophet. Although Goethe's *Mahomet* may have seemed a curious novelty in 1800 Weimar, this play was neither new, nor original; instead, it represented a German translation from a French play, adapting the work of yet another author of European renown: Voltaire. Initially staged in 1741, Voltaire's play *Le Fanatisme, ou Mahomet le Prophète* – i.e. *Fanaticism, or Mahomet the Prophet* – adapted Islamic history to deride European hierarchy, staging a drama which was immediately interpreted as "a satire-in-disguise on Christian, or more specifically on French Catholic, society and its political and religious leaders" – an interpretation given credence by Voltaire himself in his private correspondence.[1] A veiled domestic burlesque, Voltaire's play rejects an "alien" religion, even while also aiming its caustic critique at home institutions, reproaching especially the "fanaticism" of France's power hierarchies and religious hypocrisy.[2]

Adapting Voltaire's play for the Weimar theater, Goethe was motivated not by ecclesiastic satire, however, but by artistic advancement. Appealing to *Mahomet* while he pursued "the ennoblement of the German stage", Goethe's translation of Voltaire in 1799 coincides with broader efforts to modernize and broaden the theatrical culture of his native land and language; as Marvin A. Carlson notes, *Mahomet* offered Goethe "the possibility of developing an international repertoire at Weimar".[3] Yet, despite its derivative origins, Goethe's translated *Mahomet* – like all acts of translation – reflects the tastes and talents of its translator, offering a fresh interpretation through the revision of its source's form and content. Amending the tone and tenor of his original, for instance, Goethe's 1800 *Mahomet* rewrites the rigid style of Voltaire's 1741 play, refashioning its French Alexandrine meter into freer lines of German blank verse, as Stephanie Hilger has recently emphasized.[4] Infused with a new flexibility in poetic form, Voltaire's *Mahomet* serves as a surprising site for Goethe's own creative experiment, this French retrospective on Islamic origins ironically offering a vehicle for German aesthetic evolution. Mapping the divide between Enlightenment critique and Romantic artistry – between Voltaire in the 1740s and Goethe in 1800 – *Mahomet*'s stylistic evolution in German is paralleled by an evolution in its content, with the play's very title altered in translation. Dispensing with Voltaire's initial words – *Le Fanatisme* – Goethe refrains from equating Muḥammad with religious "fanaticism" from the outset, reserving his play's principal title instead merely for the Prophet's name: *Mahomet*.[5]

Reviving and revising the French literary past, the Weimar *Mahomet* gestures also to a more immediate literary past: namely, Goethe's own. While Voltaire would serve as Goethe's direct source for his 1800 *Mahomet*, the origins of Goethe's theatrical interests in the Prophet reach back nearly three decades, grounded in the very foundations of his artistic efforts. In the first years of the 1770s, while still in his early twenties, Goethe had sketched and started his own play entitled *Mahomet*, associating his prophetic protagonist not with religious imposture, like Voltaire, but rather with natural power and sublime beauty.[6] In the opening lines that survive from Goethe's aborted play, "Mahomet" himself is pictured reciting a pastoral "Hymn", singing a soliloquy as he stands "alone under the open sky":[7]

> *Teilen kann ich euch nicht dieser Seele Gefühl*
> *Fühlen kann ich euch nicht allen ganzes Gefühl*
> *Wer, wer wendet dem Flehen sein Ohr?*
> *Dem bittenden Auge den Blick?*

> [Can I not share it with you, this feeling of Soul?
> Can I not feel it with you, this sense of the All?
> Who, who turns his ear to the prayer?
> To eyes, still beseeching, a look?][8]

It is the form of these initial lines, as much as their substance, that seems striking. Speaking in sensitive questions, rather than thundering declarations, "Mahomet" is portrayed by Goethe as a lonely and sympathetic seeker, posing queries that are deeply personal. This meditative sensitivity is emphasized too by the content of the Prophet's questions, soliciting responses from his intimate audience, even as he reaches out "to share" his individual "sense". Balancing human "soul" and divine "All" – as well as first-person singular "I" ("*Ich*") and second-person plural "you" ("*euch*") – Goethe privileges an aesthetic priority in these lines, with "Mahomet" striving to translate inward "feeling" into outward expression, speaking his "prayer" in beautiful lyric. Featuring poetic repetition and assonance, these parallel German lines immediately associate the Prophet with an artistic interiority, Goethe's opening moments of this Muslim portrait reserved for poetic celebration. Merely the first quatrain of an aborted play, these initial lines nevertheless aptly merge Goethe's own creative beginnings with the beginnings of Islam, accurately anticipating an aesthetic understanding of the religion that will echo throughout his career.

II

Penned privately in the early 1770s, Goethe's aborted play *Mahomet* would soon enjoy a lyric afterlife. Resurrecting a slice of his play in the pages of a Göttingen periodical, Goethe transformed drama into poetry, publishing in 1774 a piece entitled "*Mahomets-Gesang*" – i.e. "Song to Mahomet".[9] Originally written as a sung dialogue between ʿAlī and Fāṭimah, vocalized "at the highest point of [the Prophet's] success", Goethe would denude this dialogue of all its theatrical trappings, publishing it without speech markers or stage directions.[10] The resulting poem – the 1774 "Song to Mahomet" – stands as perhaps the most powerful testament to Goethe's "romantic" appreciation of the Prophet, witnessing "a Goethe still in the grip of an early, unlimited or unbounded Romanticism", as Angus Nicholls has suggested.[11] The only piece to be published by Goethe from his original *Mahomet* drama, "Song to Mahomet" would even gain priority in Goethe's first Weimar poetry collection – published in 1778 – which features this Islamic appeal as its very first poem.[12]

Distinct in form from his aborted play, Goethe's "Song to Mahomet" seems distinct too in its content, the forceful opening lines of this poem sounding very unlike the subtle and sensitive beginning to Goethe's drafted drama. Rather than gentle interiority, interrogating the Prophet's "feeling of Soul", Goethe's poem instead begins with Promethean power, launching not with delicate questions, but with a compelling command:

> See the spring in the cliff
> Bright with joy
> Like the radiance of stars!
> Over clouds
> Its youth was nurtured
> By good spirits
> In the cliffs and scrub.
>
> Youthful freshly
> It dances from the cloud
> Down to the marble cliffs below,
> Jubilating
> To the heavens.[13]

Reflecting its early Romantic origins, "Song to Mahomet" fuses natural imagery with wild idealism, dedicating its introduction to a celestial "spring" that "dances" down "from the cloud", yet still reflects "the heavens". Overflowing with "youth", Goethe's first verses seem themselves rather wild, their irregular meter and rhyme mimicking the spontaneous "cheering" and "dancing" which forms their focus.[14] Perhaps most interesting, however, is what is *absent* from this opening to Goethe's "Song to Mahomet". If not for its Islamic title, there would be little evidence of an Islamic identity in these lines, Goethe's setting and stanzas recalling European art rather than Muslim religiosity. Instead of standard Orientalist tropes and trappings, Goethe begins his "Song" to the Muslim Prophet with naturalism, trading the stereotypical "desert and harems" for a sublime "spring", associating "Mahomet" with a familiar environment, rather than a foreign East.[15]

Eclipsing exotic clichés with domestic imagery, Goethe's opening lines anticipate his entire poem, which avoids Orientalist conventions throughout, as Frederick Quinn has recently recognized.[16] The natural "jubilation" in these initial verses instead leads to a pastoral celebration of the Prophet, with Goethe's next lines clarifying his allegory, aligning the flow of this dancing "spring" with an unnamed "young leader":

> Through the summit passes
> It chases after bright pebbles,
> And it strides as a young leader
> Pulling its brother wellsprings
> Along with it.[17]

Without naming "Mahomet" himself, Goethe mirrors the "career of the prophet" in "the course of a great river", as Nicholas Boyle suggests, portraying the Muslim Prophet not merely as a solitary hero, but also a communal actor – a "leader" who takes along his "brother[s]".[18] It is this communal significance of the Prophet which is accented in the lines that immediately follow:

> Now he steps
> On the plain resplendently silvered
> And the plain's resplendent with him,
> And the rivers from the lowlands
> And the brooklets from the mountains
> Jubilate and cry out; brother,
> Brother, take your brothers with you,
> To your age-old father,
> To the eternal ocean
> Where with outspread arms
> Us it waits for;
> Arms, alas, which open vainly
> For the ones who're yearning for him;
> For we're devoured in the barren desert
> By greedy sand[19]

Building up to a watery crescendo, Goethe's "Song" amplifies its celebration of "Mahomet" by adding mythic and messianic currents to the poem's naturalism, paralleling the Prophet with a "swelling estuary" that exultantly leads its "brothers" toward "the eternal ocean".[20] Emerging as a figure of both spiritual and social unification – synthesizing his fraternal powers, while also returning them to their "ancient father" – "Mahomet" becomes an agent of salvation in Goethe's allegory, redeeming "yearning children" from the "bleak wasteland".

The Prophet's messianic identity surfaces strongly as Goethe's "Song" reaches its climactic lines, with "Mahomet" himself immersed in aquatic allusions that increasingly seem apocalyptic. Reiterating the celestial imagery that was implied at the very opening to his "Song to Mahomet", Goethe provides an especially epiphanic conclusion:

> Come now all of you! –
> and he swells up
> More resplendent, all a tribe
> Carries a prince aloft,
> And rolling in triumph
> He gives name to countries, cities
> Spring up from his footsteps.
>
> On he rushes irresistible,
> Leaves the towers of flame-topped summits,
> Marble houses, all created
> By his abundance, all he leaves.
>
> Cedar houses Atlas carries
> On his giant shoulders, rippling
> Sails that stream high up above him
> Form a thousand confirmations
> Of his power and his splendour.
>
> Thus he carries all his brothers,
> All his treasures and his children,
> Foaming joyfully to the waiting
> Heart of their progenitor.[21]

Opening again with an exclamatory imperative – "Come now all of you!" – the final lines of "Song to Mahomet" echo its first lines, while also enlarging their allusive atmosphere, complementing natural imagery with urban imagery, and merging Islamic references with classical. Aligned with "Atlas" himself, Goethe further roots his Prophet-Messiah in European ground, infusing his "Song" with Romantic devotion to Nature, but also with a hint of the Neoclassical. It is the significance of Goethe's Hellenic analogy, however, which seems most essential, portraying the Prophet not only as a figure of tribal "triumph", but also a bearer of global burdens, with "Mahomet" credited with heroically "carr[ying] all his brothers". However, even while he reconciles the natural and the celestial, Goethe's portrait of the Prophet also appears somewhat ambivalent as it addresses success in the secular world – a theme that emerges subtly here at the conclusion of "Song to Mahomet". Not only are "towers of flame-topped summits" and "[m]arble houses" left in the "irresistible" wake of Goethe's watery hero, but his victorious progress also bequeaths "names" to "countries, cities", depicting a figure that is not only conqueror, but creator. It is, however, "joy" that above all crowns Goethe's hymn, suggesting the benefits and blessings of the Prophet's "rolling in triumph". Singing a "Song" that is Islamic in title, yet topically romantic, Goethe's fragment – adapted from his aborted play – offers a positive precedent of Islamic appeal that will rarely be matched by his Romantic successors; yet, in its own textual survival, Goethe's "Song to Mahomet" itself seems to hint at Islam's endurance as a creative catalyst for later Western artistry, its generative appeals to the Prophet anticipating the buoyancy of Romanticism's own Islamic interests.

III

Two and a half decades after publishing his "Song to Mahomet" in 1774, Goethe would herald the private performance of his translated *Mahomet*, announcing his drama adapted from Voltaire in a quiet note to his dear friend, Friedrich Schiller, dated December 17, 1799:

> The Duke and the Duchess are going to take tea with me to-day, and, as I hope, will lend a gracious ear to the recital of *Mahomet*. If you care to be present at this operation you will be heartily welcome.
>
> G.[22]

A minor exchange between major *literati*, Goethe's invitation to Schiller reflects their shared life in aristocratic Weimar, mentioning not only "the Duke and the Duchess" – Weimar's Karl August and his wife, Louisa – but also the "taking [of] tea" during a salon "recital". At the precise heart of this prosaic note, however, is the Muslim Prophet – "*Mahomet*" – an Islamic incongruity which would, however, have been unsurprising to Schiller himself. A subject of debate between the two poets in the months previous, Voltaire's *Mahomet* features regularly in correspondence during autumn 1799 between Goethe and Schiller, with the latter regularly consulted regarding the motives and mechanics of rendering the French original.[23] Attracting Schiller's advice, Goethe's translated *Mahomet* would also attract Schiller's artistry, the former's German rendition inspiring the latter's German authorship. In the first days of 1800, Schiller penned his "*An Goethe, als er den Mahomet von Voltaire auf dir Bühne brachte*" – "To Goethe, on his Staging of Voltaire's *Mahomet*" – a short dedicatory poem which features a stanza that begins "The theater's narrow space has been enlarged. / A whole world crowds into its four walls", as John Guthrie literally translates.[24] This entire stanza unfolds, in E.P. Arnold-Forster's more stylized rendition:

> A wider scene the modern stage affords,
> And all the world now populates its boards;
> No more rhetorical conceits are prized,
> What we demand is nature undisguised;
> Banished is fashion's artificial tone,

The hero acts and feels as man alone.
The freest, fullest notes from passion spring,
And real beauty to the truth must cling.[25]

Occasioned by Goethe's translated play, Schiller celebrates *Mahomet*'s significance for German drama. However, it is Goethe's earlier verses on the Prophet – his 1774 "Song to Mahomet" – that seem to echo into Schiller's verses, which also imply a link between Islamic origins and Western innovations. Invoking ideas that will become Romantic leitmotifs – merging "beauty" and "truth", celebrating "passion" and "nature undisguised" – Schiller celebrates the lyric "notes" of Goethe's play, which are "freest" and "fullest", even while commemorating a play that focuses on the founder of Islam. Perhaps most striking is this stanza's initial lines, Schiller lauding *Mahomet*'s "opening up" a fresh era of artistry, "enlarging" the "theater's narrow space", allowing "a whole world" to "crowd into its four walls". Mirroring Goethe's own transnational translation – a German rendition of a French drama with an Arabian setting – Schiller finds the dilation of European art in Goethe's act of Islamic adaptation, with *Mahomet* broadening the "narrowness" of Western "theater".[26]

While Schiller is the friendly and famous addressee of Goethe's December 1799 note, it is the other personalities in his invitation that play more pivotal roles in prompting *Mahomet*'s "staging". Goethe's first words are "The Duke and the Duchess" – a literary precedence which hints at the literal precedence of Karl August and his wife Louisa in supporting *Mahomet*'s production. While Goethe borrows *Mahomet* from Voltaire, extracting the play from its original context – the critique of French religion and society – Goethe's German translation also enters a sphere that seems no less political, ushered into Weimar society at the behest of Duke Karl himself. An audience member at a Parisian staging of Voltaire's original play in 1775, it was Karl August who initially commissioned Goethe to fashion his German translation. Attending the drama's initial and informal recital on December 17, 1799, the duke would offer advice for *Mahomet*'s improvement, but also ensure that it was the first play to be staged in the New Year, electing to have the drama coincide with his wife's birthday. Accordingly, *Mahomet* debuted in Germany's cultural capital on January 30, 1800 – the 41st birthday of Duchess Louisa – with this play on Islamic foundations becoming the foundational play to appear on the Weimar stage in the nineteenth century.[27]

The overtly political atmosphere for *Mahomet*'s debut in January 1800 reaches also beyond the "narrow space" of the local "theater", gesturing to a "whole world" of geopolitics that raged outside the "four walls" of Weimar. Promoted and quietly performed at home, Goethe's play reflects a period of turmoil abroad, his adapted drama on the Muslim Messenger emerging during days of European upheaval. The year of *Mahomet*'s translation marked Napoleon's own rise to power, his coup d'état staged in France even as Goethe was rendering this play for the German stage. This national ascent of a charismatic, yet ruthless, figure is precisely the subject of Voltaire's play, lending a sense of European timeliness to Goethe's rendition of this Islamic fiction, his 1799 translation seeming to mirror contemporary events. Indeed, even as Goethe turned towards Voltaire's French play – which itself adapts the East for its dramatic inspiration – Napoleon's own French troops would also reach eastward, campaigning in Egypt and Syria in 1798 and 1799. Returning from his invasion of Egypt in the very months that Goethe first began considering his *Mahomet* rendition, Napoleon himself seems to have understood his own mission through Muslim analogy; in an oft-quoted recollection of his North African adventures, Napoleon would assert that "I saw myself founding a religion, marching into Asia, riding an elephant, a turban on my head and in my hand the Qur'an that I would have composed to suit my needs."[28] The dizzying intersections between Napoleon's historical efforts and Goethe's literary efforts were, moreover, unmistakable for many of his contemporaries, as David B. Richards has noted; Goethe's *Mahomet* was even censored outside of Weimar, with authorities anxiously perceiving "allusions to Napoleon in the figure of Mahomet", according to Ingeborg Solbrig.[29]

This overlap between Goethe's translated *Mahomet* and Napoleon's actual exploits in 1800 would receive a more literal expression at the climax of the Napoleonic era. No longer a rising consul in 1800, Napoleon would be an ascendant emperor by 1808, convening with the Emperor of Russia in Erfurt, very near to Weimar. Offering a friendly reception to Weimar's Duke Karl August during his Erfurt sojourn, Napoleon would also meet Weimar's most exalted author – Goethe – on October 2, 1808. Recorded by Goethe in his own memoir, this encounter between two of Europe's most iconic personalities has been recurrently memorialized too by his biographers; for example, George Henry Lewes vividly recounts the scene, noting that Goethe "was summoned to an audience with the emperor, and found him at breakfast", during which:

> Napoleon, after a fixed look, exclaimed: "*Vous etes un homme*"; a phrase which produced a profound impression on the flattered poet. "How old are you?" asked the emperor. "Sixty." "You are very well preserved." After a pause – "You have written tragedies?" Here [Pierre] Daru interposed, and spoke with warmth of Goethe's works, adding that he had translated Voltaire's *Mahomet*. "It is not a good piece," said Napoleon, and commenced a critique on *Mahomet*, especially on the unworthy portrait given of that conqueror of a world. He then turned the conversation to *Werther*, which he had read seven times, and which accompanied him to Egypt.[30]

Spanning a complex series of contrasts – East and West, Europe and Africa, politics and literature – Napoleon's reception of Goethe also brings together poetic art and martial power, featuring at its very center not only *Mahomet*, but also Muḥammad – not only the play, but the Prophet himself. Comparing the drama to the man, Napoleon offers a French critique of Goethe's decision to render his French precedent, finding Voltaire's play to be an "unworthy portrait" of "that conqueror of a world". Yet, perhaps more intriguing than this literary criticism is Napoleon's literary endorsement of Goethe, embracing his most celebrated Romantic fiction, the 1774 *The Sorrows of Young Werther*. Reading it "seven times", this novel was also chosen by Napoleon to "accompany him to Egypt", Goethe's imaginative prose serving as an ally for Napoleon during his actual incursion into the Muslim world. And while Napoleon had dreamed of bringing a newly "composed . . . Qur'an" to North Africa in 1800, it is instead Goethe's own early fiction that escorts the French conqueror as he dramatically invades Muslim lands – an ironic and apt inversion of Goethe's own dramatic renewal of Voltaire's *Mahomet* in 1800, domesticating this French fiction itself built from Muslim foundations.

2

"Mohammed came forward on the stage": Herder's Islamic History

I

Six days after *Mahomet*'s private recital on December 17, 1799 for Weimar's duke and duchess, Goethe elected to host another party at his home, previewing his translated drama for a broader audience of invited guests. Mirroring the first reading of *Mahomet*, this second reading was also attended by a leading Weimar author and a prominent friend: Johann Gottfried Herder. Like Friedrich Schiller six days earlier, Herder listened to Goethe's *Mahomet* with interest on December 23, 1799 – and, also like Schiller, Herder voiced a memorable reaction to the play. However, unlike Schiller, Herder was not inspired to pen a public poem dedicated to Goethe's literary efforts, but would record instead his private disapproval, rejecting his friend's translated drama. Although recognizing that *Mahomet* "contained 'some glorious verses'", Herder was "at the same time . . . repelled by the 'inhumane' sentiments of the play", as Robert Thomas Clark notes.[1]

Herder's ambivalent reaction to Goethe's *Mahomet* reflects a broader ambivalence in the Herder-Goethe friendship, reaching back three decades to the relationship's fraught origins.[2] Although it was Goethe who helped Herder settle in Weimar – encouraging Duke Karl August to offer Herder "the posts of Superintendent, Chief Pastor, and Court Preacher" in 1776

– their relationship had soured in the years leading up to the recital of *Mahomet*.³ Yet, if Herder's unease with *Mahomet* in 1799 was symptomatic of his present "rift" with Goethe, it may have equally reflected his past work with Goethe. First meeting in 1770, the growth of the Herder-Goethe relationship was facilitated by a shared interest in the East, their correspondence in these early years consistently concerned with the literature of foreign antiquity – including Islamic texts and traditions. As Katharina Mommsen has highlighted, Herder and Goethe began exchanging ideas on Muslim sources during the early 1770s, with Arabic traditions receiving particular attention.⁴ This mutual appeal to the "*Morgenland*" – the "Morning Land", the illuminatory East – would not only form a background to their friendship, but also become foregrounded as a vehicle to express this friendship. For instance, in the same era that witnessed his composition of "Song to Mahomet", Goethe would write to Herder concerning his artistic frustrations and aspirations, remarking in a July 1772 letter that:

> Look, what sort of a musician is he who keeps looking at his instrument? . . . I might indeed pray, like Moses in the Koran: "Make me room, O Lord, in my narrow breast!" No day passes without my communing with you, and I often think, "If one could but live with him!" It will come, it will come. The youth in his coat of mail wanted to follow too soon, and you ride too fast.

Blending prophecies, sacred and secular, Goethe's exuberant passage ends by predicting his future proximity to Herder, presciently looking forward to a time in which they "live with" each other, "communing" together as neighbors. However, it is the prophetic speech that immediately precedes this personal forecast that seems most striking, Goethe anticipating his own devotion to Herder with a Qur'ānic devotion, voicing the Mosaic prayer from the scripture's sura 20: "Make me room, O Lord, in my narrow breast!"⁵ Hoping for the collapse of space between him and his friend, while also asking God to expand the space of his

own "narrow breast", Goethe transitions between intimate out-
reach and Islamic allusion, inscribing sacred Muslim speech into
his personal interactions, while also articulating his own artistic
efforts.

This fusion of intimate artistry and Islamic reference in 1772
seems also to reach far forward, receiving expression seventeen
years later with Herder's attendance of the recital of Goethe's
Mahomet in 1799. However, unlike Goethe's youthful idealism
in 1772 – quoting the Qur'ān, even while exclaiming "If one could
but live with him!" – the mature contexts of Goethe's Islamic
receptions in 1799 seem more cutting and critical. In contrast
with the personal appeal to Muslim language in his early letter to
Herder, Goethe invites Herder to view Voltaire's Muslim satire,
offering a more distant and derisive portrait of Islam. Unlike the
humane personality of Goethe's 1772 appeal to the Qur'ān, his
commissioned translation of *Mahomet* in 1799 is "inhumane";
anticipating Napoleon's critique, Herder finds Voltaire's play
"unworthy" of the Prophet, and unworthy too of Goethe's "glorious verses".[6] However, if this drama had failed for Napoleon
due to its inadequate portrait of the "conqueror of a world",
Mahomet's failure for Herder was likely due instead to its inadequate portrait of an otherworldly visionary – a visionary who
plays a pivotal role in Herder's own primary *opus*, the *Ideen
zur Philosophie der Geschichte der Menschheit* – his *Ideas for a
Philosophy of the History of Mankind*.

II

The years that followed Herder's 1776 move to Weimar – a move
which achieved Goethe's early aspiration to "live with him" –
were years of steady productivity, witnessing Herder's authorship of the four-volume *Ideen*, surfacing in print between 1784
and 1791. A seminal work of Romantic anthropology, Herder's
Ideen traces a genealogy of cultural development grounded solidly in natural history; dedicating Parts I and II to "the place

of man in the cosmos and on earth", as Frederick Beiser notes, the *Ideen*'s Parts III and IV only then turn to "history proper".[7] Emphasizing the primeval past, Herder finally reaches contemporary Europe by the conclusion of Part IV, having dedicated much of his historical overview to legacies of global antiquity. Sensitive to the aesthetic achievement and religious sentiment of the *Morgenland*, the *Ideen* stresses not only early Judaic contributions, but ranges across the ancient East, attributing a pivotal role in human "progress" also to "the Arabian". Transitioning from the "natural powers of man" to "his mind", Herder's Book VIII of his *Ideen*'s Part II argues that "Human Fancy" is "Organic and Climatic", appealing to Arabia as an example of the natural world's formative function in shaping human psychology:

> From the remotest times the deserts of Arabia have fostered sublime conceptions, and they who have cherished them have been for the most part solitary, romantic men. In solitude Mohammed began his Koran: his heated imagination rapt him to Heaven, and showed him all the angels, saints, and worlds: his mind was never more inflamed, than when it depicted the thunders of the day of resurrection, the last judgment, and other immense objects.[8]

This minor passage articulates major concerns that pervade Herder's entire *Ideen*, not only retreating back to "the remotest times", but also reading intellectual history through physical environment, advancing the *Ideen*'s "naturalist program".[9] It is the Islamic grounds for this passage's naturalism, however, that seem exceptional, recalling not Herder's historiography, but rather Goethe's lyricism. Reminiscent of "Song to Mahomet", Herder's "Mohammed" is aligned unmistakably with natural environs, surrounded by climates of lofty "conception". However, unlike the aquatic imagery of Goethe's poem, Herder's *Ideen* places the Prophet in an arid and incendiary atmosphere, with "the deserts of Arabia" fostering his "heated" and "inflamed" imagination. Perhaps most resonant for the present study, however, is the merger between Islamic origins and Romantic traits. Not only is the Prophet classed by Herder as one of those *"staunende Menschen"* – "romantic men", in T. Churchill's stylized translation – but he is also characterized by both "solitude" and "sublimity", oft-allied elements of Romanticism.[10] Associated with the aesthetic *heights*, the "imagination" of "Mohammed" is lonely and lofty, a vehicle to envision "Heaven", with the "Koran" itself "show[ing] him angels, saints, and worlds". Concluding this passage apocalyptically, Herder finds the Prophet's "mind" not only motioning upwards, but also forwards, trumpeting "the thunders of the day of resurrection" as well as "the last judgment".

In this portrait infused with awe, and perhaps even admiration, the Prophet is also treated by Herder with a telling ambivalence. Recalling his ambiguous reading of Goethe's rendered *Mahomet* as both "glorious" yet "inhumane", Herder follows his own passage above on "Mohammed" by adding a plainly pejorative statement, exclaiming "To what extent has the superstition of the shamans spread itself!"[11] Undercutting Romantic "sublimity" with shamanistic "superstition" (*"Aberglaube"*), Herder's equivocal account of Islamic origins in Part II sets a precedent for the remainder of his *Ideen*, which grapples more substantially with the advent of Islam in its concluding Part IV. Maintaining his concentration on climate, and the significance of the "solitary", Herder dedicates a section to the "Kingdoms of the Arabs" in Part IV's Book 19, very near the end of his *Ideen*. Offering a geographic survey that serves again as the grounds for psychological analysis, Herder finds "The Arabian peninsula" to be "one of the most distinguished regions of the Earth, apparently intended by Nature herself, to stamp a peculiar character on its nation", recognizing too that, "[The Arabs'] peninsula was separated from the great body of Asia by the desert, which protected them against the frequent expeditions of its conquerors; they remained free, and proud of their descent, of the nobility of their families, of their unconquered valour, and their uncontaminated language."[12] Complementing his emphasis on the "solitary, romantic men" of the "deserts of Arabia", Herder finds the Arabian "peninsula" itself a "distinguished region" – a climactic crucible that promotes a "free" people, permitting them to remain not only "unconquered", but "uncontaminated". Endowing "Nature herself" with historical intention, Herder not only extrapolates "national" effects from "natural" environs, but personifies the physical world, discovering a providential "protection" in this Middle Eastern peninsula, with "Arabian" lands allowing for a "purity" in the Arabian "language".

These musings on Eastern climate and culture lead Herder to his slow and suspenseful anticipation of Islam's own advent, transitioning from Arabian speech to Arabian spirituality. Immediately before introducing "Mohammed" in the "Kingdoms of the Arabs", Herder ruminates lyrically:

> Thus at an early period an intellectual culture arose here, which the Altai or Ural could never have produced: the Arabian language formed itself to an ingenuity in figurative eloquence and prudential apophthegms, long before they, by whom it was spoken, knew how to commit them to writing. On their Sinai the Hebrews received their law, and among them they almost always dwelt. When Christians arose, and persecuted each other, Christian sects also repaired to them. Could it be otherwise, then, that from the mixture of Jewish, Christian, and native ideas, among such a people, with such a language, a new flower in due time would appear? and when it appeared, could it fail, from this point between three quarters of the Globe, to obtain the most extensive spread from commerce, wars, foreign expeditions, and books? Thus the odoriferous shrub of Arabian fame, springing from such an arid soil, is a very natural phenomenon, the moment a man arose, who knew how to rear it into blossom.[13]

It is the form of this paragraph – its own "figurative eloquence" – that initially seems striking. Engaging his reader with extended questions and vivid imagery, Herder's prelude to the Prophet is unmistakably poetic, aligning this "man" of "Arabian fame" with a unique "flower" of the "arid soil". Expressed through natural symbols, Herder also discovers the Prophet himself to be "a very natural phenomenon" – a harvester of a historical "blossom", which is both long expected, and yet which appears in "due time". Merging messianic promise with global prospects – tracing a process not only of Arabian cultivation, but of "extensive" growth "spreading" over "three quarters of the Globe" – Herder's expectant passage reaches its resolution when "Mohammed" himself is introduced:

> In the beginning of the seventh century this man did arise; a singular compound of whatever the nation, tribe, time, and country, could produce; merchant, prophet, orator, poet, hero, and legislator; all after the Arabian manner. *Mohammed* was born of the noblest tribe in Arabia, the guardian of the purest dialect, and of the Caaba, the ancient sanctuary of the nation; a boy of considerable beauty, not rich, but educated in the family of a man of consequence.

Shortly following this report of the Prophet's physical birth, Herder adds to his portrait, by tracing his psychological progress:

> Not the dream of his celestial journey alone, but his life, and the Koran itself, evince the fervour of his imagination, and that no artfully concerted deception was necessary to the persuasion of his prophetic call. Mohammed came forward on the stage, not in the ebullition of youthful blood, but in the fortieth year of his age; first as the prophet of his house, who revealed himself only to few, and gained scarcely six followers in three years: and when, at the celebrated feast of Ali, he had announced his mission to forty persons of his tribe, he thenceforward exposed himself freely to every thing a prophet has to expect from the opposition of the incredulous.[14]

Dizzying in its dramatic abundance and amplitude, the Prophet's arrival is heralded by Herder through a succession of copious superlatives. Associated with not only the "noblest", but also the "purest", it is the margins of Muḥammad's life that are especially distinguished; a "boy" possessing "considerable beauty", the Prophet also fulfills the promise of a "man of consequence". Recalling his emphasis on Arabian exceptionalism, the Prophet is seen as "singular"; however, this singularity is itself "compound", with "Mohammed" embodying a unique mixture of "merchant, prophet, orator, poet, hero, and legislator" – a complex synthesis which complements Herder's own complex appraisal, as Ian Almond has highlighted.[15] Perhaps most resonant in the Prophet's introduction, however, is its vivid theatricality, with the various personae ascribed to the Prophet assuming a distinctly performative quality. Emphasizing the "fervour of his imagination", Herder describes the advent of the Muslim mission in aesthetic terms, with "Mohammed" coming "forward on the stage". Although he will reject Goethe's own dramatic *Mahomet* in 1799 as "inhumane", Herder himself imbues the human life of Muḥammad with a dramatic suspense more than a decade earlier, the Prophet depicted as gradually "reveal[ing] himself", gaining the "stage" in quiet steps, succeeding humbly from "his house" to an "announcement" that has consequences for the entire "Globe".

III

Herder's "compound" consideration of Islamic origins becomes more conspicuous as he shifts from the Muslim Prophet to Muslim prophecy – from "*Mohammed*" to the "Koran". Again attracting both admiration and antipathy, the Qur'ān also emerges ambivalently in Herder's section on the "Kingdoms of the Arabs", where he offers his most substantive survey of the scripture:

> His Koran, that wonderful mixture of poetry, elo-
> quence, ignorance, sagacity, and arrogance, is a mirror
> of his mind; displaying his talents and defects, his faults

and propensities, the self-deception and necessary pre-
text with which he imposed upon himself and others,
much more perspicuously, than any other Koran of any
prophet. He delivered it in separate fragments, as they
were called for by occasional circumstances, or when his
mind was rapt by contemplation, without thinking of a
written system: it consisted of the ebullitions of his imagination, or prophetic discourses of censure and exhorta-
tion, at which at other times he himself was astonished,
as something above his powers, as a divine gift entrusted
to his charge.[16]

Recalling Herder's approach to the Prophet, the "Koran" emerges
as a "wonderful mixture", comprising not a "compound" of lived
vocations, but a fusion of literary genres, embracing not only
"poetry and eloquence" but also "ignorance" and "sagacity".
This match between Islamic Messenger and Islamic message is,
moreover, no coincidence. For Herder, the Qur'ān stands as "a
mirror of his mind", with Muḥammad's "talents" and "faults"
equally reflected in the revelation. Embodying "the ebullitions
of his imagination", arising from moments in which the "mind
was rapt by contemplation", Herder concludes his sketch of the
scripture by skeptically recognizing its religious claim, reporting that the Qur'ān was regarded by the Prophet as "a divine
gift entrusted to his charge". Spanning imaginative creation and
divine assignment, Herder aptly interrupts his own account of
the "Koran" by creatively adapting this divine term for his own
purposes. Multiplying the reach of the Muslim revelation, Herder
expands the "Koran" itself, stretching this Arabic title, allowing it
to signify not a single scripture merely, but rather a sacred genre.
Juxtaposing the Qur'ān with the holy books of other religions,
Herder contrasts the Muslim scripture against "any other Koran
of any prophet" – a surprising comparative which refigures the
term "Koran" as a universal category.

This Qur'ānic comparative in Herder's account – recruiting the
Muslim revelation to illumine other cultures and communities
– itself reaches an unexpected climax as Herder brings his Book

19 to a close. Nuancing further the portrait of Islam which he has previously advanced, Herder adds a final section to Book 19, expositing the "Effects of the Arabian Kingdoms" by suggesting that:

> The religion of Mohammed imprints on the minds of men a degree of tranquility, an uniformity of character, which, though they may be as dangerous as useful, are in themselves valuable, and deserving esteem: but on the other hand, the polygamy it allows, the prohibition of all inquiry concerning the Koran, and the despotism it establishes in spiritual and temporal affairs, cannot easily avoid being attended with pernicious consequences.
>
> Be this religion, however, what it may, it was propagated in a language, the purest dialect of Arabia, the pride and delight of the whole nation. No wonder, therefore that the other dialects were thrown by it into shade, and the language of the Koran became the victorious banner of Arabian sovereignty. Such a common standard of the oral and written language is advantageous to a widely extended, flourishing nation. Had the German conquerors of Europe possessed a classic book of their language, such as the Koran was to the Arabs, their tongue would never have been so overpowered by the Latin, and so many of their tribes would not have been left in oblivion. But neither Ulphilas, nor Kaedmon, nor Ottfried, could produce, what Mohammed gave to all his followers in the Koran; which is to this day a pledge of their ancient genuine dialect, by which they are led to the most authentic documents of their race, and remain one people throughout the whole Earth.[17]

The first paragraph in this remarkable passage is bisected equivocally, with Herder's phrase – "but on the other hand" – fitly reflecting his ambivalent approach to the "religion of Mohammed". Hedging uneasily between the "estimable" and the "pernicious", Herder even finds Islam's virtues – such as its "uniformity of character" – to be "as dangerous as useful". However, it is Herder's artful and ambiguous language that ironically accents Islam's unequivocal blessing, namely its own artistic "language". Betraying his bias for aesthetic articulation – for "eloquence" – Herder seems unrestrained in lauding the Qur'ān as a linguistic ideal. A vessel for "the purest dialect of Arabia", the Qur'ān even prevails as "the victorious banner of Arabian sovereignty", verbally embodying a "pride and delight" which stands as "pledge" – a semantic sign which is visible both within the "nation" and without. These overtly political impli-cations of "the language of the Koran" also prompt Herder to invert traditional West-East hierarchies, leading him to lament his own country's lack of a "classic" Qur'ān. Jealous of "what Mohammed gave to all his followers in the Koran", Herder sur-prisingly finds the Muslim scripture a "useful" means of resisting cultural conquest and acquiring independence; as Ian Almond has previously recognized, Herder's admiring "gaze towards the Orient" in this passage seems also to embody a mixture of "envy with regret".[18]

Writing from the midst of a divided Europe, with neighboring regions in contest, Herder wistfully idealizes the Muslim scrip-ture, finding the Qur'ān to have offered an "eloquent" key to ethnic "sovereignty". Lauding its capacity to keep the Arabs as "one people throughout the whole Earth", Herder's celebration of Islamic "eloquence" offers not only aesthetic appreciation, but also political elegy, reflecting Europe's cultural strife in the mirror of the Qur'ān's synthesizing speech. And it is perhaps this "eloquent" achievement that Herder found most lacking in 1799 as he listened to Goethe's rendered *Mahomet* – a drama concerning Islamic origins, whose translation from French itself serves as a dramatic "pledge" of the dearth of German original-ity. Irritating Herder by featuring "glorious verses" which yet failed to express Islam's "humanity", Goethe's *Mahomet* also seemed to demonstrate the failure of artistic independence at home. Performing the precise problem expressed in his envy-ing the "Koran", Herder doubtless discovered in Goethe's translated *Mahomet* yet another unconscious testimony to the "German conquerors of Europe" lacking "a classic book of their language", his home theater in Weimar revealed to be "overpowered by the Latin", even as it pictured the Prophet advancing "forward on the stage".

3

"In the footsteps of Mohammed": Friedrich Schlegel and Novalis

I

After identifying the Qur'ān as "the victorious banner of Arabian sovereignty", Herder's "Effects of the Arabian Kingdoms" expands in perspective, addressing the global echoes of Qur'ānic traditions. Emphasizing especially the aesthetic "Effects" of Arabian eloquence, Herder asserts that "*Poetry*" was the "ancient inheritance" of the Arabs, adding:

> No nation can boast of so many passionate votaries of poetry as the Arabs, during their golden age: in Asia this passion spread even to the tatarian princes and nobles; in Spain, to the Christian. The *gaya ciencia* of the limosin or provencal poets was in a manner forced upon them, or inspired by their Arabian foes: and thus Europe by degrees acquired, though rudely and slowly, an ear for more refined and animated poetry.

> The fabulous part of poetry, the *romance* [*Märchen*] flourished more particularly under an orient sky.[1]

Recalling his envious wonder at the capacity of the Qur'ān's language to unify "a nation", Herder here again privileges East over West, concentrating not on linguistic comparison, however, but on literary influence. Historically indebted to Arabian poetry, "Europe" is even "rude" and "slow" in its apprenticeship, depicted by Herder as only gradually gaining "an ear for more refined and animated poetry". Chronologically and culturally in advance of the West, the Arabian "East" is also, however, the genuine home of the "*Märchen*" ("*romance*" in T. Churchill's translation), with Europe's "provencal poets" indebted to Arabian "passion". A genealogy of the "*gaya ciencia*", Herder's skeletal sketch advances from the Middle East, to Muslim "Spain", and finally to Christian Europe, with Andalucia forming the bridge between "romantic" Orient and "rude" Occident.

Finding Eastern roots for the "*romance*", Herder seems to reach back to his "romantic" characterization of the Arabian desert, which surfaced early in his *Ideen*. However, Herder's assertion also reaches forward, anticipating yet another and very different *Ideen*, authored by one of the most celebrated German Romantics: Friedrich Schlegel. Published in an 1800 issue of the iconic journal *Athenaeum*, Schlegel's *Ideen* forms a fragmentary collection of first-person insights into aesthetics and spirituality, in contrast to Herder's own weighty history, which unfolds incrementally through four volumes. However, similar to Herder's earlier compendium, Schlegel's *Ideen* also reflects a Romantic appeal to the East; interspersed amid his intellectual scatterings, for instance, Schlegel announces that "To begin with, I speak only to those who are already facing the Orient" – a cryptic claim, suggesting that Schlegel solely addresses a Western audience who are nevertheless eastward "facing".[2] This "oriental" priority resurfaces strongly at the very conclusion to Schlegel's *Ideen*, which also forms a dedication to one of Schlegel's closest friends:

> *To Novalis*: You don't stay at the threshold of things. On the contrary, your spirit is deeply suffused with poetry and philosophy. It was closest to me in these images of uncomprehended truth. What you've thought I think; what I've thought you will think or have already thought. There are misunderstandings that only serve to confirm the greatest

> shared understanding. Every doctrine of the eternal Orient
> belongs to all artists. I name you instead of all the others.[3]

An interior and enigmatic conclusion to his intellectual epigrams, Schlegel addresses this end of his *Ideen* to none other than Friedrich von Hardenberg, known to the world by his adopted pseudonym, Novalis. Espousing Romantic philosophy, but also tinged with a romantic intimacy, Schlegel not only muses on "poetry and philosophy" and "uncomprehended truth", but on personal identity, finding a mental merger between him and Novalis: "What you've thought I think; what I've thought you will think or have already thought", he asserts. Balancing individual and universal, Schlegel's fragment also shifts from his European friend to an Eastern identity, suggesting that "Every doctrine of the eternal Orient belongs to all artists", announcing that their shared mind is itself grounded in an "East", both "eternal" and "artistic".

As Schlegel's career unfolds, it will be an Indic Orient, rather than an Islamic East, that will increasingly occupy his focus. Discovering in the ancient Indian subcontinent a cultural ancestor, Schlegel will embrace Sanskritic traditions, leading him to author in 1808 his influential *On the Language and Wisdom of the Indians*. However, while this investment in India marks his maturity, Schlegel's earliest Romanticism is more distinctly Middle Eastern, as Nicholas A. Germana has noted; although "Schlegel's first reference to a cultural connection between Germany and the Orient is quite vague", observes Germana, it is certain that this connection "concerns Arabic poetic traditions rather than those from India".[4] It is in the years leading up to his *Ideen* that this Arabic "connection" would be most vividly confessed by Schlegel himself – a confession that once again connects him closely with Novalis. Writing to his friend on October 20, 1798, Schlegel characterizes his forthcoming compositions with a surprising analogy, evidencing his own "Eastern" ambitions which anticipate his *Ideen*: "The aim of my literary project is to write a new Bible and to follow in the footsteps of Mohammed and Luther."[5] Recalling Goethe's own early letter to Herder – aspiring to "pray, like Moses in the Koran"

– this confessionary letter envisions Schlegel's Romantic aspirations within an Islamic atmosphere, audaciously aligning his
literary ambitions with the achievements of the Prophet himself. However, unlike Goethe's playful tone, Schlegel's desire to
"follow in the footsteps" of Islam's founder seems somewhat
more earnest; attaching himself to the pinnacle of Arabian spirituality, as well as the archetype of European religious reform,
Schlegel strives to achieve a biblical breakthrough that will link
him equally to "Mohammed" and to Martin "Luther".

Bridging sacred and secular, East and West, Schlegel expresses
his literary aspirations in this private letter from 1798, a letter that seems especially important, and particularly poignant,
due to its specific addressee, Novalis – a friend whose own
literary aspirations will soon be cut short by tuberculosis, his
premature death only three years in the future. Curtailed due
to his condensed lifespan, and also suppressed due to censorship – as William O'Brien has emphasized – Novalis' literary
production would nevertheless succeed in gaining celebrity, his
Schriften (*Writings*) posthumously published in 1802, edited by
Ludwig Tieck, and none other than Friedrich Schlegel himself.[6]
Together with philosophical dialogues and lyric poems, the
1802 edition of Novalis' *Schriften* would include his unfinished
Heinrich von Ofterdingen – a fragmentary novel, characterized
by Dennis Mahoney as "the epitome of German Romanticism".[7]
Differing in genre from Schlegel's own writings, Novalis' fiction
yet shares with the philosophy of his friend an investment in
the Muslim East, personifying Islamic interests through imaginative creation, rather than abstract theory. Expressing Islam
through a new genre, Novalis' *Heinrich von Ofterdingen* also,
however, allows Islam to be embodied in a new gender, infusing
his German fiction with a female representative of the Muslim
religious. Rather than associating Islamic traditions with nature
and its vigorous powers – *à la* Goethe, for instance, and his
"Song to Mahomet" – Novalis instead chooses to fictional-
ize Islam in feminine terms, with the religion freshly accented
through the voice of a woman.

II

Implied in the very title of Novalis' novel is the debt owed by modern Romanticism to medieval romance. Named after a legendary poet from Germany's lyric past, *Heinrich von Ofterdingen* gestures back to traditions of the troubadour, its narrative punctuated with chivalric settings and symbols, its characters inhabiting castles and launching crusades. However, Novalis' novel seems more a philosophical allegory than an episodic adventure, dramatizing an array of political, religious, and aesthetic debates in the midst of his fiction – an intellectual range that has reciprocally invited a range of critical readings. Opening with Heinrich's dream of "the blue flower" – "*die blaue Blume*", the "famous symbol" of German Romanticism – *Heinrich von Ofterdingen* transitions from this ethereal image to an extended myth, its third chapter recounting the "Fairy Tale of Atlantis" ("*Atlantis Märchen*").[8] It is the novel's next chapter, however, that introduces more timely topics, witnessing Heinrich's encounter with an unexpected interloper. Wandering alone, outside the castle where his countrymen prepare for the crusades, Heinrich is arrested suddenly by "the tender, affecting singing of a female voice, with a wonderful, melodious accompaniment". Listening to her lonesome lyric, Heinrich hears a lament for lost homelands, the "female voice" recounting her enforced exile from a "distant . . . fatherland". Intrigued and enchanted, Heinrich draws closer, and:

> heard the sobbing of a child and a comforting voice. He went down through the thickets and found a pale, careworn girl sitting under an old oak tree. A beautiful child clung around her neck and wept; her tears flowed also, and a lute lay beside her on the grass. She was somewhat startled as she perceived the strange youth, who approached her with troubled face.
>
> "You probably heard my song," said she amiably. "Your face seems familiar to me; let me think – my memory is

getting weak, but the sight of you calls up strange recollections of happy times. O it seems to me you resemble one of my brothers who, before our misfortune, went to a famous poet in Persia. Perhaps he is still living and lamenting in song the misfortune of his brothers and sisters. If only I could remember some of the splendid songs he left us! He was noble and sensitive and knew no greater happiness than his lute."[9]

Introducing not one stranger, but two, this scene also foregrounds two distinct facets: the aesthetic and the familial. The "careworn girl" encountered by Heinrich will soon be identified in Chapter 4 as "Zulima", an exile from "Arabia", and a captive of a crusading knight; however, even before learning her exotic name or her exotic nation, readers are introduced to her "comforting voice", as well as the "lute" that "lay[s] beside her on the grass". The very first words ascribed to Zulima are also lyrically focused; invoking her absent brother, Zulima mentions his travels to "Persia" – visiting there "a famous poet" – as well as his "splendid songs", which are now regretfully forgotten. This fraternal allusion accents also the familial context of Zulima's introduction. It is not a singing "voice" merely, but also the "sobbing" of a "child" which is first heard as Heinrich enters the scene, with Zulima's maternal character offered to readers together with her musicality.

Fusing lyric artistry and familial intimacy, this initial portrait of Zulima also proves to be predictive in Chapter 4, echoing into Novalis' account of Zulima's ethnic origins; immediately following the above quotation, the novel's narrator continues:

The child was a girl ten or twelve years old, who attentively observed the strange youth, and pressed close to the bosom of the unhappy Zulima. Henry's heart was filled with compassion; he comforted the singer with kind words and asked her to tell him about her life in more detail. She appeared not unwilling. Henry sat opposite her and listened to her story, which was frequently interrupted by

tears. She lingered especially on the praise of her countrymen and fatherland. She depicted their magnanimity and
their pure, great sensitiveness to the poetry of life and to
the wonderful, mysterious charm of nature. She described
the romantic beauties of the fruitful regions in Arabia,
which lie like happy isles amid the pathless sand wastes,
like refuges for the weary and oppressed, like colonies of
paradise. She described these colonies full of fresh springs
that ripple through dense grass and over sparkling stones
among venerable old groves. She told how these groves
are vocal with gay-colored birds of melodious throats, and
attractive because of many vestiges of memorable bygone
ages.[10]

The dual elements initially associated with Zulima's person
here bleed into her native place, with "Arabia" itself expressed
through parental and artistic images. Gendered again as Zulima's
"fatherland", Arabia yet seems maternal symbolically, associated
with "fruitful regions" and "fresh springs", forming a "para-
disal" home that offers "refuges" to the "weary and oppressed".
Rather than the stark sublimity of the desert celebrated by
Herder, Novalis finds "Arabia" not merely a "sand waste", but
also soft and subtle, its oases epitomizing the "mysterious charm
of nature". Complementing its familial fertility is the sensuality
of Arabia, portrayed as a place of "rippl[ing]" sounds and "sparkling" sights, with both "springs" and "stones" equally "attractive". Mirroring the Arabian songstress herself, Zulima's Arabia
is blessed with "gay-colored birds of melodious throats", a place
where a "great sensitiveness to the poetry of life" still flourishes.

It is the narrative frame around Zulima's account, however,
which suggests its purpose, hinting at Novalis' point in accenting
the sensual and the maternal even while describing the Arabian
"singer" and her lost Arabian homeland. Before "her life" is
related, Heinrich is struck initially by the child who "pressed
close to the bosom of the unhappy Zulima" – a pitiable image
that penetrates Heinrich's own bosom, touching his very "heart".
Confronted by a foreigner from the East, Heinrich is disarmed by

a domestic feeling, Zulima's familial beauty striking him with "compassion". This process of pathos is described as unfolding within the novel, affecting the medieval dynamics of Novalis' narrated scene; however, such pathos also reaches without the novel as well, offered implicitly as a model for Novalis' modern readers. Attempting to elicit sympathy for the Arabian, Novalis presents an Eastern maiden that melts European suspicion, supplying a character of kindly maternity and congenial arts who touches the heart not only of Novalis' legendary Heinrich, but also of his living audience as well.

III

Amid the gentle nostalgia that characterizes Zulima's introduction – yearning for "romantic beauties" and "vestiges of memorable bygone ages" – a single element is subtly interwoven that seems somewhat less placid, and more problematic. Easily overlooked in Zulima's florid survey is that her "especial" concern is not the celebration of her country, but rather the "praise" of "her *countrymen*". This defense of Zulima's fellow Arabians, as well as her Arabian "fatherland", introduces into Novalis' novel an ironic juxtaposition. Sheltered near the castle where his compatriots celebrate Eastern crusades, Heinrich listens to Zulima's praise for her own Eastern compatriots, apologizing for the enemies of Heinrich's peers. This minor facet in Zulima's introduction assumes a major focus as Chapter 4 unfolds. Initially identified with her sensual voice, Zulima abruptly changes her tune, shifting from petition to accusation as she continues her speech "after a pause":

> By no means believe the stories they tell you about the cruelty of my countrymen. Nowhere were prisoners treated more magnanimously, and your pilgrims to Jerusalem were hospitably received; only they were seldom worthy of it. Most of them were good-for-nothing wicked men, who disgraced their pilgrimages with knavish deeds and

hence, to be sure, often fell into the hands of righteous vengeance. How tranquilly the Christians could have visited the Holy Sepulcher without the need of starting a terrible, useless war which has embittered everything, spread endless wretchedness, and separated the East from Europe forever. What importance did the name of the possessor have? Our sovereigns reverently honored the Sepulcher of your Holy One, whom we also regard as a divine person; and how beautifully could his Holy Sepulcher have become the cradle of a happy mutual understanding and the occasion of everlasting beneficent alliances![11]

Pivoting her attention from subtle artistry to brutal warfare, Novalis' Arabian songstress supplies his readers with a fiery censure of European "men". Defined as those who are "seldom worthy of" the "hospitality" of the Holy Land, Westerners are condemned too through contrast with Zulima's own "countrymen", who are figured not only as "magnanimous", but also as undeserving of the "terrible, useless war" prosecuted against them. Critiquing the crusades for spreading "wretchedness", it is the "separation" caused by these holy wars which Zulima most condemns, inveighing against Christian campaigns due to their division of the "East" from "Europe". Aggressively indicting the West's pillaging "pilgrims" – "*your* pilgrims" she says accusingly to Heinrich – Zulima shatters the placid surface of Novalis' novel, interrupting the dreamy romance of its initial chapters.[12] However, this scorching speech nevertheless also assumes an irresistible authority and integrity due to its speaker's affable introduction. Establishing Zulima as sympathetic – her identity equally artistic and affectionate – Novalis' soft opening to his Eastern heroine allows her harsh critique of the West to accrue significant weight, compelling medieval Henry, as well as modern readers, to commiserate with Zulima's condemnation of their own culture.

The "separation" engendered by the crusades aptly forms the crux of Zulima's sympathetic accusations – a separation that implies not only a split between nations, but also a religious schism as well. The most daring detail in Zulima's diatribe is

not her critique of discord between East and West, but her privileging of Islam over Christianity, with the former shown "to
be more accepting of other creeds", as James R. Hodkinson has
noted.[13] Blaming Christians for actively advancing religious division, Zulima credits Muslims with social and theological unity,
willing even to embrace the "Holy One" of Christianity; unlike
Europeans, whose "pilgrimages" are "disgraced" with "knavish
deeds", Zulima portrays her own people as accepting the central claims of their oppressors, celebrating Christ himself, who
"we also regard as a divine person". Shifting subtly from third-
person to first-person, Zulima initially describes her "countrymen" as "they", but, in this latter statement, modulates to "we",
explicitly including *herself* in the aggrieved party. Perhaps most
striking in Zulima's language, however, is the subjunctive mood
of her lament, musing on what *might* have been. "How beautifully could his Holy Sepulcher have become the cradle of a happy
mutual understanding", Zulima declares, suggesting that Christ's
tomb might even serve as the source of "everlasting beneficent alliances". Merging complementary strands already associated with
Zulima, this exclamation balances the aesthetic and the domestic, emphasizing the potential "beauty" of blessed "alliances"
between Islam and Christianity, even while celebrating the transformation of a barren "sepulcher" into a maternal "cradle" – a
place of nurturing, a site for the rebirth of religious "mutuality".
This spiritual nostalgia for lost brotherhood between Christians
and Muslims also offers a poignant parallel for Zulima's own
personal nostalgia, with Novalis' female refugee from Arabia
now serving as an allegory for family dysfunction between the
Abrahamic faiths.

Supplying a fleeting ideal of Arab domesticity in Novalis'
novel, Zulima disappears at the end of his Chapter 4, never again
to resurface in *Heinrich von Ofterdingen*; bidding farewell to her
at the castle of the plotting crusaders, Heinrich gives Zulima his
mother's "veil", even as Zulima gives him a "ribbon" inscribed
with her name in her "mother's tongue" – an exchange which
balances the familiar intimacy and cultural foreignness that
has characterized their brief encounter.[14] And yet, despite this

disappearance at the end of Chapter 4, Zulima's presence will reemerge in a postscript to Novalis' unfinished novel, appended to the posthumous edition published by Tieck and Schlegel in 1802.[15] Hinting at a broader Islamic "sympathy" that was to evolve through Novalis' later narrative, this editorial addendum suggests the intended directions for the unfinished *Heinrich von Ofterdingen*. Working from Novalis' own notes, the postscript hints at the novel's hopes of returning to Zulima's "family", with Heinrich's envisioned future including the following:

> After becoming acquainted with the heroic age and with antiquity, he visits the Holy Land, for which he had felt so great a longing from his youth. He seeks Jerusalem, and acquaints himself with Oriental poetry. Strange events among the infidels detain him in desert regions; he discovers the family of the eastern girl (see Part I.): the manners and life of nomadic tribes. – Persian tales, recollections of the remotest antiquity. The book during all these various events was to retain its characteristic hue, and recall to mind the blue flower: throughout, the most distant and distinct traditions were to be knit together, Grecian, Oriental, Biblical, Christian, with reminiscences of and references to both the Indian and Northern mythology.[16]

Although not named in these point-form plans, it is clear that Zulima is the personality to whom Novalis had planned to return, labeled here in this editorial summary merely as his "eastern girl" – a reductive reference, consistent with the designation too of her "people" as "infidels". More consistent with Novalis' sympathetic portrait of Zulima, however, is the novel's aspirations to address both "Oriental poetry" and "Persian tales" (*"Persische Märchen"*) as part of Heinrich's continued adventures, as well as Heinrich's discovery of the "family" of Zulima – elements that echo the artistic and domestic characteristics of the Arabian during her brief appearance in Novalis' actual novel.[17]

Most pivotal in this postscript, however, is simply the suggestion that *Heinrich von Ofterdingen* was slated to enter the

East itself. Projecting a voyage that was to "recall to mind the blue flower" – Novalis' central Romantic symbol – this Oriental arrival was also to produce the reconciliation of religious "traditions", allowing a range of global legacies to be "knit together", including "Grecian, Oriental, Biblical, Christian". In reaching the "Holy Land", and touring "Jerusalem", Novalis reportedly aspired to synthesize the "most distant and distinct" in his Eastern adventures, an ideal that aptly echoes Zulima's own aspirations voiced in Chapter 4. Recalling Zulima's hopes to make her homeland "the cradle of a happy mutual understanding", linking East and West, Novalis himself had hoped that his novel would reach realms of religious reconciliation, dramatizing a mythic "knitting together" of discrete spiritualities on Oriental soil. However, just as Zulima's own imperative for such a blessed "alliance" remains in the subjunctive only – an unfulfilled "could have" – Novalis' novel too never authentically reaches its "Holy" destination, his fiction abandoned as a fragment at his untimely death, leaving mere traces of its yearning for a more wholesome totality. Due to the edition prepared by Tieck and Schlegel, however, the first readers of *Heinrich von Ofterdingen* nevertheless were offered the faint possibility, the skeletal plans, for such a reunion, finding an endnote that envisions Novalis' unrealized return to his domestic "source" in the "East", seeking "alliances" both "everlasting" and "beneficent". And as it was Schlegel who had articulated his own Romantic ambitions to Novalis in 1798 through Muslim allusion – attempting to "follow" the model of not only "Luther", but "Mohammed" – it is fitting that Schlegel and Tieck's edition of Novalis reciprocally hints at the Islamic afterlife which his German novel had aspired to attain. Ever waiting its fulfillment, Novalis' own *Heinrich von Ofterdingen* itself tracks Eastern "footsteps" towards a Romantic reconciliation in its posthumous publication, with Western audiences offered Novalis' blueprint to arrive at an "alliance" only possible under "an orient sky", where the "countrymen" and descendants of "Luther" may yet walk in pursuit of "Mohammed".

4

"Allāh is the best Keeper":
Joseph Hammer's Ḥāfiẓ

I

An unrealized fiction with Eastern aspirations, Novalis began his *Heinrich von Ofterdingen* at the same time that another Romantic young man would realize his own Eastern aspirations. Departing his native home in Austria in May 1799, Joseph Hammer soon arrived in Istanbul, beginning his service as a *Sprachknabe* ("language boy"), a diplomatic translator at the Turkish court.[1] Crossing the pivotal divide between continents and centuries – Europe and Asia, eighteenth century and nineteenth – the Eastern arrival of Joseph Hammer is a negligible moment in the protracted history of Austrian-Ottoman relations. Minor in its political outcomes, Hammer's stay in Istanbul would, however, have major literary consequences, his diplomacy in the East helping to reshape Western poetry, exercising a formative impact on Romantic Orientalism. In the very month that he reached Turkey, June 1799, Hammer would begin working with copies of, and commentaries on, Ḥāfiẓ's celebrated verse collection – his *Divan*.[2] Completing a German rendition of this Persian original by 1806, Hammer ultimately published his two-volume translation in 1812 and 1813, tackling more than five hundred of Ḥāfiẓ's *ghazals*, as well as numerous ancillary pieces. Proudly announced as an unprecedented effort, Hammer's translation would bear the fulsome title: *Der Diwan des Mohammed Schemsed-din Hafis*.

Aus dem Persischen zum erstenmal ganz übersetz, claiming to "translate" for the "first time" Ḥāfiẓ's "entire" poetry collection "from Persian".³

Arising from Hammer's worldly diplomacy, his German *Diwan* would itself spark a series of global imitations, inspiring a range of leading authors, from Europe, to England, to America. Enjoying its greatest influence on Germany's greatest author – J. W. Goethe – Hammer's *Diwan* also helped launch the literary celebrity one of America's most prominent authors – Ralph Waldo Emerson – with the Austrian's Eastern translation soon reaching the most Western frontiers, echoing transatlantically from its origins in Istanbul to New World receptions.⁴ Such international impact was, of course, entirely unforeseen by the unknown youth who first disembarked at Istanbul in the early summer of 1799; however, by the time Hammer published his *Diwan*'s first volume in 1812, he had some intimation of its potential significance. Grounding this historic translation in his own personal history, Hammer prefaces his *Diwan* by confessing that Ḥāfiẓ's "current Germanization" was "begun in Constantinople in 1799", and completed over a period of "seven years".⁵ Paralleling his life's progress with his poetic translation, Hammer's introduction to his *Diwan* begins with his own experiences abroad; it ends, however, by considering his audience at home. Apologizing for his translation's tendency to retain Ḥāfiẓ's "original" tropes, Hammer concludes his Preface by defending his conservation of Persian "color" in his *Diwan*, refusing to adapt Ḥāfiẓ to the "colder imagination of Westerners" ("*kältere Fantasie des Abendländers*").⁶ This robust defense of his *Diwan* concludes with Hammer's own climactic purpose in translating Ḥāfiẓ; speaking of himself in the third person, Hammer asserts that "he wished less to translate the Persian poet [for] the German reader, than the German reader [for] the Persian poet".⁷ Justifying his own strategy of rendition, Hammer turns his efforts in translation from Eastern writings to Western audience, refusing to revise the former for the latter's tastes. Rather than render Ḥāfiẓ – "the Persian poet" – Hammer hopes instead to render his own "German reader", enlarging domestic perspectives and amending home prejudices.

Making his audience the very object of his translation, Hammer proposes to "carry across" (*translatio*) his reader to new climes and cultures; rehearsing his own early experiences of eastward travel, Hammer's *Diwan* seeks to import its European audience into Muslim lands, even as Hammer himself had "begun" his Ḥāfiẓ translation "in Constantinople in 1799".[8]

Hammer's aspiration to translate his Western readers, articulated in the Preface to his Eastern translation, seems also faintly prophetic, his *Diwan* proving successful in reshaping audiences in Europe and America, exercising an influence, both immense and immediate. It is not the published foregrounds to Hammer's *Diwan*, however, but its personal backgrounds, that most vividly suggest Ḥāfiẓ's capacity to translate European identities. Widely circulated in the West after its 1812–1813 publication in German, Ḥāfiẓ's *Diwan* had first attracted Hammer "in Constantinople", where the young diplomat developed a taste for foreign manuscripts, which he would collect through his lifetime. Stamped inconspicuously inside some of these acquired texts is a small oval seal, Hammer embossing his Middle Eastern assets with a customized insignia, imprinted in black ink. Serving as a hallmark of Hammer's ownership, such stamps are standard among book collectors; Hammer's stamp, however, seems rather non-standard in its content, its inscription composed entirely in Arabic:

السياح السامر

يوسف حامر

[*as-Sayyāḥ as-Sāmir*
Yūsuf Ḥāmir]
[The Itinerant, the Night Converser
Joseph Hammer][9]

Surprising in its foreign script, this stamp is most surprising in its foreign description of a familiar subject – Joseph Hammer himself – identifying the Austrian by an Arabic name. Rechristened as "*Yūsuf Ḥāmir*", Hammer's seal brands his own book, but also rebrands himself, his name transformed in both script and sound. It is the initial two terms of Hammer's imprint, however, that suggest both the playful, and the profound, implications of his new name. Assonant and alliterative, the first words of Hammer's seal – *"as-Sayyāḥ as-Sāmir* – establish a rhyme with his Arabic name, the term *"as-Sāmir"* aurally anticipating *"Ḥāmir"*. Fashioning his new persona in poetic terms, this seal is not only innovative in style, however, but also in spirituality, characterizing Hammer as "The Itinerant, the Night Converser" – terms that seem to typify the Austrian as a wandering dervish, engaging in holy rambling and repartee. Self-describing as a mystic traveler and talker, Hammer's stamp itself travels into new regions of religion, speaking a fresh Sufi identity through a complex act of code shifting. Echoing and extending the Preface to his 1812–1813 *Diwan*, Hammer no longer renders his German reader in the pages of his Muslim translation, but instead renders his own German name into Muslim expression, with Europe's translator of Sufi poetry himself translated into a slice of Sufi poetry. Celebrated for importing Islamic verse into the West, Hammer imports his Western self into Islamic verse, rendering his own most intimate text, his very name, into Arabic eloquence – a stunning reversal of religious authorship which anticipates a Romantic life infused by Islamic adaptations.

II

The spirit of religious reconciliation suggested in Hammer's bibliographic stamp reflects not only his solitary Romanticism, but also his romantic relationships. Born in Graz, Austria in 1774, Hammer has been characterized as a "conservative Catholic"; however, he would eventually in 1816 elect to marry Caroline Henikstein, daughter of Joseph von Henikstein – prominent patron of the Austrian arts, and Jewish convert to Catholicism.[10] Wedding a woman of Jewish ancestry, Hammer's personal life holds an interreligious resonance which will parallel his interreligious publications. During his nearly three decades of marriage to Caroline, Hammer pursued an eclectic literary program, embracing a wide cultural and spiritual range; in addition to his influential ten-volume *History of the Ottoman Empire* (1827–1835), Hammer would tackle more esoteric interests as well, producing an extended account of the legendary "Assassins", for instance, as well as a chronicle of the Mithraic cult.[11] The intellectual latitude suggested by this miscellaneous career would be facilitated by Hammer's promotion up the ladder of Austrian society, culminating in his inheritance of the land and lineage of the prominent Purgstall family in 1835. Elevated to the aristocracy, Hammer assumed another new name with this 1835 inheritance, becoming a baron in this year, and subsequently known as Joseph von Hammer-Purgstall. Adopting the Purgstall title and rank, Joseph and Caroline also relocated to the Purgstall "Palace" in south Austria, with their marriage embracing yet another hybrid and hyphenated identity, becoming the Von Hammer-Purgstalls of Schloss Hainfeld.[12]

This complex trajectory in Hammer's life would reach a tragic crisis in 1844, with the sickness and untimely death of his beloved Caroline on May 15. It would be this conjugal loss, however, that provoked another of Hammer's hybrid religious projects. In the year of Caroline's passing, Hammer published his *Zeitwarte des Gebetes in Sieben Tageszeiten* – a collection of prayers arranged temporally, structured according to "seven periods of the day", stretching from dawn through to night. Not only coinciding with his wife's death, Hammer's 1844 *Prayerbook* was meant also to serve as her memorial; printed prominently on its first page, Hammer frames his *Prayerbook* as a requiem, dedicating it to the "memory of my blessed and most beloved spouse".[13] Immediately following this intimate introduction, Hammer opens his *Prayerbook* with his first petition to God, launching with a lyric prayer:

> *In Namen Gottes, des Allbarmherzigen und Allerbarmenden.*
> *Die Eröffnerinn.*
> *Lobpreis sei Gott dem Herrn der Welten!*
> *dem Allbarmherzigen, dem Allerbarmenden,*
> *dem Inhaber des Tags der Rechenschaft,*
> *Dich beten wir an und Dich rufen wir um hilfe an . . .*

[In the name of God, the All-Merciful and All-Forgiving.
The Opener
Praise be God, the Lord of the worlds!
The All-Merciful, the All-Forgiving,
the Owner of the Day of Judgment,
You do we worship, and You do we call on for help . . .][14]

Reserving his first page for a potent petition – appealing to God through his mercy and sovereignty – Hammer's sparse and stark introduction seems significant, but also startlingly familiar. Rather than offer an original invocation, Hammer begins by translating liturgical lines, initiating his *Prayerbook* with Islam's most recognizable prayer – the first chapter of the Qur'ān. Situating these initial words of the Muslim scripture on his own initial page, Hammer opens with the Qur'ān's own "Opener" – the *Fātiḥah* (*Die Eröffnerinn*) – merging his interior life of prayer with Islamic praxis. Placing the Qur'ān's invocation immediately after his conjugal dedication, Hammer juxtaposes his final memorial to his wife with the first prayer of the Muslim sacred book, his last tribute to Caroline situated in close contact with the Qur'ān's leading petition.

Fusing Catholic translator, his wife of Jewish ancestry, and an act of Islamic translation, Hammer's *Prayerbook* holds yet another surprise, fusing two books in one: German and Arabic. Beginning from both directions – opening from the front and the back – Hammer's *Prayerbook* is split in half, its German prayers serving as translations of Arabic originals, these alternate languages mirrored at alternate ends of this 1844 collection. Identical in content, yet inverse in form, the Arabic half of Hammer's *Prayerbook* also features a title page which differs markedly from its German counterpart (Figure 3, below).[15] Blending supple script within a spherical design, this Arabic insignia is elaborate in its inlaid patterns, its text encased within dramatic peaks and fluid curves. Written in ornamental design, Hammer's title is itself poetically ornate, reading in Arabic: *Mīqāt aṣ-Ṣalāt fī Saba'a Awqāt* – i.e. *The Fixed Times of Prayer in Seven Periods*. Offering a pleasing sound to complement its pleasant shape, the lithe letters of Hammer's Arabic title also comprise an embellished lyric, pairing together *"Prayer"* and *"Periods"* – i.e. *"Ṣalāt"* and *"Awqāt"* – twinning these terms in assonant rhyme.

Balancing religion and art, prayer and poetry, this Arabic title seems an apt opening to the Eastern end of Hammer's Western *Prayerbook*, its floral design reflecting another balance that is maintained in its pages: namely, that of life and death. Published during his wife's final sickness, and dedicated to her memory, Hammer also highlights in his *Prayerbook*'s final lines that this collection was also completed on Caroline's birthday. Prepared

Figure 3 Arabic title design of Joseph von Hammer-Purgstall's German-Arabic *Prayerbook* (1844).

for printing during the very days that witness Caroline's fatal exit, Hammer's dual-language *Prayerbook* appeared on the anniversary of her entrance into the world, accomplished precisely on the "22nd of July", which marked "Caroline's forty-eighth birthday", as Hammer himself notes.[16] A gift commemorating both her birth as well as her death, this *Prayerbook* features an Arabic title that seems both a floral bouquet presented for Caroline's birthday, but also a garland for her tomb. Universal in span – stretching from death to birth – Hammer also seems to have envisioned his *Prayerbook* as straddling a religious universality as well, with these Islamic prayers befitting his wife, whose own genealogy straddles Judaism and Christianity. According to Hammer's memoir, his *Prayerbook* was meant to offer ecumenical petitions that would be "suitable to be prayed by members of all religions".[17] Recalling the feminine protagonist of Novalis' novel – his fictional Zulima – the *Prayerbook* dedicated to Hammer's actual wife becomes a complex site of religious crossing, a domestic "cradle" and a reconciliatory tomb, which itself "knits together" schismatic divides. Arising from a deeply personal act – a romantic gift for his dying wife – Hammer's *Prayerbook* targets a broad commonality, seeking to be "suitable" for "members of all religions"; although speaking in specifically Islamic language, the *Prayerbook* ironically appeals to a global spirituality, reflecting not only the interreligious marriage of Joseph and Caroline, but also a marriage of all religious adherents as well.

III

The hybrid life shared by Joseph and Caroline culminates with the 1844 *Prayerbook*, this Islamic memorial crystallizing their unusual romance. However, it is the daily life of this couple, rather than Caroline's untimely death, that best exemplifies their Romantic adoption of Muslim expression. Not restricted to title pages merely, the Islamic sacred will form the very façade of the

Hammers' home, not inked in literary imprint, but carved into the stone of their shared life. Acquiring aristocratic title and an aristocratic estate in their last years together, Joseph and Caroline assume a new identity in 1835, adding "Purgstall" to their name. However, the Purgstall estate would also receive a new identity in its inheritance by the Hammers, altered to reflect its fresh inhabitants. Situated in Feldbach, thirty miles east of Graz, Schloss Hainfeld still stands today, its antique past witnessed in the turrets which rise proudly at the castle's four corners. It is not its sixteenth-century architecture, however, but the improvements made by the Hammers in the nineteenth century, that are most conspicuous when approaching the estate grounds. Greeting visitors with a vivid sign of the hybrid spirituality of its former occupants, Schloss Hainfeld features an arresting insignia immediately above its grand gateway, prominently displaying a plaque whose carved letters read:

الله يحرس مجدك
العالي فسر
في حفظه
فالله خير
حافظا
١٢٥٢

Welcoming strangers by identifying itself as a stranger in south Austria, Schloss Hainfeld announces itself in Arabic, the lone estate in this European region to advertise in Eastern script. Confessing its foreign character, Hammer's former home seems even more foreign when its doorway is deciphered, his estate's exterior offering a message that complexly marries the diverse strands which have defined his interior life, its Arabic text signifying:

> May *Allāh* protect thy renown,
> sublime, thus go
> in His keeping
> For *Allāh* is the best
> Keeper

Opening with *Allāh*, Hammer first offers a hospitable supplication, pleading for God's protection in Arabic as he welcomes visitors to his Austrian home. Turning from invocation to imperative, Hammer's inscription next urges his guest to "go" in God's "keeping" – a statement itself strengthened by Hammer's assurance that "*Allāh* is the best Keeper". Orienting the pilgrim as they enter his historic estate, Hammer offers also a religious reorientation, speaking not only in an Eastern language merely, but also in Eastern liturgy. This last line of Hammer's sign is itself a Qur'ānic quotation, cited from the Muslim scripture's twelfth chapter, a chapter which fittingly shares Hammer's own Christian name, "The Chapter of Joseph": *Sūrat Yūsuf* (Q. 12:64).[18] Cementing a link between Austrian estate and its Arabist owner, this sacred passage forms a literal passageway into Hammer's domestic identity, with Islamic expression from "The Chapter of Joseph" comprising a keystone that links the "Palace" with its possessor, Joseph Hammer.

However, in the Qur'ānic quotation that concludes Hammer's inscription there is another pun which emerges, one more explicit and more universal. Communicating God's protective "keeping", characterizing Him as the "best Keeper", Hammer alludes to *Allāh* as the supreme *Ḥāfiẓ* ("حافظ") – a term of rich resonance, etymologically implying a "guard", a "keeper", a "memorizer". A divine epithet, sacred to the Qur'ān, this name is more famously a poetic pen-name, a secular shorthand for Hammer's own beloved Persian poet, Muḥammad Shamsuddīn Ḥāfiẓ. Exploiting this term's rich ambiguity – "*Ḥāfiẓ*" implying not only a memorizer of the Qur'ān, but also God in the Qur'ān, the deity who "remembers" and preserves his creatures – Hammer subtly reminds his own guests of his literary achievements, recalling his 1812–1813 translation of Ḥāfiẓ's *Divan*, even as friends pass through his door. Inscribing Ḥāfiẓ's name into the façade of his own house, even as Ḥāfiẓ's name is inscribed into his own biography, Hammer deepens the domestic import of his Islamic adaptations, finding a fresh way to inhabit Muslim textuality. Revising the Austrian estate he inherited in 1835, Hammer translates this home Qur'ānically, living within actual walls built from this scripture's holy "keeping", perpetually reminded and retained in the house of "Ḥāfiẓ".

Opening with *Allāh* and ending with *Ḥāfiẓ*, Hammer's Arabic reception to his castle spans the boundaries of Islamic spirituality, from the Qur'ān to Sufi poetry. However, while its verbal content concludes with "*Ḥāfiẓ*", a few final marks are also visible under this inscription, recording a simple date: "١٢٥٢", i.e. "1252". Corresponding to the year 1836, but expressed through Arabic numerals and calendar, Hammer dates his home according to Islamic, rather than Christian, history. Relinquishing the standard *Anno Domini* (1836), and instead accepting *Anno Hegirae* (1252), Hammer remakes his home as Islamic spiritual space, but also according to Islamic spiritual time, recalibrating his domestic life in light of a sacred moment in Muslim history.[19] In this temporal re-visioning, Hammer's castle allows him ultimately to complete a return voyage, retreating back to his earliest encounter with "Ḥāfiẓ" in Ottoman lands, renovating this familiar residence in Austria to recall more foreign experiences. Orienting the territory and time of his Occidental life and locality, Hammer continues to pioneer a home for Ḥāfiẓ in the West, while also building an Eastern abode for his own "itinerant" identity, constructing a fit household of religious "remembering" in this habitation of Islamic "keeping".

5

"In no other language": Goethe's Arabic Apprenticeship

I

VON HAMMER

Every part of my little book demonstrates how much I owe
to this worthy man.[1]

Thus begins a section from Goethe's *Noten und Abhandlungen
zu besserem Verständnis des West-östlichen Divan* – Goethe's
Notes and Essays, published as a prose accompaniment to his
1819 poetic *Divan*. Supplying an explanatory background
for his "little book", tracing the historical foregrounds to his
Islamically-inspired *Divan*, Goethe seeks to instill a "better
understanding" in his domestic reader ("*besserem Verständnis*"),
even as they grapple with his poem's foreign form and content.
Appealing to an international range of scholars and scholarship
– German, British, French – Goethe's *Notes and Essays* reserve
the above accolade for an Austrian, suggesting that "every part"
of this new collection betrays the influence of Joseph "VON
HAMMER". Especially indebted to Hammer's 1812–1813 edition of Ḥāfiẓ, Goethe acknowledges that it was this *Diwan* that
had first allowed him to "grasp the inner nature" of Ḥāfiẓ's
poetry "with a special affinity", enabling Goethe to "establish
a relation to [Ḥāfiẓ] through my own production".[2] Erecting
a creative bridge that spans continents and cultures, the east-

ward reach of Goethe's own *Divan* finds a fitting foundation in "VON HAMMER". Not only is Goethe's artistry "owed" to Hammer's academics, but the interreligious character of the German *Divan* also seems to recall unconsciously the Austrian's own intimate embrace of Muslim expressions and identities, as surveyed in the last chapter.

Although apt, an irony also haunts Goethe's tribute to Ḥāfiẓ's Austrian translator. Even while preparing his own *West-Eastern Divan* for publication in 1819, Goethe will strive to transcend translation altogether, resisting the necessity of reading Western renditions, seeking instead to learn Middle Eastern languages himself. Aspiring to acquire not only Arabic, but also Persian, Goethe endeavored to approach Muslim sources without mediation, freeing himself from all debts "owed" to other "worthy men". Indeed, this desire for direct encounter with Eastern literatures reaches back to Goethe's earliest years and intellectual efforts. More than a half century before he published his *West-Eastern Divan*, Goethe had gravitated initially towards philology as an undergraduate, hoping to study Semitic tongues at university; dissuaded by his father, however, Goethe settled on the study of law at Leipzig instead. Commencing his authorial career in the 1770s, Goethe would again return to his Arabic interests, making minor progress in the language even as he drafted his fragmentary drama – *Mahomet* – and published his 1774 "Song to Mahomet". Abandoned while still an unknown youth, Goethe's investment in Middle Eastern languages would reawaken at the peak of his renown, with Ḥāfiẓ and Hammer's translation again playing a pivotal role. Inspired by his reading of the latter's German *Divan* in 1814, Goethe would be spurred to taste the source languages submerged under the literary brilliance implied by Hammer's rendered Persian.[3]

Returning to Arabic and Persian in the wake of Hammer's translation, Goethe's literary celebrity helped facilitate his fresh attempts at language learning, offering him the opportunity to rely on his own nation's leading philologists. Assisted by scholars in Jena, Tübingen, and Heidelberg – early Orientalist pioneers, including J. G. Eichhorn, H. E. G. Paulus, G. W. Lorsbach and J. G. L. Kosegarten – Goethe would renew his study of Semitic languages, spending days scripting the Arabic alphabet, and practicing Persian calligraphy.[4] By the beginning of 1815, Goethe would reflect on his motivations for these linguistic efforts in a letter to his friend, Christian Heinrich Schlosser; writing on January 23, 1815 – in the midst of his composing poems for his 1819 *Divan* – Goethe confesses to Schlosser his aspirations to "learn Arabic", as well as "practice" its script, concluding that "In no [other] language, perhaps, is spirit, word and script so primordially bound together" (*"In keiner Sprache ist vielleicht Geist, Wort und Schrift so uranfänglich zusammengekörpert"*).[5] Situated at the crux of linguistic study and literary authorship, Goethe's letter links his two most recent acts of writing, with his 1815 "learn[ing] Arabic" established as a precedent and a parallel to his poetic *Divan*. More important, however, is Goethe's suggestion that these two contemporary pursuits are twin acts of synthesis. While his literary authorship will produce a *West-Eastern* work – binding together religions and regions in his *West-östlicher Divan* – Goethe's linguistic approach to Arabic is equally a task that is "bound together". For Goethe, Arabic is a medium that merges not only "script" and "word", but also "spirit", a vehicle that moves from physical, to verbal, to metaphysical. However, while Goethe's *Divan* artificially marries cultural traditions, merging hyphenated opposites through his artistry, Goethe finds Arabic to be a marriage that is "primordial", a "binding" of discrete worlds that is organic and innate. An essential Romantic concern, Arabic's "primeval" nature seems to reflect Goethe's own priorities and principles, with this language – better than any other – building a seamless ladder from visible "script" to invisible "spirit". This intrinsic originality of Arabic reflects Goethe's own established interests, leading him to pursue years of personal apprenticeship in Islam's liturgic language, forming a hidden linguistic foreground to his public literary enterprise.

II

Celebrated regularly as "the greatest of German men of letters", Goethe's attraction to Middle Eastern "letters" naturally seems significant.[6] Yet, Goethe's private research only rarely emerges in accounts of his famous publications. Submerged below Goethe's daily schedules, the "learn[ing of] Arabic" becomes a domestic "practice" – as Goethe himself suggests to Christian Schlosser – this extraordinary language forming a mere facet of his ordinary routine. Patiently penning its organic script, Goethe's Arabic pedagogy will itself be organically contoured, forming a living experiment which remains provisional and temporary, progressive yet tentative. Sifting through the many manuscripts inscribed by Goethe in the years leading up to his *Divan*'s publication, numerous witnesses to his "Arabic learning" materialize. The collaborative and conditional character of Goethe's "practice" is especially evident, however, in a single exercise sheet authored during the autumn of 1815. Produced during his September stay and study in Heidelberg, this manuscript – labeled "Bl. 126" – finds Goethe training under the prominent theologian and Orientalist, H. E. G. Paulus (d. 1851). Rehearsing and refining his Arabic by following an expert's example, Goethe's pen strokes appear both beside and beneath Paulus' own; a selection from "Bl. 126" is reproduced below, with Goethe's Arabic appearing in grey, and Paulus' Arabic appearing in black:[7]

بسم الله الرحمن الرحيم

قل أعوذ برب الناس
ملك الناس
إله الناس   إله
من شر الوسواس الخناس

بسم الله الرحمن الرحيم
قل   الرحيم الرحيم

Modeling himself after his mentor's example, Goethe mimics Paulus in the margins, simulating samples of his Arabic. Visually performing the pedagogic process, this manuscript exemplifies the linguistic exchange between aged poet and younger professor, the former following the latter's lines of Semitic script. Perhaps most interesting is the repetitions and revisions apparent in Goethe's own writings, rehearsing at his page bottom "الرحيم" (*ar-raḥīm*) – "the Compassionate" – seeking to improve his Arabic hand through manual "practice", inscribing this same term three separate times.

A moment of informal instruction, this intimate exchange seems especially significant when its Arabic content is considered – content that is derived from the Qur'ān itself. The material which Goethe mirrors from the pen of Paulus represents the very conclusion of the Qur'ān, excerpted from the Muslim scripture's brief and final Chapter 114. Rendered into English, "Bl. 126" reads as follows, with Paulus' contribution again in black, and Goethe in grey:[8]

> In the name of God, the Merciful, the Compassionate
> Say: "I take refuge with the Lord of men,
> the King of men,
> the God of men,   God
> from the evil of the slinking whisperer

> In the Name of God, the Merciful, the Compassionate
> the Compassionate the Compassionate   Say

Scripting a sacred source for Goethe's imitation, Paulus copies out the final words of Islamic revelation, allowing his pupil to begin his Arabic studies at the very end of the Qur'ān. In targeting this particular Qur'ānic chapter for Goethe's textual training, Paulus' selected source for linguistic study seems both apt and ironic. The closing words of the Qur'ān themselves imply an imperative "practice", demanding the reader to engage in oral repetition. Opening with a command – "Say!" ("قل") – this chapter of the Qur'ān seems highly conscious of its own performance, directing its audience to repeat and rehearse its content. Appearing to appreciate its authority, this very imperative is obeyed by Goethe, who reiterates a single term multiple times – "الرحيم" (*ar-raḥīm*; "the Compassionate") – after he himself inscribes the command to "Say!" ("قل"). Heeding divine directive at his page bottom, Goethe's interest is also drawn to the Divine Himself at page right; tracing a lone term alongside Paulus' inscription, Goethe here gravitates to "God" – "إله" (*"ilāh"*) – dedicating this single line in the margins to *Allāh* alone.

However, perhaps the most potent irony implied by the Arabic practice of Goethe's "Bl. 126" is simply its partial and fragmentary form. Copying and recopying Chapter 114, Paulus and Goethe engage in a Qur'ānic conversation that serves to open up the termination of the Muslim canon. Appealing to the scripture's definitive conclusion, Paulus and Goethe each offer an indefinite impression of this canonical climax, neglecting to complete the Qur'ān's own completion. Stopping two verses short of finishing Chapter 114, Paulus serves as an example for Goethe, who himself fails to copy out fully Paulus' own incomplete content, selecting only a few words from these sacred sentences to reproduce. Privileging process over production, "Bl. 126" reflects the tentative aims first expressed by Goethe in his 1815 letter, aspiring to "learn Arabic", yet admitting that his pedagogy will comprise mere "practice" (*"üben"*). In harmony with the "fragmentary imperative" associated with Romanticism more broadly, Goethe's imperfect attempts at Arabic – copying the very climax of the Qur'ān inconclusively in his own hand – also serves as an apt introduction to his own poetic practices, offering a fluid Arabic anticipation of the definitive Arabic opening to Goethe's *Divan*.[9]

III

Goethe's quiet and covert attraction to Arabic, renewed in 1814 and 1815, will receive an urgent and unmistakable announcement in 1819, emerging proudly on the very title page to his *West-östlicher Divan*. Advertized on the cover of his verse collection, Goethe's collaborative study of Arabic surrenders its private seclusion, occupying instead the most public of spaces. Ascribed a prominence and a profile very unlike his personal papers, the Arabic inscribed on the face of Goethe's *Divan* does recall his "Bl. 126", however, in its conversational character, featuring dual voices that are poised in uneven interview. Anticipating the twin title pages that will preface Hammer's *Prayerbook* in 1844, Goethe's 1819 *Divan* features a frontispiece with two distinct titles:

(Left-Hand Page)	(Right-Hand Page)

(Right-Hand Page)

West-oestlicher
DIVAN
von
GOETHE
Stuttgard
in der Cottaischen Buchhandlung
1819

الديوان الشرق
للمؤلف الغربي

Facing title pages of Goethe's 1819 West-östlicher Divan

Doubly named, the *Divan* opens with two sides and two languages, framed by both a German and an Arabic title.[10] However, it is the dueling content of these dual titles, rather than their distinct languages, that seems most surprising. Goethe's German title, printed on the right, supplies the most well-known label for his 1819 work, i.e. *West-östlicher Divan* (*"The West-Eastern Poetry Collection"*). Not customarily cited, however, is Goethe's facing title in Arabic, whose left-hand text reads:

الديوان الشرقي / للمؤلف الغربي

The Eastern Poetry Collection / of the Western Author

A fresh act of cultural overlap, Goethe offers an alternate Arabic title to his poetry collection, this unique language of "fusing together" here recruited at the *Divan*'s opening to offer a unique fusion of "East" and "West". However, in this synthesis of language and label, a surprising asymmetry also surfaces. Although mirrored together on right and left, Goethe's two titles clearly mistranslate each other, welcoming readers into a work with not one, but rather two, distinct identities. In the language of the West, the poem is heralded as a hyphenated marriage of *West* and *East* ("*West-östlicher*"). However, in the language of the East, the "Collection" is "Eastern", while the "Author" is "Western"; according to his Arabic title, Goethe's "*Divan*" is from the East ("الشرقي"), while he himself is from the West ("الغربي"). Bearing an "Occidental" title of synthesis, as well as an "Oriental" title of separation, the *Divan* offers itself to readers as an uneasy balance, with labels of coalition and partition tensely aligned in its opening two pages.[11]

Recalling the millennial monument subsequently inspired by Goethe's *Divan* – Weimar's *Goethe-Hafis Denkmal*, opened in 2000 – his 1819 *Divan* itself seems a shrine that straddles plurality and unity, its diverse languages suggesting confrontation and exchange. Prefacing his German poem with an Arabic title, it is Goethe himself who is implied in linguistic difference, his familiar text presented as a foreign agent, with creator and creation alternately juxtaposed as representing Occident and Orient. However, amid its complex significance, it is easy to overlook that Goethe's Arabic title page also lacks significant details. While Goethe's "Western" title grounds itself in person, place and publisher – "Goethe"; "Stuttgard"; "Cotta", adding too the *Divan*'s date, "1819" – these mundane descriptors melt away in Goethe's "Eastern" title, its stylized Arabic script erasing all sense of this text's published contexts. Identified generically and grandly as "the Western writer", Goethe's Arabic persona is free of personal specificity and signature, solely defined as the author of an "Eastern *Divan*". Subtly anticipating the Arabic façade of Hammer's Austrian home – Schloss Hainfeld – the Arabic frontispiece of Goethe's poem recalibrates calendar and context, not by adding an Islamic date, but by removing all European detail. Inspired by Hammer's own 1812–1813 translation, a more specific debt to Hammer emerges in the dual title pages of Goethe's 1819 *Divan*, justifying further the lavish tribute to "VON HAMMER" articulated in his *Notes and Essays*. Revising its own cultural identity through Arabic inscription, the 1819 *Divan* does indeed seem beholden in "every part" to Hammer's example, with Goethe's "little book" recalling the multilingual monuments that punctuate the Austrian's own biography, rehearsing not only the scholarly sources, but also the personal pursuits, of "this worthy man".

6

"Is the Qur'an from eternity?": Goethe's *Divan* and the "Book of Books"

I

Advancing beyond the *Divan*'s dual title and reaching its core text, readers find Goethe's bilingual facade bleeding into the body of his poem.[1] A collection of more than two hundred discrete pieces, the 1819 *Divan* is structured loosely into twelve "books", each of which features *two* titles, representing East and West, written in Persian and German. The *Divan*'s initial book, for instance, is doubly branded as both *Moganni Nameh* and *Buch des Sängers* – i.e. "Book of the Singer" in transliterated Persian, and German translation.[2] Organized under such linguistically diverse labels, the *Divan*'s poems also seem suitably diverse in their literary form. From quatrains to couplets, from regular stanzas to irregular rhymes, Goethe experiments with prosodies and personae in his *Divan*, interspersing a range of styles and speakers throughout his lyrics. Establishing an epic conversation between identities across scriptures, mythologies, and histories, Goethe's verses feature an ample cast of characters, voicing their own cultures and commitments. Dialogues between divergent figures infuse the *Divan*'s twelve books, pairing together Persian poets, Qur'ānic patriarchs, and even the Muslim Prophet himself. Although ostensibly a poetry collection, the *Divan* occasionally reads like a drama, with distinct personalities performing discrete parts. Recalling his

earlier approaches to Islam, Goethe again offers a theatrical portrait of the East in his 1819 poem, with the *Divan* proving a more
successful, and more sympathetic, stage upon which Muslim identities interact and address his German audience.

This theatricality in the *Divan* emerges most urgently in its
second book, Goethe's "Book of Hafiz" – "*Hafis Nameh / Buch
Hafis*". As it is Ḥāfiẓ who factually served as Goethe's dialogic
partner in his authoring the *Divan*, it is apt that the *Divan*'s "Book
of Hafiz" also develops a fictive dialogue, setting the German and
Persian poets in lively debate. Included at the beginning of this
second book is a poem entitled "Surname" ("*Beiname*"), which
features two characters in conversation: "Hafiz" and "The Poet",
the latter often understood as a surrogate for "Goethe himself".[3]
A call and response, mirroring his collection's broader strategies
and structure, "Surname" finds Goethe interrogating his Persian
predecessor directly, with the *Divan* giving a distinct voice to
Ḥāfiẓ, even as Ḥāfiẓ had helped the *Divan* gain its own poetic
voice. Opening with invocation and interrogative, it is Ḥāfiẓ's
very name that supplies Goethe's focus from his beginning lines:

> Poet
> Tell me why, Muhammad Shamseddin,
> you are "*Hàfiz*" to
> Worthy folk.
>
> Hàfiz
> For asking, you
> Merit thanks. I answer, then:
> Legacy of the Qur'an
> I unaltered carry on
> Hallowed in my memory
> And, by acting piously,
> Daily every injury
> Ward away from me and those
> Who the Prophet-word and seed
> Treasure and their duty heed.
> So my name the people chose.

Poet
Hàfiz, it would seem to me
That I needn't yield to you:
Like another I will be
When I think as *he* would do.
We are quite alike, I see.
Taking in an image of
Value from the Book I love –
As upon a cloth that He
Image of the Lord impressed –
I revived in quiet breast
(Quelling foe, denier, thief)
With the image of belief.[4]

A dramatic dialogue passing between distinct personae, this dialogue also dramatizes issues of very personal concern, interrogating the identity of Ḥāfiẓ himself. Recalling his earliest efforts to parse Islamic language, Goethe's "Poet" opens by querying how best to read Ḥāfiẓ's pen-name: "why", Goethe asks, was *"Hàfiz"* so named by his "folk"? This external query quickly turns inward, however, defining not only the interviewee, but also the interviewer, with Goethe's own identity illuminated through his interrogation of Ḥāfiẓ. Reflecting the dual title pages and the bilingual books of the *Divan* as a whole, Ḥāfiẓ's explanation of his Eastern name leads the Western poet to assert that "We are quite alike". Mirrored as tandem twins, German and Persian poets occupy opposing positions in this cultural dialogue, yet they also emerge as identical in their nominal substance.

At the crux of this cross-cultural symmetry, however, is a holy source, with the Muslim scripture forming the "heart" of Ḥāfiẓ's own "surname". Appealing to the actual etymology of "Ḥāfiẓ", Goethe accurately links the "Persian poet" to the "legacy of the Qur'an", suggesting that it is Ḥāfiẓ's "unaltered carrying" of the sacred book of Islam which accounts for the "name" his "people chose", with the term "Ḥāfiẓ" implying a "memorizer" or "keeper", as emphasized in Chapter 4. Ironically, however, it is precisely this Islamic specificity that accounts for Ḥāfiẓ's

Western appeal. Possessing his holy "Book" by heart, Ḥāfiẓ becomes a Muslim mirror for the European poet, whose own "breast" is equally "imprinted" by a biblical "image". Inscribed with Western sacred writ, Goethe emerges as a German "Ḥāfiẓ", with both poets meriting this shared "name" due to their mutual memory and scriptural "retention". At the textual core of this West-East correspondence is the Qur'ān, the Muslim scripture marrying discrete identities through shared recollection. Reminiscent of its dialogic role in his Arabic pedagogy – with the Qur'ān and its calligraphy exchanged between Goethe and Paulus in 1815 – Islam's holy book now promotes dialogue with Persian poetry, allowing Goethe and Ḥāfiẓ to mirror each other in 1819. A primer for his personal study, the Qur'ān reaches back to Goethe's earliest preparations for the *Divan*; yet, the Qur'ān equally reaches forward, its influence unfolding in the imaginative outcomes of the *Divan*'s poetry.

II

Emerging in his early correspondence, the Qur'ān was of creative interest to Goethe from his career's very first years, citing sura 20 in his 1772 letter to Herder even while musing on his authorial aspirations. Initially tied to his artistic efforts, the Qur'ān continues to be aligned closely with aesthetic concerns for Goethe. Nearly a half century after surfacing in his personal correspondence, the Qur'ān is again aesthetically contextualized in Goethe's 1819 *Notes and Essays* – his critical accompaniment to the *Divan*, where Goethe describes the Qur'ān as a text of effective eloquence. Accenting the scripture's "style", Goethe describes the Muslim scripture as "austere, grand, fearsome, and in places truly sublime" – a style that also entirely befits its lofty "content and purpose".[5] However, Goethe also advances beyond mere abstract appreciation of the Qur'ān in 1819, constructing his *Divan*'s practical poetics from Qur'ānic adaptation, selecting "sublime" verses from the ancient scripture to serve as the

basis for his own German lyrics. Appealing in "Surname" to
Ḥāfiẓ's "carrying" of the Qur'ān, Goethe will follow his Persian
predecessor by "carrying" the Qur'ān over into new literary contexts, seeking to translate the scripture into his fresh secular lines.
However, unlike the "unaltered" retention of the scripture attributed to Ḥāfiẓ, Goethe will not merely "keep" Qur'ānic content,
but will opt instead to amend and add to its language, reshaping
Arabic origins to suit his Weimar modernity.

This revisionary process surfaces early in Goethe's collection,
informing the *Divan*'s introductory verses. Situated near the
beginning of his first book – "Book of the Singer" – are two poems
in tandem, Goethe's "Freethought", followed immediately by his
"Talismans" (i.e. "*Freisinn*" and "*Talismane*"). Emphasizing
natural beauty and supernatural wonder, and speaking in a "sublime" style, these dual poems offer an apt introduction to the
Divan, reflecting traits and themes that pervade Goethe's entire
collection. Aligned in their order and their expression, the final
stanza of "Freethought" and the first stanza of "Talismans",
which appear successively in the sequence of Goethe's 1819
Divan, are reproduced below:

Er hat euch die Gestirne gesetzt	[He set the stars, that you may guide
Als Leiter zu Land und See;	Your course, by land and sea;
Damit ihr euch daran ergötzt,	That you may take delight, beside,
Stets blickend in die Höh.	Looking up, steadily.
Gottes ist der Orient!	To God belongs the Orient!
Gottes ist der Okzident!	To God belongs the Occident!
Nord- und südliches Gelände	The Northern and the Southern lands,
Ruht im Frieden seiner Hände.	Resting, tranquil, in His hands.][6]

Spanning horizons of divine sovereignty, these two stanzas stress God's providential care, stretching from high to low, far to near, touching both "sky" and "sea", "East" and "West". Although sourced from discrete poems, a seamless transition seems to link the final lines of "Freethought" and the first lines of "Talisman". However, these two quatrains are connected not only through shared concern, but also through their sacred origins. It is not poetic coincidence, but rather Qur'ānic influence, that allows these stanzas to mirror each other, with the conclusion of "Freethought" and the introduction of "Talismans" both adopting and adapting language from the Muslim scripture. Each of these stanzas dedicates its initial two lines to Qur'ānic paraphrase. For instance, lines 1 and 2 from the final quatrain of "Freethought" – "He set the stars, that you may guide / Your course, by land and sea" – clearly recall the Qur'ān 6:97, which begins: "It is He who has appointed for you the stars, that by them you might be guided in the shadows of land and sea". Similarly, the initial couplet of "Talismans" opens with "To God belongs the Orient! / To God belongs the Occident!", two emphatic exclamations which seem mere extensions of the Qur'ān's own "To God belong the East and the West" (Q. 2:115).[7]

Informing the substance of his verses, the Islamic scripture also aids Goethe in shaping their structure and style, with his rhymes and rhythms determined by these translated quotations from the Qur'ān. Forming the first half of each stanza, Qur'ānic allusions set the aesthetic pace for Goethe's quatrains, suggesting assonances and alliterations that echo through the following lines. In "Freethought", for instance, Goethe's opening quotation from the Qur'ān 6:97 – "*Er hat euch die Gestirne gesetzt*" ("He set for you the stars") – establishes a determinative rhyme scheme, with its line-final "*gesetzt*" finding fulfillment in line 3's "*ergötzt*" ("take delight"; emphasis added). Alternately, in "Talismans", Goethe begins by stretching a single statement from the Islamic scripture into two lines: "*Gottes ist der Orient! / Gottes ist der Occident!*" ("To God belongs the Orient! / "To God belongs the Occident!") – an opening that invites him to innovate a pair of complementary lines, completing his quatrain with:

"Nord- und südliches Gelände / Ruht im Frieden seiner Hände" ("The Northern and the Southern lands, / Resting, tranquil, in His hands"). Matching the meaning of his lines 1 and 2, Goethe also dilates their divine directions, completing the Qur'ān's compass through adding "North" and "South" to "East" and "West". Establishing a call and response between sacred source and secular verses, this mirroring between Qur'ānic content and German creation seems to perform the very "likeness" that was first heralded between Goethe and Ḥāfiẓ, the former following the latter not only in "carrying over", but also in surveying new climates for, these Qur'ānic fragments.

The series of Islamic allusions interwoven throughout the *Divan* – exemplified succinctly in the successive stanzas which link "Freethought" with "Talismans" – often introduce Western audiences to the Qur'ān covertly, Goethe merging the scripture quietly and without comment into his own composition. Enjoying lines in their own language, Weimar readers would not likely have recognized their actual origins, unaware that while reading Goethe's "little book" they read verses derived from Islam's holy book. The Qur'ān's implicit contribution to the *Divan* is, however, occasionally made more explicit, with the scripture supplying Goethe's primary subject, as well as his secondary source. In the *Divan*'s ninth book, more than a hundred and fifty pages after his "Freethought" and "Talismans", Goethe includes a piece that openly addresses the Qur'ān; untitled, and cited solely by its initial verse – "Is the Qur'an from eternity?" ("*Ob der Koran von Ewigkeit sei?*") – Goethe's poem launches with the following lines:

> Is the Qur'an from eternity?
> That, I will not ask.
> Might the Qur'an created be?
> No answer – a thankless task.
> That it the Book of Books need be
> My Muslim faith made clear to me.[8]

Recalling "Surname" near the start of the *Divan*, "Is the Qur'an from eternity?" again situates the Muslim scripture at the center of Goethe's poetic questioning. However, unlike this earlier piece, Goethe's latter poem opens not with an interrogative, but rather with a refusal to "ask", declining to satisfy its own lead query regarding Qur'ānic origins. Similarly, while "Surname" had twinned German "Poet" and his Persian counterpart through their shared devotion to their divergent scriptures – the Qur'ān and the Bible – it is only the former which now surfaces in Goethe's "Is the Qur'an from eternity?" Silent as to the Bible's status, the German poet privileges the Qur'ān here as the "Book of Books", insisting on the Qur'ān's canonicity, ironically voicing this assumption of his "Muslim faith". Fanciful and playful, this confession of Qur'ānic fidelity nearing the end of the *Divan* also recalls Goethe's original aspiration to become "like" Ḥāfiẓ, helping him to realize his initial desire, mirroring the Persian poet's own commitment to the Qur'ān. The potency of Goethe's faithful allusion to the "Qur'ān" is heightened by its surfacing in a debate concerning "creation" in his *Divan* – a work which has itself engaged in audacious acts of Qur'ānic creation, building its own artistry from the foundations of Muslim scripture. Addressing issues directly which have previously been performed quietly, the *Divan* here declares its Qur'ānic debt, Goethe's "little book" acknowledging itself as a mere offspring of a superlative bibliographic class – a created successor to the "eternal" and elative "Book of Books".[9]

III

Writing from Weimar to Karl Ludwig von Knebel on February 22, 1815, Charlotte Schiller offered a report on recent events at home, including a "small" and "genial" soirée hosted by Weimar's duchess, Louisa. Occupying the center of this friendly company in 1815 would be a familiar presence – J. W. Goethe himself – the aged poet lecturing to this cozy assembly on his latest "engagement with the Orient". Intrigued by his efforts, Charlotte Schiller observes excitedly to her friend that "Persian poetry is extremely remarkable", recalling how "Goethe read to us from Firdawsi's poem, which has 120,000 verses, and 60,000 distiches". Completing her account, Schiller closes by expressing her hopes for future instruction, predicting and projecting Goethe's return to the salon in the coming weeks. "We are to hear also something from the Koran", she insists to Knebel, adding that "The Duchess is very excited for this reading, and all [the rest of] us not any less".[10]

As the wife of Friedrich Schiller, Charlotte's 1815 account of Goethe's Islamic "lectures" inevitably recalls a similar reading given by Goethe a decade and a half earlier. Delivered to an aristocratic and intimate elite, Goethe's recital of Persian poetry offers a striking parallel to his previous "recital" of his translated *Mahomet*; however, rather than Friedrich Schiller and the Duke Karl August, it is their wives that instead form Goethe's target audience, sharing his Islamic efforts with distinguished women, not only Charlotte Schiller, but Duchess Louisa herself. And while in 1800 Goethe's source text would represent a French satire on the Muslim Prophet, in 1815 he is requested to recite from the Muslim scripture itself, no longer producing mere European burlesque, but performing the actual Qur'ān. Expressing the wish of her select company to "hear something from the Koran", Charlotte's desire was apparently fulfilled in the subsequent days, Goethe returning to Weimar's regal household to lecture from the Muslim scripture for this close-knit gathering.[11]

Surprising as it is to find Islamic sources enduring as an interest of the Weimar elite, it is even more surprising to find this progressive interest following a regressive pattern, gravitating to more authentic and more original Islamic moments even as Goethe and his circle move onward towards European futures. While Goethe had staged for the Duchess a belated play on the Prophet in January 1800, Goethe returns in 1815 to deliver a reading of Islamic authenticity, no longer reciting mere interpretive theater, but instead, pronouncing the religion's own revelation. Paralleling his Arabic efforts from precisely this time – writing to Schlosser also during the first days of 1815, confessing his wish to approach Arabic's organic and original "script" – Goethe nears Islamic beginnings even as his life nears its own end, pursuing a genealogy of Eastern return that culminates in old age. Perhaps most importantly, it is again the Qur'ān which plays a pivotal role in Goethe's retrograde progress – a text that he will not only lecture on in 1815, but which continues to occupy his literary focus as he approaches death in 1832. Five years before his demise, Goethe would republish his *Divan*, offering readers not only a revised edition, but also an expanded one, enlarging his 1819 collection to include fresh, original poems. Appearing for the first time in this 1827 edition would be another untitled piece on the Qur'ān – a poem which also situates the scripture at the heart of temporal processes, positioned between prophecy and memory:

> Of old the sacred Koran did they cite,
> They named the verse and chapter ever blest,
> And each good Muslim, as was but right,
> Reverenced, and felt his conscience was at rest.
> The modern Dervish nothing better knows,
> But prates of old and new with endless zest;
> Each day our most admired disorder grows.
> O sacred Koran! O eternal rest![12]

Newly revising and reviving his *Divan* in advanced age, it is fitting that Goethe pens this poem that itself balances "new" and "old". Nostalgically recalling an earlier era, in which "Muslim" scripture was distinctly "named" – its "verse and chapter" precisely cited – Goethe's poem also critiques the "modern", lampooning contemporaries as they "prat[e] of old and new with endless zest". It is the suggested remedy to these worsening conditions, however, that seems most striking in Goethe's poem; confronted "each day" with the "growth" of "disorder", the poet takes refuge in a climactic invocation, exclaiming finally: "O sacred Koran! O eternal rest!"

Offering this new extension to his earlier *Divan* – a *Divan* which itself revises antiquity, remaking the original *Divan* of Ḥāfiẓ

– Goethe dramatizes the tensions between progress and memory, even while gesturing to an "eternal" scripture, the Qur'ān attributed to a time outside of time, transcending incremental development and inevitable decay. Interrogating literary evolution, even while his own literary efforts evolve, Goethe laments a bygone time, when "verse and chapter" was "named" with ease, authoring an elegy on scriptural memory which itself recalls the Qur'ān, returning to remember this "sacred" Muslim source in its very last line. Recalling the progress of Goethe's own biography, and its imminent end, this untitled poem seems too to anticipate Goethe's own "eternal rest", marking a poignant moment before his own death, articulating a valediction which bewails, yet ultimately breaks from, both "old and new". If retrograde in perspective, this Islamically-informed poem more subtly points forward to Goethe's own Islamic afterlives, gesturing to the millennial memorial that will be dedicated to Goethe's multicultural memory in the streets of Weimar – a memorial in which Goethe is materially married to Ḥāfiẓ, confronting the very "keeper" of the "sacred Koran" himself, the German's "eternal rest" mirrored in a Persian poet whose own title derives from his capacity to "cite" the "verse and chapter ever blest".

7

"The Flight and Return of Mohammed": S. T. Coleridge and Robert Southey

I

In the middle months of 1799, Goethe began crafting Voltaire's *Mahomet* for the Weimar stage, translating this French *Tragedy* while consulting his close friend and neighbor, Friedrich Schiller. During these very same months, a parallel partnership surfaced in Britain, pairing two of England's most prominent Romantics, drafting together their own theatrical treatment of "Mahomet". Initiated in the late summer and early fall of 1799, Samuel Taylor Coleridge and Robert Southey would collaborate to produce a lyric poem on the Muslim Prophet, seeking to reimagine Islamic origins in English verse. Provisionally entitled "The Flight and Return of Mohammed", this epic in embryo was exchanged between Coleridge and Southey even as Goethe and Schiller exchanged letters on *Mahomet* – a striking coincidence in time and topic, stretching across Romanticisms, European and British.[1]

This international overlap seems less surprising in light of shared trends shaping the literary worlds of British and German authors on the verge of the nineteenth century. Fascinated by Napoleon's forceful incursion into Egypt, invading Alexandria exactly a year earlier – in July 1798 – Romantic poets reveled in both Revolutionary and Oriental themes, picturing the Prophet's career as an ambivalent allegory for Napoleon's conquests.[2] For

British authors, however, 1798 would signal not only political revolution abroad, but also literary revolution at home, witnessing the most iconic of Romantic collaborations: Wordsworth and Coleridge's *Lyrical Ballads*, printed in August 1798. And yet, it is German climates, as much as British contexts, that seem to link the parallel Islamic appeals of Goethe-Schiller and Coleridge-Southey. During the summer of 1799, the very months that the British "Flight and Return of Mohammed" first surfaced, Coleridge had himself just "returned" to Britain, completing his formative sojourn in Germany, begun the year before. Exposed to a heady mix of German philosophy, biblical criticism, and Orientalism, and breathing an artistic atmosphere impressed by Goethean influence, Coleridge arrived back in Britain in July 1799, and soon started a poem on the Muslim Prophet, working with Southey at home in Somerset, while doubtlessly brooding on his recent journeys abroad.[3]

Equipped with such complex foregrounds – personal and historical, Eastern and European – the British "Flight and Return of Mohammed" nevertheless failed to take wing; abandoned by the end of 1799, the poem progressed no further than mere sketches and selections. Drafted during the same period that finds Coleridge possibly revising his most famous Oriental fantasy – his "Kubla Khan" – the collaborative "Flight and Return of Mohammed" seems to share little with such sibling poems, comprising "a fragment" that is now mostly forgotten, not merely overshadowed by more advanced pieces, but largely overlooked by later critics.[4] What remains of this aborted effort, however, testifies to an Islamic influence on British Romanticism that intriguingly echoes earlier German receptions. The lone lines that survive from Coleridge's own contribution to "The Flight and Return of Mohammed" form the poem's intended introduction, launching "The Flight" with the following verses:

> UTTER the song, O my soul! the flight and return of
>   Mohammed,
> Prophet and priest, who scatter'd abroad both evil and
>   blessing,

Huge wasteful empires founded and hallow'd slow
      persecution,
Soul-withering, but crush'd the blasphemous rites of the
      pagan
And idolatrous christians. – For veiling the gospel of
      Jesus,
They, the best corrupting, had made it worse than the
      vilest.
Wherefore heaven decreed th' enthusiast warrior of
      Mecca,
Choosing good from iniquity rather than evil from
      goodness.
Loud the tumult in Mecca surrounding the fane of the
      idol; –
Naked and prostrate the priesthood were laid – the people
      with mad shouts
Thundering now, and now with saddest ululation
Flew, as over the channel of rock-stone the ruinous river
Shatters its waters abreast, and in mazy uproar
      bewilder'd,
Rushes dividuous all – all rushing impetuous onward.[5]

Mimicking a Miltonic mood, Coleridge opens with a blank-verse preface, introducing this prophetic poem with an epic invocation, summarizing its argument and sketching its initial action. Rather than seek support from an external Muse, Coleridge starts instead with an inward imperative, urging his own "soul" to "Utter the song". Searching his Romantic interior for Islamic exteriors, the Prophet's story begins with Coleridge's own personal space, finding this foreign religion reflected in his familiar spirit.[6]

   Such complexities and contrasts seem also to multiply through these initial lines, Coleridge playing with the polarities suggested by the poem's title, balancing not only "flight" and "return", but also "prophet" and "priest", "evil" and "blessing". This ambivalence emerges too in Coleridge's depiction of Islam itself; although associated with "[s]oul-withering", the Prophet's mission is also portrayed more sympathetically, "crush[ing]", for instance, "the blasphemous rites of the pagan". Identified as a religious reformer, "Mohammed" is seen struggling against those who "veil" the "gospel of Jesus", with Coleridge high-lighting a critique of "idolatrous christians" that mirrors his own concerns at the end of the eighteenth century – a period in which Coleridge's attraction to Unitarianism too resists tradi-tional Christian teachings, a connection which Humberto Garcia has recently emphasized.[7] Most familiar in this brief selection, however, is its conclusion, recalling not Coleridge's own priori-ties, but his German predecessors. In a complex series of aquatic conceits, Coleridge characterizes the Meccan "people" as a "rushing" of "waters", seeming to echo Goethe's own "Song to Mahomet", associating Islamic origins with a "river" that surges irresistibly onward. However, while Goethe finds "Mahomet" a sublime stream, it is Muḥammad's opponents that are defined by Coleridge as a river both "ruinous" and "impetuous" – a simile that again privileges the Prophet, yet inverts Goethe's marine metaphors. Recalling earlier Continental imagery, as much as early Islamic history, Coleridge's brief introduction to the abandoned "The Flight and Return of Mohammed" hints at the ambivalent awe that will catalyze Romantic representations of the Prophet as the British century comes to a close – represen-tations that seem most to recall not Goethe's satiric *Mahomet: A Tragedy* in 1799, but rather his sublime "Song to Mahomet" twenty-five years before.

II

Increasingly attracted to other projects through the fall of 1799, Coleridge's concern with "The Flight and Return of Mohammed" soon waned. The project enjoyed more sustained interest, how-ever, from Coleridge's collaborator, Robert Southey. Britain's future poet laureate, Southey had only just begun to win recogni-tion in 1799, authoring recent successes such as *Joan of Arc: An*

Epic Poem (1796, 1798) which had garnered Southey "a modest degree of fame".[8] A pivotal period for his career, marking the midway between relative anonymity and national celebrity, the very middle of 1799 finds Southey engaged not with his own advancement, however, but rather with Islamic origins. Previewing his collaboration with Coleridge, Southey's personal correspondence in the summer of 1799 evidences his Islamic interests, writing to John May from Minehead in Somerset:

> Of the few books with me I am most engaged by the Koran: it is dull and full of repetitions, but there is an interesting simplicity in the tenets it inculcates. What was Mohammed? self-deceived, or knowingly a deceiver? If an enthusiast, the question again recurs, wherein does real inspiration differ from mistaken? This is a question that puzzles me, because to the individual they are the same, and both effects equally proceed from the first Impeller of all motions, who must have ordained whatever he permits. In this train of reasoning I suspect a fallacy, but cannot discover it.[9]

Anticipating the ambivalence that pervades Coleridge's introduction to the "Flight and Return" are Southey's own "questions" concerning "Mohammed", "puzzling" over the Prophet, posing query after query regarding his "mistaken" motives. This confused "train of reasoning" opens not with the Prophet's character, however, but with "the Koran" – a text which stands at the root of Southey's ambivalence, depicted as entirely "dull", yet persistently "interesting". A mirror for his own reflections, Southey's "Koran" is "full of repetitions", even as Southey's own "question[s]" continue to "recur", endlessly "engaged" by this repetitious source. Haunted by a question laden with Romantic resonance, Southey's queries are centered in the problematic "difference" between "real inspiration" and the "mistaken" – a difference between subjective illusion and truthful subject, between mere madness and genuine revelation. Reductively associating the Prophet with a dichotomy between deception and self-deception,

Southey is yet still compelled to grapple with a single question of "interesting simplicity", namely "What was Mohammed?" – a question that "recurs" not only in Southey's 1799 correspondence, but which will prove a "repetitious" interest for British Romanticism more broadly.

From personal correspondence to collaborative poetry, Southey's simple question concerning "Mohammed" emerges also at the very opening to his own draft material for "The Flight and Return of Mohammed". More substantial than Coleridge's aborted introduction, Southey penned over a hundred lines for their prophetic poem, launching his own verses with a query:

> Cloakd in the garment of green, who lies on the bed of Mohammed,
> Restless and full of fear, yet semblant of one that is sleeping?[10]

Recalling his informal letter, Southey's formal poetry begins with a question of intimate identity, asking "who" occupies the Prophet's most personal place: "who lies on the bed of Mohammed"? Befitting its epic aspirations, Southey's meager fragment starts *in medias res*, opening in the midst of the Prophet's mission, at the very moment of his "flight" from Mecca.[11] However, it is not "Mohammed", but rather his trusted son-in-law – 'Alī – that here wears "the garment of green"; bravely serving as the Prophet's surrogate in order to hide his escape, 'Alī is the "semblant" of the "one that is sleeping". Dramatizing a moment from sacred history, this opening substitution also seems to hint at Southey's own puzzlement at the Prophet, mirroring Southey's vain struggles to "discover" the Islamic founder. Not merely "cloakd", but entirely absent, from this opening, the Prophet eludes the English poet himself, these lines reflecting Southey's own "restless" attempts to distinguish "real" character from "mistaken", yet continually misled by a mere "semblant" of "Mohammed".

These first lines launch a pursuit of the Prophet that evolves both within and without Southey's poem as its dramatic action unfolds. After depicting 'Alī's courageous deception,

Southey broadens perspective to consider diverse reactions to Muḥammad's "flight" from both his opponents and adherents. Focusing first on the Prophet's Meccan oppressors, Southey pivots in the middle of the passage below, shifting to consider Muḥammad's early Muslim community:

> Follow, follow the Chosen one's flight! – they rush from
>   the city
> Over the plain they pursue him, pursue him with cries &
>   with curses
> Sound that rung over the plain & rung in the echoing
>   mountain
> And Mecca received in her streets the din of their clamor-
>   ous uproar
> But the voices of the Moslem, the silent prayer of the
>   faithful
> Rose to the throne of God, & tears of the heart
>   overflowing
> Interceded for him whom they lovd & believed his
>   Apostle.[12]

Offering his reader contradictory "voices", Southey contrasts the "cries" and "curses" of the Prophet's enemies with "the silent prayer" whispered by the Muslim "faithful". Divided by antagonism and appreciation of the "Apostle", these lines are equally divided aesthetically, recruiting opposing styles to convey their significance. Describing the hostile hunters of the "Chosen one", Southey's opening verses are packed with "rushed" repetition, from line 1's "Follow, follow", to line 2's "pursue him, pursue him", reaching also line 3's "rung over ... & rung in". Alternately, the style of the passage's second half is itself "serene", slower and "flowing" as it describes the Muslim response. Implicitly inverting his 1799 letter – which had critiqued Islamic scripture as "full of repetitions" – Southey here associates the anti-Islamic with raucous repetition, contrasting the "din" of the Meccan's "clamorous uproar" with the solemn "tears of the heart" that afflict Muḥammad's followers. Offering content that seemingly sympathizes with "Moslem" over non-Muslim, Southey's style also subtly emphasizes Islamic "serenity", contrasting the mad "restlessness" of Muḥammad's enemies, who rush vertically "over the plain", with the silent ascent of the "faithful", whose prayers "rose" horizontally to the sedate "Throne of God" itself.

III

This aesthetic empathy with the "Moslem" community amplifies as Southey's poem reaches its actual subject: the Prophet himself. Surfacing finally in line 56, "Mohammed" assumes the stage again through an act of interrogation, Southey still surrounding the "Chosen one" with personal queries. However, instead of asking questions *concerning* the Prophet, Southey now asks questions *of* the Prophet, interrogating him directly; discovering "Mohammed" as he hides from his enemies – the "Koreish" – the poet asks:

> Was thy Spirit shaken, Mohammed:
> When in the depth of the rock thou heardest the voice of the Koreish?
> He who was with thee trembled, the sweat on his forehead was chilly,
> And his eyes in alarm were turnd towards thee in the darkness.
> Silent they sat in the rock, nor moved they, nor breathd they, but listend
> Long to the sound of the feet, their fainter & fainter sounding
> Died in the distance now, – yet still they were silent & listend.
> Abubeker first, as his fear gave faith to the echo
> Fresh in his sense alarmd – "hark! hark! I hear them returning

"They are many & we but two! –" he whisperd in terror.
"There is a third," aloud replied the Son of Abdallah
  – "GOD."[13]

Concealed in a cave with his close ally, "Abubeker", the Prophet occupies a tableau of quiet "terror", its deep interior "silence" contrasted with the external "voice of the Koreish". This "silent" scene opens, however, with an emphatic interrogative, Southey's narrator querying the hero of his narration, asking his protagonist even as he faces peril "Was thy Spirit shaken[?]" – a question that again echoes Southey's prior puzzlement, debating the Prophet's psychic state. However, unlike his previous letter to John May, Southey's poetic lines offer an oblique answer to his repeated questions. Shifting from interior "spirit" to exterior "reply", rising from deep "silence" to speech "aloud", Southey's passage concludes with resounding capitals; confronting his companion's "alarmd" assertion, the Prophet offers reassurance, testifying to the unseen attendance and assistance of "GOD". Juxtaposed with the "terror" and "tremble" of "Abubeker" – with his "chilly ... forehead" and "eyes in alarm" – Southey presents a Prophet who is assured of providence, ironically answering not only doubts expressed within the drama, but also the doubts experienced without, allowing Southey's own poem to address its poet's skepticism.

This confidence displayed by "Mohammed" is itself tested, however, as Southey's fragment reaches its conclusion. Informed that his wife "Cadijah" has fallen ill – that she "Lies on her bed of pain" – the Prophet is depicted as distraught, debating whether he should return to Mecca despite its obvious dangers. Urged by 'Alī to remain away, Southey's draft closes with the following lines:

Mohammed heard & he bowed his head & groand for his
  exile.
"Tell her," at length he cried, "to trust in the Lord her
  Creator,
"In me his apostle. tell her the way of Death shall be
  pleasant,

"For she was faithful on earth, & the gates of Paradise
   open.
"Bid her rejoice in her God. – but is it not long to the
   morning?
"Perhaps unseen I can enter the city & bless her
"Ere she departs."
   "Not so! it were death," said Ali "to venture
"Prophet of God remain! thy duty is self-preservation.
"Remember thy lofty task!¹⁴

Confronted now with his wife's suffering, not threats to his own
safety, the Prophet is no longer able to voice "aloud" in confidence, but instead gives vent to his distress through "groaning"
and "crying". However, this final scene also recalls the Prophet's
first scene, terminating again with celestial "trust"; blessing his
wife from afar, Muḥammad assures "Cadijah" that her "way
of Death shall be pleasant". Even as the prayers of the Muslim
"faithful" had "risen up" to "the throne of God" at the beginning of Southey's poem, its conclusion "opens" up the "gates of
Paradise", shifting perspective from trials "on earth" to heavenly
rewards above.

The abrupt last line of Southey's poem reflects its unfinished state. And yet, an unintended completeness and coher-
ence seems suggested in this suspenseful conclusion. Mirroring
the very first lines of his poem, Southey's final lines of "The
Flight and Return of Mohammed" again center on "Ali", who
no longer preserves the Prophet through aiding his escape, but
preserves the Prophet through pressing him to "remain". And
while Southey's fragment never reaches the victorious "return"
heralded in its title, its "exilic" ending is aptly Romantic, picturing a Prophet who is "unseen" in the streets of the "city", yet
feels impelled to "enter & bless". Perhaps most promising and
prescient is 'Alī's valediction to Muḥammad, "Remember thy
lofty task!" – an Islamic imperative that caps not only Southey's
unfinished poem, but an Islamic imperative that will enjoy its
own unfinished afterlife, echoing through Romanticism's poetic
futures. Coleridge and Southey's "The Flight and Return of

Mohammed" will be gradually forgotten as 1799 ends and 1800 begins; however, the poem's "lofty task" of portraying the Prophet will be vividly "remembered" by Southey himself, receiving expression in his next poem – a poem with its origins also in 1799, composed during the very same time as his "Flight of Mohammed", and covertly offering its own literary means of the Prophet's "Return".

8

"The all-beholding Prophet's aweful voice": Southey's *Thalaba the Destroyer*

I

Writing to Coleridge on December 5, 1799, Southey offered a lively report on his recent literary efforts, eagerly announcing the progress of his latest project, prospectively entitled *Thalaba*. "It will be a good poem", Southey declares, "I know it".[1] With "half the fifth book" now completed, yet asserting that "it must extend to twelve", Southey acknowledges to Coleridge the obscurity of his title character ("Thalaba" himself), adding breathlessly: "Thalaba is not quite so popular a name – but he will not be found wanting when weighed in the balance. – Mohammed occupies a corner of my brain – one of the chambers – my heart is in the hexameter business."[2] Advancing forward to poetic futures, engaged in his evolving *Thalaba*, Southey yet gravitates back to poetic pasts, still reluctant to relinquish "Mohammed" – a project of "hexameter[s]" long ago abandoned by Southey's collaborator and correspondent, Coleridge. Recalling the brief fragments that survive from their aborted "Flight and Return of Mohammed", Southey's own "Mohammed" still survives here in literary fragments, surfacing between informal dashes in this hurried letter to Coleridge. No longer buried in the "depth of the rock" in Southey's poem, the Prophet is now buried in the poet's own psyche, "occupying a corner of" Southey's "brain". Previously fleeing to hide in Southey's dramatic verses, "Mohammed" is now hidden within Southey's own "heart", secreted in "one of the chambers" of his remote interior.

Perhaps more significant than the persistent "return" of "Mohammed" for Southey is this project's fresh associations, here twinned with a new "name": "Thalaba". Privately anxious about the "popularity" of this identity in 1799, Southey's *Thalaba* will indeed prove unpopular, rejected by critics soon after its 1801 publication. Appearing as the twelve-book *Thalaba the Destroyer*, Southey's epic would quickly come under attack, critiqued most famously in the *Edinburgh Review* by Francis Jeffrey, who regarded Southey suspiciously as "one of the leaders of a new poetic school": Romanticism.[3] Yet, as Southey presciently predicted in his letter to Coleridge, *Thalaba* would ultimately "not be found wanting when weighed in the balance", playing a profound role in promoting Romantic Orientalism, impacting not only Southey's British friends and successors – e.g. Coleridge and Percy Bysshe Shelley – but also leaving transatlantic traces, influencing American authors such as Edgar Allan Poe.[4] However, if "weighty" in its literary influence, Southey's *Thalaba* does initially seem somewhat "imbalanced" in its literary composition, uneasily negotiating a range of poetic commitments. Formulated by Southey while working on other projects – including his unfinished "Flight and Return of Mohammed" – *Thalaba* marks a shift in Southey's approach and attention, moving away from religious history and towards mythic fantasy. Inspired not by Islamic origins merely, but also by Orientalist adaptations, *Thalaba* is indebted especially to Robert Heron's *Arabian Tales, or, A Continuation of the Arabian Nights Entertainments* – a 1792 English translation of a French fiction. As Tim Fulford recognizes, it was from this "collection of Oriental tales" that Southey borrowed the story of "the Dom Daniel" – a den "under the deepest abysses of the ocean" that serves as "the seminary of the evil magicians".[5] A significant setting for Southey's "metrical romance", *Thalaba* ultimately concludes in "the Dom Daniel" den, where Thalaba himself vanquishes the epic's primary villains.

Despite its mythic depths, Southey's December 1799 letter to Coleridge suggests a kinship between *Thalaba* and their "Mohammed", with the religious concerns of their prophetic poem filtering into the core of Southey's fiction. The Islamic foregrounds to *Thalaba* – implied by Southey's letter two years before its publication – would be concretely articulated by Southey many years after *Thalaba*'s appearance. Writing retrospectively in 1838, Southey recalls that his 1801 *Thalaba the Destroyer* "was professedly an Arabian tale", seeking to highlight "the best features of the [Muslim] system of belief and worship", while also "placing in the most favorable light the morality of the Koran". Indeed, Southey even traces his authorship of *Thalaba* to an Islamic appeal: "I began with the Mahommedan religion, as being that, with which I was then best acquainted myself, and of which every one who had read the Arabian Nights' Entertainments possessed all the knowledge necessary for readily understanding and entering into the intent and spirit of the poem."[6] Starting with neither literary setting nor literary symbol, *Thalaba* instead "began" with "religion" – indeed, "with the Mahommedan religion" – the poem's "spirit" emanating from a historical faith. However, this factual foreground for *Thalaba* is itself colored with creative fantasy, Southey suggesting that the fictive "Arabian Nights' Entertainments" had furnished his audience with ample "understanding" of the poem's "Mahommedan" motives. Recalling his previous correspondence with Coleridge – marrying the abandoned "Mohammed" with mythic "Thalaba" – Southey's later reflections seem to imply a similarly rich hybrid, merging religious research and imaginative invention, a merger that will climax conclusively in the final lines of *Thalaba the Destroyer*.

II

A classic quest narrative, Southey's twelve books trace the episodic trials of Thalaba, whose story of heroic sacrifice would lead Southey to liken him to "a male Joan of Arc".[7] Undertaking a "divinely-appointed mission to destroy the idolatrous enemies of his religion", as Fulford asserts, Thalaba traverses foreign countries and grapples with fantastic characters, defeating magicians and defending maidens.[8] Universal in its mythic themes, *Thalaba* nevertheless centers on images that are specifically Islamic, traversing distinctly Muslim settings and scenery. Invoking Arabic names original to Islamic scripture – including people, such as "the Prophet Houd", and places, such as "the Garden of Irem" – Southey also features characters from Muslim literary culture, including "the Simourg", the celestial bird who resides on Mount "Kaf".[9] And while Southey "began with the Mahommedan religion", assuming his audience's "possession" of "all the knowledge necessary", *Thalaba* nevertheless finds it "necessary" to furnish its reader with a myriad of learned endnotes, striving to explain its exotic referents with English annotations. Again merging fiction and fact, Southey supplements his creative verses with notes that emphasize historical verity, shading his subjective artistry with a sense of academic objectivity.[10]

Indeed, it is in comparing *Thalaba*'s primary text to its secondary notes that Southey's straddle between religious history and fictive fantasy becomes most urgently apparent. In Book VII, for instance, Thalaba pledges the destruction of an enemy sorcerer, "Aloadin", uttering the following lines:

> "Now for this child of Hell!" quoth Thalaba,
>   "Belike he shall exchange to day
>   His dainty Paradise
>   For other dwelling, and the fruit
>   Of Zaccoum, cursed tree."[11]

The initial lines of this passage should present no problem for Southey's readers, with Thalaba's rant relatively free of foreign reference. The final words uttered by Southey's hero, however, enter unknown territory, invoking an expression which is entirely alien: "Zaccoum". An unmistakably exotic borrowing, Southey anticipates his audience's confusion, appending an explanatory note to ensure their accurate understanding:

> The Zaccoum is a tree which issueth from the bottom of Hell: the fruit thereof resembleth the heads of Devils; and the damned shall eat of the same, and shall fill their bellies therewith; and there shall be given them thereon a mixture of boiling water to drink; afterwards shall they return to Hell. *Koran, Chap. 37.*[12]

Not a clarification merely, but rather a citation, Southey explains his literary usage through supplying his readers with a scriptural translation, quoting from the 37th chapter of the *"Koran"*. Seemingly a simple tool for parsing this Arabic term, Southey's citation recruits the Qur'ān as a proof text for his own poetry, infusing his own English verse with verses from Islamic revelation. Although Southey will describe *Thalaba* as situating "the morality of the Koran" in "the most favorable light", it is the *"Koran"* which here enlightens Southey's *Thalaba*, the hellish "tree" of his fictive lyrics cultivated from fertile Islamic soil.

Replanting his own reference to "Zaccoum" back in the Muslim scripture, Southey again blurs the lines between British myth and "the Mahommedan religion", with sacred terms from Muslim sources surfacing in the centers and margins of his poetic pages, infusing both *Thalaba's* body text and its endnotes. Recruiting the Qur'ān for his creative purposes, Southey performs a literal and literary rendition, offering an actual translation of this Islamic text in his own paratexts, even while cultivating new contexts for the *"Koran"* in his own epic narrative. Grafting "Zaccoum", the "cursed tree", into his own growing stanzas, this Qur'ānic term plays a pivotal role in Southey's poetic scheme, not only offering a vivid image, but also helping to satisfy the poem's irregular meter, fulfilling the six syllables required in this particular line. Providing the roots for his mythic poetry even while rooting himself in the spiritual world of Muslim scripture, Southey's own note itself "issueth from the bottom" of his verse production, his *Thalaba* ingesting this fruitful allusion from the Qur'ān, even as

Thalaba himself threatens his enemy with a taste of his promised perdition.[13]

III

Such tensions between *Thalaba*'s Islamic origins and its Orientalist innovations – between Southey's poetic text and his Qur'ānic paratexts – leads to a dramatic collision in the romance's dénouement. Allusions to Muslim sources surface throughout Southey's twelve books; however, it is the allusive last lines of *Thalaba*'s last book that seem most complex, ironically recalling the poem's own beginnings, and its "Mahommedan" backgrounds. The end of Southey's epic envisions its hero's "destructive" victory, with Thalaba's odyssey coming to a close as he overcomes "Okba", one of the "magicians" of "Dom Daniel". Reaching the poem's final episode, Southey portrays his protagonist as he confronts this "desperate wretch" who has "spread" his vanquished "bosom to the stroke":

> "Old man, I strike thee not!" said Thalaba,
> "The evil thou hast done to me and mine
>   Brought its own bitter punishment.
> For thy dear Daughter's sake I pardon thee,
> As I do hope Heaven's pardon. For her sake
> Repent while time is yet! Thou hast my prayers
> To aid thee; thou poor sinner, cast thyself
> Upon the goodness of offended God!
> I speak in Laila's name, and what if now
> Thou canst not think to join in Paradise
> Her spotless Spirit, . . . hath not Allah made
> Al-Araf in his wisdom? where the sight
> Of Heaven shall kindle in the penitent
> The strong and purifying fire of hope,
> Till at the day of judgement he shall see
>   The Mercy-Gates unfold.[14]

Neither condemning nor cursing his enemy for his past deeds, Thalaba instead reaches forward as he counsels repentance, hoping for "Heaven's pardon", and positing a purgatorial afterlife. It is the range of Islamic referents that punctuate this passage, however, that seem most significant, with Thalaba's refusal to "strike" his enemy articulated through Arabic allusions, gesturing not only to "Allah", but also to "Al-Araf" – a locale original to Islamic eschatology, forming a limbo between Heaven and Hell. A Qur'ānic term, which even serves as the title to the scripture's seventh chapter, "Al-Araf" is invoked by Thalaba to give "hope" to the villainous Okba – a promised place of "strong and purifying fire", where "the penitent" might yet ascend to Heaven.[15]

The clemency of Thalaba's refusal to act, and the clemency of his active speech, are both reflective of *Allāh*'s "goodness", his human mercy mirroring the very "Mercy-Gates" of God Himself. The Islamic accents of Thalaba's forgiveness are unmistakable; however, they are amplified exponentially through a surprising intervention in the poem's culmination, which Southey adds immediately after the above:

> The astonished man stood gazing as he spake,
> At length his heart was softened, and the tears
> Gushed, and he sobbed aloud.
> Then suddenly was heard
> The all-beholding Prophet's aweful voice,
> "Thou hast done well, my Servant!
> Ask and receive thy reward!"
>
> A deep and aweful joy
> Seemed to distend the heart of Thalaba;
> With arms in reverence crost upon his breast,
> Upseeking eyes suffused with transport-tears
> He answered to the Voice, "Prophet of God,
> Holy, and good, and bountiful!
> One only earthly wish have I, to work
> Thy will, and thy protection grants me that.
> Look on this Sorcerer! heavy are his crimes,

> But infinite is mercy! if thy servant
> Have now found favour in the sight of God,
> Let him be touched with penitence, and save
> His soul from utter death."
>
> "The groans of penitence," replied the Voice
> "Never arise unheard!
> But for thyself prefer the prayer,
> The Treasure-house of Heaven
> Is open to thy will."[16]

Spontaneously erupting into this final episode of *Thalaba* is none other than the "Prophet of God" himself, Southey's "Mohammed" no longer hiding "beneath" or "in the rock", but rather descending from above, speaking "aloud" even as Thalaba searches for him with "upseeking eyes". Akin to the *deus ex machina* of Greek drama, Southey reserves a conclusive context for the Prophet's dramatic appearance within his poem; intervening only once in *Thalaba's* twelve books, "Mohammed" materializes here at this climactic moment of compassion. Recalling his identity in Islamic traditions as "a mercy to the worlds", the Prophet emerges in Southey's poem not amid its many episodes of violent strife and struggle, but only as Thalaba elects to show "mercy" to his enemy, with the Prophet descending to announce his approval: "Thou hast done well".[17] Yet, this "sudden" surfacing of the Prophet also remains ethereal and elusive, with neither his image nor body available to Southey's readers or his characters, presented instead as a merely audible presence, offering his benediction as an "aweful voice". This exclusive orality is accented further in the final lines of the above passage, with the Prophet no longer associated merely with his visionary "voice", but identified simply as "*the* Voice" – the "Voice" who guarantees that our "groans of penitence" will never go "unheard". Complicating and complementing the Prophet's invisibility is his own identity as "the all-beholding", Southey portraying Muḥammad as entirely unseen, yet capable of seeing entirely.

Southey's visionary portrait of the Prophet leads to the last lines of *Thalaba*, which dilate out into a dizzying pageant of apocalyptic imagery, initiated by Thalaba's reply to the "Prophet of God":

> "Prophet of God!" then answered Thalaba,
> "I am alone on earth.
> Thou knowest the secret wishes of my heart!
> Do with me as thou wilt! thy will is best."
>
> There issued forth no Voice to answer him,
> But lo! Hodeirah's Spirit comes to see
> His vengeance, and beside him, a pure form
> Of roseate light, the Angel mother hangs.
> "My Child, my dear, my glorious, blessed Child,
> My promise is performed . . . fufil thy work!"
>
> Thalaba knew that his death-hour was come,
> And on he leapt, and springing up,
> Into the Idol's heart
> Hilt-deep he drove the Sword.
> The Ocean-Vault fell in, and all were crushed.
> In the same moment at the gate
> Of Paradise, Oneiza's Houri-form
> Welcomed her Husband to eternal bliss.[18]

Sketching an eclectic survey of eschatological symbols, Southey's poem reaches a religious crescendo, with Thalaba's lost beloved – "Oneiza" – returning to the poem finally to welcome "her husband" to Heaven. Complementing this ecstatic obscurity, Southey's conclusion insists on the Prophet's own conspicuous "silence"; although Thalaba "answers" the Prophet promptly, Southey asserts that the "Voice" returns no "answer", with the Prophet fading to imperceptibility, not only concealed from sight, but now also unheard. Replacing Southey's removed "Voice" is "Hodeirah", the "spirit" of Thalaba's father, accompanied also by his "Angel mother" – a shift in character that also marks a shift away from compassion, with the Prophet's "mercy" giving way to "vengeance". Encouraged to strike suicidally at "the Idol's heart", Southey's hero destroys not only the "Dom Daniel" den, but also himself, a devastation that yet leads to a surprising restoration. Although "all were crushed", Thalaba is ushered into a distinctly Muslim "Paradise", reunited with his beloved Oneiza, who has been recreated as a Qur'ānic maiden – a "Houri".[19] This iconoclastic climax, balancing between old "idolatry" and new "forms", serves to accent the formlessness of the Prophet himself, with Thalaba's demolition of the tyrannical image anticipated by his "upseeking" eyes which search for the imageless Muḥammad. Most resonant in Southey's conclusion, however, is the ephemeral quality of the Prophet's "Voice", which not only enters "suddenly", but just as suddenly exits. Surpassing his unfinished epic on "Mohammed", Southey's polished *Thalaba* also seems to be overcome by this earlier fragment, not only featuring the climactic "return" of the Prophet, but also his quick "flight" away, with "Mohammed" no longer fleeing enemies, but instead elevated through a celestial ascent. At the conclusion of this Romantic poem, Southey's readers – like Thalaba himself – still find themselves pursuing the Prophet – a figure who is susceptible to "repeated" questions, but who resists final comprehension, whose likeness is heard but not seen, heralding "mercy" yet retreating beyond the unattained "Mercy-Gates".

9

"The Prophet, who could summon the future to his presence": Landor's Eastern Renditions

I

I take with me for the voyage your poems, the Lyrics, the Lyrical Ballads, and Gebir; and except a few books designed for presents, these make all my library. I like Gebir more and more: if you ever meet its author, tell him I took it with me on a voyage

God bless you!

Yours affectionately,

R. S.[1]

Writing this letter to Coleridge on April 1, 1800, Southey concludes "affectionately", but also informally, signing off simply as "R. S.", even as he sends "blessings" to his dear friend. Preparing to embark "on a voyage", Southey dispatches this letter just days before departing Bristol, leaving England to spend his next year in Portugal, where he will complete *Thalaba*, submitting it for publication at home while still abroad.[2] It is not Southey's own poetry that accompanies him to Portugal alone, however, but the poetry of others. In tandem with "the Lyrical Ballads", penned by Romantic pioneers – Wordsworth, and Coleridge himself – Southey also mentions less celebrated lyrics, adding an anonymous work: "Gebir". Carried away by his praise for this poem of unknown origins, Southey merely mentions Coleridge's own "Lyrics", while lavishing praise on "Gebir", which he finds he "like[s . . .] more and more". Launching his "voyage" abroad, Southey also launches a quest to "meet [*Gebir*'s] author", urging Coleridge to inform the nameless writer that "I took it with me". This enthusiastic review of *Gebir* in Southey's private letter was moreover anticipated in his published criticism; celebrating *Gebir* in the September 1799 issue of the *Critical Review*, Southey advertizes the poem as "abounding with such beauties as it is rarely our good fortune to discover".[3]

These early appreciations of *Gebir* will lead Southey to accomplish the very imperative he gives to Coleridge, not only ascertaining the identity of "its author", but, in 1808, actually meeting the man himself: Walter Savage Landor. As implied by his 1800 letter, however, Southey's poetry – including *Thalaba* – would be greatly influenced by *Gebir* long before meeting Landor, as Southey himself later recalled. "'Gebir' fell into my hands," Southey reminisces in an 1837 Preface to his collected poetry, "and my verse was greatly improved by it, both in vividness and strength. Several years elapsed before I knew that Walter Landor was the author, and more before I had the good fortune to meet the person to whom I felt myself thus beholden."[4] Still unknown and unseen, Landor becomes a writer "to whom" Southey is "beholden"; although *Gebir*'s author is yet invisible in 1800, *Gebir* succeeds in strengthening the "vividness" of Southey's "verse". This phantom benefit exercised by *Gebir* itself anticipates Southey's later "good fortune" in "meet[ing]" Landor in "person". Developing a friendship after their 1808 introduction, Landor would support, and even offer to subsidize, Southey's subsequent artistic efforts; serving as poetic inspiration for Southey's 1801 *Thalaba*, Landor proposed to promote materially Southey's *The Curse of Kehama*, published in 1810 – yet another Orientalist fantasy, which anticipated Southey's elevation to British poet laureate in 1813.[5]

The irony of Landor's early anonymity – his *Gebir* exercising pivotal influence despite its author's absence – is heightened by the ephemeral origins of *Gebir* itself. An unstable platform to launch Southey's practical and poetic journeys in 1800, Landor's 1798 *Gebir* anticipates the 1801 *Thalaba* by borrowing its primary materials from a complicated line of compromised transmissions. Relying on an English translation of a French translation of a supposed Arabic original, *Gebir* tells the story of an ancient "prince of Spain" ("Gebir") who falls in love with his adversary, the Queen of Egypt ("Charoba") – a story suggested to Landor by the 1785 *Progress of Romance*, a collection authored by Clara Reeve, which includes an episode advertised as "The History of Charoba, Queen of Ægypt", authored "in Arabic" by "*the Reverend Doctor Murtadi*".[6] Spanning only seven short books, yet utilizing epic style and substance, Landor published his *Gebir* anonymously in 1798, offering a Preface that acknowledges the poem's "Oriental" provenance, confessing that *Gebir*'s "subject was taken, or rather the shadow of the subject, from a wild and incoherent but fanciful Arabian Romance".[7] Aptly vague in naming his textual inspiration, the unnamed Landor identifies his own Romantic tale as ambivalently inspired by an "Arabian Romance" – a work that is "wild", but also fertile in its "fanciful" character. It is this "Arabian" source that offers Landor a "subject" ripe for reformulation, transforming this lost Eastern tale into an anonymous English Romance. The tentative deferral at the heart of Landor's description – suggesting that his "Arabian" source provided not *Gebir*'s "subject", but a "shadow of the subject" – is perhaps most telling, anticipating the ephemeral influence enjoyed by his shadowy poem on Southey, as well as the epic mysteries which are inscribed into *Gebir*'s own opening lines.

II

I sing the fates of Gebir. He had dwelt
Among those mountain-caverns which retain
His labours yet, vast halls and flowing wells,
Nor have forgotten their old master's name
Tho' severed from his people: here, incens'd

By meditating on primeval wrongs,
He blew his battle-horn, at which uprose
Whole nations; here, ten thousand of most might
He call'd aloud, and soon Charoba saw
His dark helm hover o'er the land of Nile.
What should the virgin do?[8]

Meditating "more and more" on these opening lines of *Gebir* in the spring of 1800, Southey discovered the launch of a southward adventure, even as he launches his own adventure south to Portugal. Bridging European and Eastern, *Gebir* begins with an international invasion, recounting the story of a Spanish prince who seeks to redress "primeval wrongs" by invading the "land of the Nile". This hemispheric conflict is expressed not only in the content of Landor's poem, however, but also in its composition, which straddles divergent schools and styles. Published as a thin octavo in 1798, the very first phrases of *Gebir* betray Landor's investment in Latinic models, his "I sing the fates of Gebir" heavily echoing Virgilian epic, rather than Orientalist "romance".[9] Contextualized through classical "fate", it is equally clear, however, that Landor's hero is etymologically Eastern, owning a name with Arabic origins. Probably intended by Landor to evoke "Gibraltar", as Mohammed Sharafuddin has suggested, the name "Gebir" derives instead from the Arabic root "*j-b-r*" ("جبر"), which forms verbs such as "to compel" and "to force" – an apt etymology for the poem's archetypical "conqueror".[10] Less conspicuous, and less conscious, are the faint Orientalist echoes in Landor's aquatic imagery; recalling the "swelling" portrait of the Prophet first advanced by Goethe, Landor's Gebir is equally saturated with rising water, not only the "flowing wells" of his native homeland, but also "the Nile" of his targeted conquest.

The complex literary genesis of *Gebir* – bridging East and West, North and South – reflects too its complex linguistic genealogy. Landor would later admit in a retrospective Preface that "many parts" of *Gebir* "were first composed in Latin, and I doubted in which language to complete it" – a surprising confession, which is substantiated by Landor's publication of a Latin version of his own poem.[11] Printed in 1803, and entitled *Gebirus*, this rendition of Landor's Arabian Romance into a romance language adds yet another layer to his culturally complex poem. Only reaching Landor after a cascade of receptions – from Arabic, to French, to English – Landor himself produces dual versions of *Gebir*, giving fresh life to this "Oriental" story in two languages, one from modern Britain, and one from Roman antiquity. Keenly aware of such complex foregrounds, Landor seems to have felt compelled also to defend his own creativity, anxiously asserting the "originality" of his poem. In a "Prose Postscript to *Gebir*" – which was subsequently "suppressed" – Landor lashes out at a reviewer who had accused his *Gebir* of being "nothing more than the version of an Arabic tale".[12] "I repeat to him in answer", asserts Landor "what I asserted in my preface, that, so far from a *translation*, there is not a single sentence, not a single sentiment, in common with the tale."[13] Landor adds: "I have not changed the scene, which would have distorted the piece, but every line of appropriate description, and every shade of peculiar manners, is originally and entirely my own".[14] Anticipating his audience's criticism, deflecting claims that his poem is merely a "*translation*", Landor offers yet another "shady" story of *Gebir*'s origins. Rather than emphasizing here that he borrowed "the shadow of the subject" for *Gebir*, as he does in its Preface, however, Landor now asserts in his Postscript that "every shade of peculiar manners" which emerges in *Gebir* "is originally and entirely my own" – an ironic claim considering the poem's compromised mix of classical borrowings and "Arabian" origins.

This ardent defense against "*translation*" seems even more ironic, however, considering the very next work that Landor will undertake, his 1800 *Poems from the Arabic and Persian*. Appearing just two years after *Gebir*'s initial publication, this brief pamphlet of fourteen pages proudly announces itself as a compendium of Middle Eastern translations, its nine "Arabic and Persian" *Poems* supposedly accessed through an intermediary French version. However, as Sidney Colvin long ago noted,

Landor's later critics have been unable to find such a French version, nor have Arabic and Persian "originals" for Landor's *Poems* been located. Instead, an "autograph note added [by Landor] in old age to his own copy" of *Poems from the Arabic and Persian* certifies this volume instead to be his own creation, Landor confessing that "I wrote these poems after reading what had been translated from the Arabic and Persian by Sir W. Jones and Dr. Nott".[15] Thus, while he would assert that the 1798 *Gebir* was "originally and entirely my own" – despite its pastiche of poetic adaptation – Landor's 1800 *Poems from the Arabic and Persian* is indeed his own, despite its supposed origins in the Middle East.

Heightening the ironic inversion between Landor's *Gebir* and his *Poems from the Arabic and Persian* is the inverted "Orientalism" that also emerges in the two works. While *Gebir* claims Eastern origins – deriving ostensibly from an "Arabian Romance" – its style and content conforms more often to classical conventions; alternately, Landor's *Poems from the Arabic and Persian*, despite being original to the English author, feature frequent reference to settings and symbols that seem native to the East. In the collection's "Persian" poems, for example, Landor makes conspicuous reference to "the gardens of Schiraz", the "gulph of Hormuz", and "Samarcand", as well as tropes that are typical of Persian literature, including "pearls", the "nightingale", and "jonquils".[16] Similarly Landor's "Arabic" entries in his *Poems* – supposedly authored by "the son of the unfortunate Sheik Daher" – chart a broad map of the East, ranging from "Damascus", to "Busrah", to "Ispahan", mentioning too an "Egyptian well".[17] Each of these poem clusters – Persian and Arabic – also feature linguistic markers that falsely suggest their Middle Eastern origins; for example, Landor's final poem is "Addressed to Rahdi", invoking in this title an imperfect transliteration of the common Arabic word for "well-pleased" (i.e. "*rāḍī*").[18]

Most relevant in these original "translations", however, is Landor's reach towards the religious, highlighting not only Middle Eastern terrains and terminology, but also Middle

Eastern spiritual traditions. Consistently "Oriental" in their imagery, Landor's poems also occasionally imply Islam specifically. Paired as a two-poem sequence near the end of this brief collection is Landor's "On His Wife's Affliction" and "On His Wife's Death", the latter poem concluding with a poignant final stanza:

> God is great! repine not, O child and mourner of dust!
> The Prophet, who could summon the future to his
>   presence,
> Could the Prophet himself make the past return?[19]

Opening with words that echo Islam's essential doxology – "*Allāhu akbar*", "God is great[er]!" – Landor shifts seamlessly in his second line to "The Prophet", thereby connecting the dual dimensions of the Muslim creed. Bridging these spiritual polarities, Landor's poem bridges also temporal and spatial polarities, linking "future" and "past", as well as "presence" and absence. Lamenting the loss of a departed wife, emphasizing the impossibility of her "return", Landor's speaker places the Prophet at the very crux of romantic grief, with the Muslim Messenger serving as a nostalgic analogy for the irretrievable beloved. Anticipating Southey's own artistic approach to "Mohammed", Landor finds the Prophet balancing between the beloved's presence and absence, even while he also forms the focus of the poem's concluding question: "Could the Prophet himself make the past return?" – a query which allows the founder of Islam to embody both the promise of a prophetic "future", as well as a lament for the limits of an irrecoverable "past".

III

The line drawn by Landor between translated past and future return unfolds as his own literary efforts cross the line between eighteenth and nineteenth centuries. Invoking the Prophet, and his "summoning of the future" in the 1800 *Poems from Arabic and Persian*, it will be Landor's own *Gebir* and its afterlife that best embodies the prophetic potential of his poetry. Greeted by Southey's enthusiasm after its 1798 appearance, *Gebir* would merit republication in 1803; however, this five-year span also prompted Landor to modulate his poem significantly, adjusting *Gebir* to its nineteenth-century contexts and climates. Initially published "in the same month, July 1798, that Napoleon invaded Egypt", as C. C. Barfoot notes, Landor's 1798 poem has long been read as a prophetic allegory, and expectant celebration, of Napoleonic conquest, appearing "at a time when the victories of Napoleon were in many minds associated with the hopes of man".[20] However, like so many of his Romantic generation, Landor discovered Napoleonic promise turn to the peril of tyranny, leading Landor to shift not only his politics, but also his poetics. Disillusioned by 1803, Landor adds a fresh Preface to *Gebir*'s second edition, reframing the poem's significance, insisting that "In the moral [of the poem] are exhibited the folly, the injustice, and the punishment of Invasion, with the calamities which must ever attend the superfluous colonization of a peopled country".[21]

Offering an indictment of Napoleon's 1798 invasion of Egypt, which coincided precisely with *Gebir*'s first publication, Landor's revised edition in 1803 seems to reject its own original circumstances and allegiances. This polemical inversion of *Gebir*'s politics receives emphasis not only in Landor's new Preface, however, but also in new paratexts, his 1803 republication even including a footnote that explicitly names Napoleon himself, condemning the "great changes" which "Bonaparte" has forced on societies and "institutions" by means of "violence".[22] Updating its prophecy – reflecting its new present and lamenting its lost futures – *Gebir* retains a timely significance in 1803, but also assumes a new layer of critical irony, with its gestures to an Eastern past now serving to reject Napoleon's invasion of the present-day East. As Humberto Garcia has most recently noted, Landor's poem itself begins with a veiled reference to the Qur'ān, gesturing to the "city of Irem", which Landor found featured in George

Sale's annotations to his 1734 *Koran*.[23] Such Qur'ānic contexts
fit the 1798 edition of Landor's poem perfectly, recalling *Gebir's*
own claim of indebtedness to an "Arabian Romance". However,
in the poem's revised edition in 1803, such appeals to the Qur'ān
seem not merely to reach back to an ephemeral Egyptian antiquity, but also forward to a concrete Egyptian modernity, with
allusions to Islamic prophecy serving now as ominous prophecies
of Napoleon's actual "violence" in Islamic lands. Newly implicated in a dizzying act of circular allegory, *Gebir's* gestures to
Muslim revelation in its revised edition seem to reveal contemporary crimes against Muslim peoples, Landor's prescient poem of
Eastern conquest refigured as a caustic condemnation of France's
eastward incursions.[24]

Landor's reach back to the Islamic past even while reflecting
on the European present is a strategy that itself "returns" as he
approaches his career's most celebrated and sustained work. First
inspired by Southey himself, Landor's literary efforts through the
1820s culminated in his five-volume *Imaginary Conversations*, a
series of fantasy dialogues between factual figures, reconstruct-
ing real history through fictional exchanges.[25] In his second series
– *Dialogues of Sovereigns and Statesmen*, published first in 1824
– Landor turns to subjects which are specifically Islamic, dramatizing a dialogue between "Mahomet and Sergius", as well
as between "Soliman and Mufti".[26] And while the former seems
flatly satirical, simply mocking Muslim identities, the latter conversation appears more complex, addressing the Qur'ān and its
translation. Set in the court of "Soliman", Landor records the
Sultan's desire to have his scripture rendered for his people:

SOLIMAN.
My intention is, to enlighten the dim-sighted, by
ordering the Koran to be translated into the languages
of all nations.
Why dost thou raise thine eyes, Mufti?[27]

As suggested by the final line of the above, Landor's "Soliman" is
resisted by his own "Mufti" – the court's orthodox expert – who

marshals a myriad of reasons against the Qur'ān's universal rendition. Arguing that "if every man reads, one or two in every province will think", the Mufti insists on reserving religious authority for the ruling elite, keeping the Qur'ān away from "the vulgar".[28] Ultimately dissuaded from his original "intention" by such cynical arguments, Landor's "conversation" concludes with his Sultan suspending the "order" to have "the Koran" undergo widespread "translation". However, more significant than this conclusion is simply to find these topics – translation and Islamic sources – returning to haunt Landor's maturity, meditating again on Muslim rendition several decades after his earliest poetry. Gesturing to its promises and problems, Islamic translation occupies a surprisingly stable space in Landor's discursive "imagination", his Romantic *Conversations* in 1824 recalling actual conversations with fellow Romantics more than twenty years previous. Still approaching Muslim origins through defective or deferred rendition, Landor continues an ironic debate concerning the recuperation of Islam's textual antiquity, questioning whether the Qur'ān indeed could "enlighten" global futures, yet denying this prophetic text its chance to "make the past return", both recommending and suspending the scripture's advance "into the languages of all nations".

10

"I blush as a good Mussulman": Byron's Turkish *Tales* and Travels

I

Viewed with detached distance by Landor, Islamic sources would gain greater proximity to the most iconic poet of Britain's next Romantic generation: Lord Byron. Appealing to Islam not only imaginatively, but experientially, Byron would tour actual Muslim lands, first visiting Ottoman Albania in the autumn of 1809. The poetic and personal impact of such Eastern travels potently echo through the remainder of Byron's literary career and his adult life; as Lady Annabella Byron recalled, "the East" would hold a lasting allure for her famous husband:

> He often spoke of a mysterious necessity for his return to the East, and vindicated the Turks with a spirit of Nationality, admiring above all their complete predestinarianism. He would say "The East – ah, there it is," . . . and he has two or three times intimated to me that he abjured his religion there. In the autumn in London, he said with a shudder of conscious remembrance, "I was very *near* becoming a Mussulman." He preferred the Turkish opinions, manners & dress in all respects to ours. This idea of his conversion to their faith having occurred to me at Halnaby, derived some confirmation from his composing at Seaham that part of the Siege of Corinth which relates to Alp's

assumption of the Turban, and also from a paper which
he then wrote at the commencement of a Critique upon
Leake's work, afterwards reviewed in the Edin[burgh
Review] by Hobhouse.[1]

This suggestion of Byron's "*near*" conversion – almost abandon-
ing "his religion" and "becoming a Mussulman" – is startling,
both amplifying and altering Romantic investment in Islam.
Reflecting a broader shift in generation and personality, Byron
shares with British predecessors a profound interest in Islam, yet
occupies an opposite pole as he engages with the East. While his
peers will stay at home, adventurous Byron sallies abroad; unlike
Landor, Byron does not merely imagine "conversations" between
Muslims, but converses with Muslims directly, donning Ottoman
"dress", while also adopting Ottoman "opinions", entering an
alternate "spirit of Nationality".

Cryptically alluding to his "mysterious necessity" to "return
to the East", it is Byron's Eastern authorship that firmly suggests
to Lady Byron her husband's "near" acceptance of Islam. Rather
than Byron's travels merely, it is his "composing" travel writings that offers "confirmation" of his "idea of conversion", his
"*Siege of Corinth*" cited by Lady Byron as supplying an imaginative witness to Byron's hidden spiritual biography. Associated
with a foreign religion, such poems which reflect Byron's Eastern
experiences will become familiar classics, his so-called *Turkish
Tales* – beginning with *The Giaour* in 1813 and reaching *The
Siege of Corinth* in 1816 – occupying an influential place in later
British Romanticism.[2] However, such mature representations of
the "East" are also quietly anticipated in Byron's earliest years;
intimations of his Islamic "admiring", for example, are evident as
early as 1807, when the nineteen-year-old Byron privately drew
up a "list of different poets, dramatic or otherwise, who have
distinguished their respective languages by their productions" – a
list that included the following entry:

Arabia. – Mahomet, whose Koran contains the most sublime poetical passages far surpassing European poetry.[3]

Confessing his early admiration of the "Koran", Byron attributes the scripture to both a nation and a name, connecting the Qur'ān to both "Arabia" and "Mahomet". A witness to Byron's early interest in Islamic prophecy, this passage itself proves prophetic, foreseeing Byron's specific attraction to the Muslim scripture as "poetical", celebrating its sacred text as an example of the literary "sublime". Privileging Islamic revelation over "European poetry" – praising the Eastern scripture as "far surpassing" Western verse – Byron also ironically anticipates his own literary dependence on the Qur'ān, looking forward to his later *Turkish Tales* which will fashion some of Romanticism's "most sublime poetical passages" through appealing to the "Koran".

Byron's highly personal attraction to "the East" – voicing his private preference for "Turkish opinions, manners & dress" after returning from his Ottoman travels – also finds an early mirror in Byron's youth, witnessed in his domestic preparations to depart. And while it is his wife (Annabella Byron) who recalls Byron's Eastern nostalgia, it will be his mother (Catherine Byron), who first hears his plans to embark eastward. Musing on the best time to launch his Oriental adventures, Byron writes an erratic letter to his mother in the fall of 1808, just a year after reflecting in his journals on the Qur'ānic "sublime", which begins:

Newstead Abbey, Notts. October 7. 1808.

Dear Madam,

I have no beds for the H ** s or any body else at present. The H ** s sleep at Mansfield. I do not know, that I resemble Jean Jacques Rousseau. I have no ambition to be like so illustrious a madman – but this I know, that I shall live in my own manner, and as much alone as possible. When my rooms are ready I shall be glad to see you: at present it would be improper and uncomfortable to both parties. You can hardly object to my rendering my mansion habitable, notwithstanding my departure for Persia in March (or May at farthest), since *you* will be *tenant* till my return.[4]

Confronted by a confusing mix of "madman" facts, the reader witnesses the young Byron as he responds to a host of requests and remarks from his mother, deferring her present wish to have guests stay with him at "my mansion", as well as the suggestion that Byron himself "resemble[s] Jean Jacques Rousseau". This jumble of domestic details leads to Byron's parenthetical mention of his determined "departure", planning to leave for "Persia" in the coming spring. Mixing his tentative travels abroad with problematic tenants at home, Byron's lack of "beds" in Britain melts into his mention of Oriental adventures, this letter balancing personal intrigues and Persian plans, even while Romantically insisting that "I shall live in my own manner, and as much alone as possible". Reflecting Byron's fusion of Eastern aspirations and household issues, it is such early interweaving that also anticipates his own Turkish travels, as well as his *Turkish Tales*; echoing his early correspondence with his mother, and anticipating the later "remembrance" of his wife, Byron's Eastern efforts are enveloped with the most personal and the private, concerned with feminine confidence and domestic arrangements.

II

Byron launched his first sojourn to the East in 1809, a year that launched too the most fertile decade of British literary engagement with Islam. During the next ten years, Byron would not only acquire his Ottoman experiences, but also publish each of his primary *Turkish Tales*. However, this same decade also witnessed Orientalist contributions arising from Byron's fraternal circle, with male friends such as Thomas Moore and Percy Bysshe Shelley similarly inspired by Muslim models.[5] Reflecting Byron's own personality and personal life, however, it is women who loom largest as he directs his authorial attentions to the East. Sharing his plans for Persian travel with his mother, and his Eastern nostalgia with his wife, women will also supply central concerns for Byron's *Turkish Tales*, including the first, his 1813 *The Giaour*.[6] Borrowing its title from the Turkish term "*gavur*" – ultimately derived from the Persian, "*gabr*" ("infidel") – Byron's tale opens with a prefatory letter that characterizes his "story" as not only indebted broadly to "the East", but specifically grounded in "the adventures of a female slave".[7] Eventually identified as "Leila" – the captive concubine of the Turkish "Hassan", who executes Leila for her love affair with "the Giaour" himself – Byron's enslaved heroine will form the crux of his *Tale*, with feminine concerns serving as the center of his first *Turkish* fiction.

Prominently featuring a female Muslim character, *The Giaour* also views Muslim religiosity through a definitively feminine lens; recalling Novalis' *Heinrich von Ofterdingen* and its portrait of Zulima, Byron ambivalently approaches Islam through a womanly representative. Beginning in line 473, *The Giaour* offers its first extended description of Byron's heroine, cataloguing Leila's facial features, pausing first to consider her eyes:

> Her eye's dark charm't were vain to tell,
> But gaze on that of the Gazelle,
> It will assist thy fancy well;
> As large, as languishingly dark,
> But Soul beam'd forth in every spark
> That darted from beneath the lid,
> Bright as the jewel of Giamschid.
> Yea, Soul, and should our prophet say
> That form was nought but breathing clay,
> By Alla! I would answer nay;
> Though on Al-Sirat's arch I stood,
> Which totters o'er the fiery flood,
> With Paradise within my view,
> And all his Houris beckoning through.
> Oh! who young Leila's glance could read
> And keep that portion of this creed,
> Which saith that woman is but dust,
> A soulless toy for tyrant's lust?[8]

Although reflecting the strong Islamic accents of Byron's *Turkish Tales* as a whole, the span and scope of this particular passage is nevertheless surprising, incorporating an ample range of Muslim allusions. Celebrating Leila's beauty in his initial lines, Byron recalls a rich tradition of Sufi lyric, likening her "eyes" to the "jewel of Giamschid", while also capitalizing on an innate English pun between "gaze" and the "Gazelle" – a standard trope in Persian poetry.[9] From physical beauty to spiritual bounty, Byron quickly transitions away from poetic symbols and towards religious references, interweaving expressions that are not only Arabic in origin – for instance, the divine name: "By Alla!" – but which are also distinctly Qur'ānic. Even while supposedly paraphrasing the Muslim "prophet", Byron's passage includes specific terms such as "Al-Sirat" ("the bridge", "the path") and "Houris" ("celestial maidens"), both of which are borrowed from Islamic eschatology, and ultimately, the Qur'ān.[10]

It is the particular import of this passage, however, rather than its broad allusiveness, which enriches the religious gestures it contains. Despite its heavy indebtedness to Islam, Byron's passage also seems an Islamic critique, depicting Leila as condemned by the "creed" of her very own culture – a creed which supposedly asserts that woman's "form was nought but breathing clay", adding that "woman is but dust, / A soulless toy for tyrant's lust". Dramatizing a tension between physical surfaces and spiritual depth – between feminine "form" and soulful substance – this passage also features a tension between Islamic dependence and Islamic deprecation.

Paralleling its contrast between the outward beauty of women and their allegedly "soulless" interiors, these lines rely on Muslim expression yet reject Muslim traditions. These contradictions are somewhat resolved by Byron himself, however. Recognizing that women's "soullessness" is certainly *not* the teaching of the Muslim "prophet", Byron himself confesses the creedal error of his own poetry, adding a footnote to the conclusion of this passage. Clarifying for his British readers that such misogyny contradicts Muslim scripture itself, Byron suggests that the view which his own verses advance is "A vulgar error: the Koran allots at least a third of Paradise to well-behaved women; but by far the greater number of Mussulmans interpret the text their own way, and exclude their moieties from heaven."[11] Establishing a dialogue inside his English poem on Islam's outer reality, Byron's censure of "Mussulman" treatment of "women" is accomplished through appealing to "the Koran" itself, which Byron understands as more correct than its own religious communities. Recruiting Muslim writ to critique supposed Muslim customs, Byron adopts Islamic revelation as his own familiar proof, allowing him to condemn foreign Islamic practices. Inscribing an ironic interiority within his edition's paratext, Byron raises his informal voice to defend both Muslim women, as well as the Muslim "creed", which are equally impugned in his formal verse. Allowing the Qur'ānic citation in his footnote to resist his own body text, the Islamic "soul" of Byron's British prose emerges from the bottom of the poetic page, rising to contradict the "soulless" allegations of his poetry.[12]

III

Published in the spring of 1813, *The Giaour* would prove an instant success, provoking both Byron's exaltation, as well as his anxiety. Encouraged by the poem's brisk sales and multiple editions, Byron would begin another *Turkish Tale* by November; however, as suggested by his correspondence during this fall of 1813, Byron also felt ambivalence regarding *The Giaour*'s immediate success. Pushing forward with the second of his Oriental fictions, Byron elected not only to feature a woman at the center of his tale, but to feature her in its title, producing next his *The Bride of Abydos*, which appeared in print in December 1813.[13] However, even while evidencing his investment in these *Turkish Tales* – literary, economic, and personal – Byron also deprecates the style and poetic "measure" of his most recent efforts, writing excitedly to Lord Holland on November 17, 1813:

> My head is full of Oriental names & scenes – and I merely
> chose that measure as *next* to *prose* to tell a story or
> describe a place which struck me – I have a thorough &
> utter contempt for all measures but Spencer's stanza and
> *Dryden's couplet* – the whole of the Bride cost me *four*
> *nights* – and you may easily suppose that I can have no
> great esteem for lines that can be strung as fast as minutes.
> – I have here & there risen to the couplet when I meant to
> be *fine* – but it is my story & my *East*.

Continuing on to relate a host of miscellaneous details regarding
his *Bride*'s composition, Byron also adds that:

> The very *wild* Stanzas are more like Southey or King David
> – 'By the waters of Babylon' &c. than anything English – but
> that is thoroughly Eastern – & partly from the Koran.[14]

Overwhelmed by an "Oriental" atmosphere – his own "head"
colonized by Eastern "names & scenes" – Byron seems contradictory in his self-criticism. Recalling the tension between body text
and footnotes in his first *Turkish Tale – The Giaour –* Byron here
criticizes the "couplets" and rapid composition of his second *Tale
– The Bride of Abydos –* both boasting and lamenting that "the
Bride cost me *four nights*" merely. Announcing that he "can have
no great esteem for lines that can be strung as fast as minutes",
Byron nevertheless hurriedly continues his letter by informing
Lord Holland that these fast and fresh "lines" claim an ancient
and exalted background. First situating his "stanzas" in relation
to "Spencer", and "Dryden", and finally "Southey", Byron initially identifies British precedents for his *Bride.* However, in seeking to account for the "wild" nature of his work, Byron reaches
more wildly afield. Instead of "anything English", Byron stretches
back to biblical antiquity, invoking "King David" and his iconic
Psalm 137 ("By the waters of Babylon"). At the conclusion of the
above, however, Byron fulfils his own youthful projections from
six years earlier, positing a final precedent for his poetry, recognizing that his *Bride*'s style and substance derive "partly from the
Koran" – an artistic admission that recalls his early celebration

of the Qur'ān as superseding all "British poetry", even while his current "British poetry" seeks to build for itself a "thoroughly Eastern" background.

A pastiche of global influences that yet seems highly personal and individual, Byron not only appeals to a range of source texts – from modern English to ancient "Eastern" – but also emphasizes his own idiosyncratic ownership of his *Turkish Tales*. These Islamic fictions, as well as their Islamic origins, emphatically belong to Byron, he suggests; "but it is my story", Byron insists "& my *East*". Such an intimate investment in his Eastern authorship continues to unfold as 1813 nears its end; even while preparing *The Bride* for publication, reviewing the proofs for his second *Turkish Tale*, Byron writes to his publisher, John Murray, on December 3, 1813, to request that he:

> Look out in the Encyclopedia article *Mecca* whether it is there or at *Medina* the Prophet is entombed – if at Medina the first lines of my alteration must run –
>
> "Blest – as the call which from Medina's dome
>
> Invites Devotion to the Prophet's tomb
>
> &c.
>
> if at "Mecca" the lines may stand as before. – Page 45. C[ant]o 2d. – Bride of Abydos.[15]

Confessing his urban confusion – mixing up "Mecca" and "Medina" – Byron suggests his literary "devotion" to Arabian topics, but also his actual distance from Arabian topography, with Islam's most sacred places finding an uncertain position in Byron's mental map. Anxious to establish accurately the Prophet's area of interment – seeking to entomb the Muslim founder respectfully in his English verse – Byron follows up this December 3 note with yet another note to John Murray, repeating his question just a few hours later, articulated now with increased urgency:

> Did you look out? is it *Medina* or *Mecca* that contains
> the *holy* sepulchre? – don't make me blaspheme by your
> negligence – I have no book of reference or I would save
> you the trouble I *blush* as a good Mussulman to have con-
> fused the point.
>
> yrs. B[16]

Playfully raising the stakes in this ensuing note, it is "blasphemy"
that worries Byron now, with the accuracy of his poetic reference to the Prophet's "*holy* sepulchre" conceived as a potential
spiritual crime. Unmistakably sardonic in tone, it is not Byron's
insistence and interrogation of John Murray that seems most
important here, however, but rather the intimacy of his expressions. Self-identifying as a "Mussulman" – indeed, as a "good
Mussulman" – Byron's memo is surely meant to provoke a smile
from Murray. Yet, this comic suggestion of Byron's own conversion offers an eerie echo of Lady Byron's own reminiscence,
suspecting her husband of earnestly entertaining his own "conversion to their faith" – a parallel bolstered by Byron's own
"blushing" at his mixing of "Mecca" and "Medina". An act of
physical confession, Byron no longer "shudders" as he testifies
to his "*near*" conversion to Islam, but rather "blushes" at his
Islamic "confusion", involuntarily exhibiting an external marker
of his own interior regret. Offering a perplexed confession that
aptly reflects his own *Turkish Tales* and travels, Byron announces
that "I *blush as* a good Mussulman", anxiously appropriating a
conflicted signature of feminine modesty, even while he searches
to locate the Prophet's own most personal place of final rest.[17]

11

"Beautiful beyond all the bells in Christendom": Byron's Aesthetic *Adhān*

I

Confessing to Lord Holland the Qur'ānic foreground to his *The Bride of Abydos* – insisting that his poem is belatedly derived "partly from the Koran" – Byron suggests the impact which the Arabic scripture exercised on his English "stanzas". The influence of the Qur'ān seems most evident not in the style of Byron's poem, however, but in the substance of his *Bride*. In the fifth section of the poem's second canto, Byron pictures his eponymous heroine – "the Bride", Zuleika – as she waits in her "lone chamber", running her "fairy fingers" over "fragment beads of amber":

> Near these, with emerald rays beset,
> (How could she thus that gem forget?),
> Her mother's sainted amulet,
> Whereon engraved the Koorsee text
> Could smooth this life and win the next;
> And by her comboloio lies
> A Koran of illumined dyes;
> And many a bright emblazon'd rhyme
> By Persian scribes redeem'd from time;
> And o'er those scrolls, not oft so mute,

> Reclines her now neglected lute;
> And round her lamp of fretted gold
> Bloom flowers in urns of China's mould;
> The richest work of Iran's loom,
> And Sheeraz' tribute of perfume;
> All that can eyes or sense delight
> Are gather'd in that gorgeous room:
> But yet it hath an air of gloom.[1]

Implied in Zuleika's single bedroom is a broad span of Eastern ethnicities, her scattered possessions suggesting a rich national survey, not only reflecting its Ottoman setting, but roving from "China" to "Iran". Complementing its geographic reach is this tableau's aesthetic diversity, with Zuleika's distinct objects appealing to the reader's discrete faculties, presenting a veritable "banquet of the senses", as Mohammed Sharafuddin has suggested.[2] Embracing smell and sight, hearing and touch, Byron successively touches on the Bride's "amulet", her "lute", her "flowers", her "lamp", as well as her "perfume", providing an intoxicating and overwhelming atmosphere which is rooted in "sense delight".

Intersecting this sensual catalogue of secular objects, however, is a conspicuously sacred exception: the "Koran". Naming the scripture in general, Byron also cites a specific selection – "the Koorsee text" – a reference to the Qur'ān 2:255, so named as it celebrates God's "*Kursī*" (His "Throne"), which "comprises the heavens and the earth".[3] Realizing that this Arabic term – "Koorsee" – and its Qur'ānic context, would be unfamiliar to his audience, Byron elects to parse this Islamic verse in a footnote, which he appends to this passage; explaining this "text" engraved on Zuleika's "amulet", Byron clarifies for his British readers that: "The Koorsee (throne) verse in the second cap. of the Koran describes the attributes of the Most High, and is engraved in this manner, and worn by the pious, as the most esteemed and sublime of all sentences."[4] Echoing his youthful celebration of the "Koran", Byron here associates the Muslim scripture not only with "piety", but also with artistry, the

"Koorsee verse" visible in its "engravings", but also verbally "sublime" in its inscribed "sentences". Reflecting the sensory span of Byron's poetic passage from his *Bride of Abydos*, the Qur'ān emerges too as a "text" that is not only read, but also heard, "engraved" in "illuminated dyes", but also spoken in "emblazon'd rhyme". A source of audition, the Qur'ān is further-more associated with other audio sources in Byron's poem, sub-tly merged with the Bride's own musical interests. Immediately after mentioning Zuleika's "Koran of illuminated dyes", Byron adds that "And o'er those scrolls, not oft so mute, / Reclines her now neglected lute"; marrying together secular instrument and scriptural manuscripts, the Bride's opposing media are affili-ated in being "not oft so mute", this qualifying phrase bridging Qur'ānic "scrolls" and Zuleika's "lute". Reaching back to the aesthetic approach to the Muslim scripture, articulated first in Byron's 1807 journals, this passage from *The Bride of Abydos* also embodies an auditory motif that echoes throughout the *Turkish Tales*, with the sounds of the Islamic sacred resonat-ing in Byron's lines, seeking to vocalize the religion's "sensory delight" in his English verse.

II

This overlap between Islamic acoustics and Byron's female pro-tagonist – his musical Bride affiliated with Muslim "scrolls, not oft so mute" – is not arbitrary, but increasingly seems an essen-tial element of *The Bride of Abydos* as the poem unfolds. After Zuleika is found alone with her aesthetic objects and sacred scrip-ture, she is joined by her prospective lover, Selim; celebrating his beloved's "long-loved voice" in a passionate plea, Selim praises Zuleika's vocal "tone" through a complex series of similes:

> Blest – as the Muezzin's strain from Mecca's wall
> To pilgrims pure and prostrate at his call;
> Soft – as the melody of youthful days,

That steals the trembling tear of speechless praise;
Dear – as his native song to Exile's ears,
Shall sound each tone thy long-loved voice endears.
For thee in those bright isles is built a bower
Blooming as Aden in its earliest hour.[5]

The hazy nostalgia of this poetic passage assumes a clearly Islamic color, Selim articulating an "exilic" yearning for a range of religious homes, from "Mecca" – the birthplace of the Prophet – to "Aden" – the Edenic paradise, the "perpetual abode" of the faithful.[6] However, these melancholic and meandering lines also assume a definitively musical accent, amplifying their Muslim texture with a wistful "melody", merging the "Muezzin's strain" with the "native song" addressed "to Exile's ears". This oral impulse in Byron's lines leads to the object of Selim's encomium: the "tone" of Zuleika's "long-loved voice". Although an entirely expected theme of Romantic poetry – praising the vocal beauty of the beloved – this "voice" in Byron's poetry assumes a deeply religious resonance, likened first to "the Muezzin's strain from Mecca's wall", an analogy that serves to spiritualize Zuleika's own "strain". As "blest" as the sacred call to prayer – the Muslim *adhān* – Byron again synthesizes spirituality and sensuality, fusing a "lone" female's voice with the "call" of the "Muezzin", welcoming "pilgrims pure and prostrate" to "Mecca".

Merging the music of the "Muezzin" with the "long-loved voice" of his fictional beloved, Byron harmonizes opposing identities, shifting seamlessly between sacred prayer and secular poetics. Surfacing in his description of Zuleika's voice, Byron's interest in Islamic aurality returns to haunt Zuleika's final silence, with the tragic death of his Bride also amplified through sacred sounds. In the poem's penultimate section, Byron's narrator laments Zuleika's death – after her "heart hath burst" – invoking the heroine directly:

Zuleika! last of Giaffir's race,
    Thy destined lord is come too late:

He sees not – ne'er shall see thy face!
   Can he not hear
The loud Wu-wulleh warn his distant ear?
   Thy handmaids weeping at the gate,
   The Koran-chanters of the hymn of fate,
   The silent slaves with folded arms that wait,
Sighs in the hall, and shrieks upon the gale,
   Tell him thy tale![7]

This pivotal passage, reporting the funeral rites of Zuleika, is attended not only by Muslim mourners, but also by Muslim music. Grieving with bereaved tones, the lamentations for Byron's lost "Bride" are vividly "loud", with even the "silent slave" enveloped by "sighs" and "shrieks". In the midst of this cacophony, however, is once again "the Koran" – a sacred intervention at the conclusion of the *Bride* which recalls Zuleika's "chamber" at the beginning of the poem's second canto. While "chanters" of the scripture here attend Zuleika's public death, "the Koran" had first occupied Zuleika's private life, her "lute" which "reclined" near Qur'ānic "scrolls" now answered by a Qur'ānic "hymn of fate". Perhaps most potently, it is these "loud" sounds of Muslim lament that rhetorically stand as a "signal" of Zuleika's passing from life to death; it is the "loud Wu-wulleh" and the "Koran-chanters" which are meant to "tell" the "tale" to "distant ear", reporting the demise of Zuleika to her doomed lover, who has "come too late".[8]

Emphasizing the elegiac sounds of the Muslim sacred, Byron seeks to deepen both the artistic and the spiritual import of his poetry – a strategy that transcends the tragic end to Byron's *Bride*, and survives into his later *Turkish Tales*. For example, in Byron's *The Siege of Corinth* – the poem cited by Lady Byron as evidencing her husband's "*near*" conversion – readers are offered perhaps the most impressive fusion of Islamic sound and Romantic sensibilities; in a powerful symphony of piety and dark beauty, Byron describes the "grand army of the Turks" as it besieges "Corinth" at "midnight":

> And the wide hum of that wild host
> Rustled like leaves from coast to coast,
> As rose the Muezzin's voice in air
> In midnight call to wonted prayer:
> It rose, that chanted mournful strain,
> Like some lone spirit's o'er the plain;
> 'T was musical, but sadly sweet,
> Such as when winds and harp-strings meet,
> And take a long unmeasured tone,
> To mortal minstrelsy unknown.[9]

A litany of Romantic tropes and topics crowd these dense lines, from the mysterious to the "mournful", from the "lonesome" to the lyrical. As so characteristic of Byron's art, this passage's elusive pleasure is once again clearly centered in auditory experiences. Beginning with the flat "hum" of the Ottoman "host", this section ends with a "long unmeasured tone", this latter sound itself synthesizing polarities, intersecting natural and supernatural, hovering between earth and heaven. Rising like a "lone spirit" which sails "o'er the plain", Byron's "tone" is produced by marrying "air" and artistry, likened to the sound which is triggered "when winds and harp-strings meet". It is the Islamic source of these thoroughly Byronic lyrics, however, which identifies this passage as original to his *Turkish Tales*. Breaking up the confused "rustling" in his initial lines is the clear "call to wonted prayer", the "Muezzin's voice" launching this "midnight" meditation. A sound that is "musical, but sadly sweet", Byron again appeals to the *adhān* even while synthesizing the ethereal and the exilic, this Muslim "call" to prayer serving as the superlative symbol for his Romantic designs.[10]

III

Byron's repeated return to the sounds of the Islamic sacred reflects the Romantic priorities of his own art. However, this poetic interest itself has deeply personal origins, rooted in Byron's biography. Described as his "revolutionary confessional poem" by Jerome McGann, Byron's *Childe Harold's Pilgrimage* would see its first volume appear in 1812, preceding his first *Turkish Tale* by a full year.[11] Mirroring Byron's actual memories through the travels of his protagonist – Harold – the *Pilgrimage* is the first work to translate Byron's own tour of Islamic lands into lyric poetry; in the second canto of its first volume, Byron's *Pilgrimage* finds Harold journeying through Albania, where the sound of the *adhān* is heard:

> Hark! from the mosque the nightly solemn sound,
> The Muezzin's call doth shake the minaret,
> "There is no god but God! – to prayer – lo! God is great!"[12]

More specific in its Islamic audio, Byron's passage supplies an actual translation of the "solemn sound" that is "nightly" announced, condensing the entire "call" to prayer down to a single line of English verse: "There is no god but God! – to prayer – lo! God is great!" This poetic moment – like many moments in Byron's *Pilgrimage* – reflects personal experience; unlike most, however, this moment is specified in its place and time for Byron's later readers. In the 1832 edition of the *Pilgrimage*, this stanza would be contextualized by footnote quotations from Byron's travelling companion, John Cam Hobhouse, revealing these lines to reflect their "arrival at Tepaleen", where he and Byron "lodged in the palace" of Albania's ruler, Ali Pacha, during "Ramazan" in October 1809.[13] Historically grounded in season and surroundings, Byron's poetry accrues new relevance and resonance, his "Muezzin's call" that "doth shake the minaret" shaking too the division between artistic representation and lived experience, this moment of Islamic audition resounding within *Childe Harold's Pilgrimage*, but also reaching without, offering a distinct echo of Byron's own biography.

This explicit fusion of Byron's personal life with his Islamic poetry is performed not only through recollections supplied by his friend Hobhouse, however, but also through Byron's own recollections. Returning to the end of his *The Giaour* – the first of his *Turkish Tales* – Byron describes the spot where the poem's antagonist, Hassan "the Turk", has been vanquished:

> A turban carved in coarsest stone,
> A pillar with rank weeds o'ergrown,
> Whereon can now be scarcely read
> The Koran verse that mourns the dead,
> Point out the spot where Hassan fell
> A victim in that lonely dell.
> There sleeps as true an Osmanlie
> As e'er at Mecca bent the knee;
> As ever scorn'd forbidden wine,
> Or pray'd with face towards the shrine,
> In orisons resumed anew
> At solemn sound of "Alla Hu!"[14]

Stringing together a series of Eastern allusions, Byron saturates this passage with essential *orientalia*, turning initially from a generic "turban" to images more specific to Islam, including the "Koran", "Mecca", and even God's name in Arabic: "Alla". Anticipating his *Bride of Abydos*, Byron's investment in the Muslim sacred encompasses distinct media, both visual and oral, with "the Koran" depicted as both "carved" and "sounded"; however, Byron again seems to privilege Islamic sounds over Islamic sights. While the Qur'ān's inscription "can now be scarcely read" – obscured by "weeds o'ergrown" – the "sound of 'Alla Hu!'" is, by contrast, always "resumed anew", still fresh through unfolding years of "orisons". Byron's interest in this Islamic "sound", which seems merely implied in his verses, is explicitly amplified by a footnote which he appends to this passage; parsing the foreign phrase – "Alla Hu!" – Byron explains to his British readers that:

> "Alla Hu!" the concluding words of the Muezzin's call
> to prayer from the highest gallery on the exterior of the
> Minaret. On a still evening, when the Muezzin has a fine

voice (which they frequently have), the effect is solemn
and beautiful beyond all the bells in Christendom.[15]

Blurring the lines between poetic character and historical poet
– between his fictional portrait and a factual moment – Byron
identifies his own historical experience as the source for this
imagined scene in his *Turkish* poem. Shifting from the religious
rites associated with Hassan's death, readers are transported
back to Byron's biography, privy to his own individual impressions of the "Muezzin's call to prayer", with "Alla Hu!" rever-
berating from a "still evening" in his actual life.

Contrasting sunset "stillness" and sounded "voice", this footnote to *The Giaour* is perhaps most arresting in its juxtaposition
of the Islamic and the Christian, privileging the Muezzin's "call"
over "all the bells in Christendom" – an inter-sectarian judgment
based not on Byron's religious bias, but on his religious aesthetics.
While recognizing the "solemn" quality of the *adhān*'s "effect",
it is the artistic impact of the *adhān* that receives Byron's final
emphasis, finding the Muslim call to prayer to be "beautiful",
its singular broadcast sounding "beyond" all Christian "bells".
Merging again the sensual and the spiritual, it is an aesthetic
criterion that lifts the Islamic over the Christian for Byron, the
performed sound of the Muslim sacred compelling Byron to opt
for this cross-cultural "preference". And although Byron remains
only "very *near*" to "becoming a Mussulman" in his religion – as
he admits to Lady Byron – it is his artistic sensibilities which
prompt him to "abjure" his own Christian origins, converting
him to the sounds of Islam in the texted pages of his own *Turkish
Tales*. Voicing his musical devotion to the Muslim "sublime",
Byron's mysterious exclamation to his wife – "The East – ah,
there it is" – falls short of authentic "conversion"; however, this
cryptic comment points to a deeper devotion to Islamic aesthetics
which is yet audible in the "conscious remembrance" of his own
autobiographical romances.

12

"The orient moon of Islam rode in triumph": Percy Bysshe Shelley as "Islamite"

I

"Sale, the translator of the Koran, was suspected of being an Islamite, but a very different one from you, Shiloh."[1]

Casual and caustic, this remark was reportedly spoken by none other than Lord Byron, addressed to his personal friend, and poetic peer, Percy Bysshe Shelley. Transcribed by Thomas Medwin – friend and biographer of both British Romantics – Byron's quip surfaced in a conversation just months before Shelley's untimely death in 1822, as the two friends sojourned together in Italy.[2] Affectionately nicknamed "Shiloh" by his friend, it is Shelley's flexible religious identity that seems most to interest Byron. Recalling his own *"near"* conversion to Islam, Byron's comment raises the peril and promise of Shelley's Islamic adherence; rather than Byron almost "becoming a Mussulman", it is Shelley who is now "suspected of being an Islamite". This witty remark, aimed sarcastically at Shelley, assumes a weightier significance, however, when we recall that Shelley's longest poem had appeared just a few years previously, and had featured on its title page the very name of the Muslim religion, published in 1818 as *The Revolt of Islam*.[3]

Accusing Shelley of harboring Islamic sympathies, Byron sardonically compares his friend with George "Sale" – the esteemed "translator of the Koran" into English – bridging Britain's key scholar of Islam and Britain's key Romantic poet. This comparison is framed, however, as a contrast, Byron joking that Sale and Shelley are inverse in their identity, "suspecting" Shelley to be an "Islamite", but a "very *different* one" from the sincere academic, George Sale. And consistent with such a contrast, the "Islam" which emerges in Shelley's English verses does indeed significantly diverge from the "Islam" presented in earnest English scholarship. Interested not in Eastern religion, but in Western politics, Shelley's own *Revolt of Islam* recruits Muslim terminology as an exotic mirror to reflect on Europe. Indexing the progress of his revolutionary commitments, Shelley's 1818 poem prominently alludes to *Islam*, but only as a vehicle to give "his radical ideas an airing", as Roderick Cavaliero notes.[4] Reflecting his early embrace of the French Revolution, and his subsequent disillusionment, Shelley's *Revolt* opens with a canto simply entitled "France", whose first lines express political regrets, rather than interreligious engagement:

> When the last hope of trampled France had failed
> Like a brief dream of unremaining glory,
> From visions of despair I rose[5]

Despite its foreign title, Shelley's poem presents a crisis familiar to his Romantic readers in 1818, lamenting in his first-person voice the "unremaining glory" of European revolution. More overtly than Voltaire's *Mahomet* – the French "tragedy" translated by Goethe in 1799 – Shelley's *Revolt of Islam* critiques domestic nationalism under the banner of Orientalism, this supposedly "Islamic" poem opening with "trampled France" articulating "the lessons of the French Revolution".[6] Sarcastically suggesting Shelley's own Islamic conversion, Byron's comment seems especially applicable to Shelley's *The Revolt of Islam* – a poem which itself arose through textual conversion, remade from an earlier Shelley poem. Published in the previous year, Shelley's 1817 *Laon and Cythna; or, the Revolution of the Golden City: A Vision of the Nineteenth Century* was quickly condemned by critics, who were offended by the poem's "forthright attack on the Christian religion as complicit with oppressive political power", as well as its "representation of incestuous love", as Jack Donovan observes.[7] Electing to revise and rapidly reissue *Laon and Cythna*, Shelley's *The Revolt of Islam* appeared in January 1818, representing a thinly veiled remake of Shelley's withdrawn original.

The Islamic conversion of *Laon and Cythna* – like the Islamic conversion of Shelley himself, suggested by Byron – are equally facetious, with both writer and his writing remaining staunchly European in interest, and Romantic in purpose. However, if Shelley's *Revolt of Islam* has very little do with the Muslim religious, it would be a mistake to assume that Shelley was not interested in the religion altogether; while his critics correctly distance Shelley's political poetry from Islam per se, it is dangerous to widen this distance too far, risking neglect of Shelley's substantive engagement with Muslim sources. During the very time that he began the poem that would eventually be converted to his *Revolt of Islam*, Shelley also authored, for instance, a piece of unfinished prose, dedicated to "The Moral Teaching of Jesus Christ". In the first words of his essay, Shelley begins by addressing Christianity through a surprising Islamic comparison, contrasting the careers of the Messiah and Muḥammad. Emphasizing similarity and difference between these religious founders, Shelley asserts: "The preachers of the Christian religion urge the morality of Jesus Christ as being itself miraculous and stamped with the impression of divinity. Mahomet advanced the same pretensions respecting the composition of the Koran and, if we consider the number of his followers, with greater success."[8] A telling ambivalence in Shelley's treatment of "Mahomet" here emerges. Identifying an interreligious commonality, recognizing "the same" claims advanced by both Islam and Christianity, Shelley nevertheless credits the former with persuading more "followers", the Muslim mission advanced with "greater success". Casting doubt on Islam's authenticity – pejoratively alluding to the Prophet's "pretensions" concerning "the Koran" and its "composition"

– Shelley also seems to admire "Mahomet", marveling at his ability to attract a higher "number" of adherents than the "preachers of the Christian religion". Anticipating Byron's ironic epithet for his "Islamite" friend, Shelley here reflects on religious "conversion" through contrast, sketching "sameness" and "difference" between Christianity and Islam, while also belying their religious credibility. And yet, despite this irony and infidelity, this short selection also reflects an indebtedness to Islam that will persist through Shelley's writings, suggested not only by the "Islamic" conversion of *Laon and Cythna,* but also by a series of more substantive allusions in his later poetry. Demonstrating an awareness of the superior "success" of Islam, this religion will succeed too in sustaining Shelley's own later engagement; surfacing especially in the years before his premature death, Shelley ultimately proves to be a "follower" of Islamic interests, even while producing his final Romantic writings.

II

On the eve of my departure from Bombay, in October 1818, I met in the bazaar, at a Parsee book-stall, with a copy of *The Revolt of Islam*. It has been shipped with other unsaleable literary commodities . . . I was astonished at the greatness of [Shelley's] genius, and made the volume the companion of my journey, delighting to trace in it the elements of his young mind down to their complete development, as in a chart we love to follow the course of some river whose source we have visited. On my return he was the first person I wrote to, and found that he had not forgotten the companion of his boyhood.

Thomas Medwin[9]

Returning from his military service in colonial India, Thomas Medwin's final evening in "the Orient" introduces him to

Shelley's own Orientalist Romance, discovering "a copy of *The Revolt of Islam*" while Medwin frequents "a Parsee book-stall". Tracing a curious circle of transmission, Shelley's Eastern poem is "shipped" eastward, grouped with "other unsaleable literary commodities", only to find a reader from the West – a reader who elects to make this "volume" the "companion" of his own westward "journey" home. A vehicle of literal and literary "return", the *Revolt* leads Thomas Medwin not only back to Europe, but also back to a "companion of his boyhood"; inspired by the "genius" of his *Revolt of Islam*, Shelley is "the first person" that Medwin "wrote to" after reaching European shores. Charting his actual voyage home across foreign waters, Medwin's *"Islamic"* reading allows him also to "trace" Shelley's "young mind down" to its "complete development", as one would "follow the course of some river" on "a chart".

Cousin and fellow student of Shelley's – first attending school together at Syon House Academy – Thomas Medwin is prompted by Shelley's Eastern poem of English "genius" to find his friend again in the fall of 1820.[10] Joining Shelley in Italy, and also later meeting Byron there, Medwin is sufficiently impressed by this season of "companionship" to write prominent biographies and recollections of both Romantics in the coming years.[11] However, reflecting the "Islamic" impetus which leads Medwin to locate Shelley in 1820, it will also be Islamic interests that infuse their interactions during this autumn. Transcribing Byron's lighthearted quip, accusing Shelley "of being an Islamite", Medwin's sojourn in Italy will also promote Shelley's more earnest engagements with Muslim sources. Writing to his friend, Thomas Love Peacock, on November 8, 1820, Shelley reports from Italy that "A schoolfellow of mine from India is staying with me, and we are beginning Arabic together" – linguistic efforts that Medwin and Shelley pursued throughout the fall.[12] Catalyzed by Medwin's arrival, Shelley's "beginnings" in "Arabic" find him appealing to a range of friends for assistance, writing also to Claire Clairmont in Florence, seeking to procure not only "an Arabic Grammar and Dictionary" but "any other Arabic books, either printed or Manuscript".[13] Living together in the native region of Romance

– in Italy – Shelley and Medwin nevertheless turn their collective attention not merely to romance languages, but to Islam's liturgical language, with Arabic punctuating their daily journals and correspondence.

According to Medwin, however, his time in Italy with Shelley would be occupied not only with Eastern linguistics, but also with Eastern literature. In his *The Life of Percy Bysshe Shelley*, Medwin recalls that:

> We seldom read new works of fiction, but made an exception in favour of Antar, which we borrowed from Byron, and found greatly interesting. This Jack-the-Giant-Killer romance, abounds with vivid and picturesque, but overcharged descriptions of the scenery and manners of the tribes of the Desert, and [Shelley's] "Lines from the Arabic" were almost a translation from a translation in that Oriental fiction.[14]

Suggesting Byron's own influence in Shelley's Orientalism, Medwin notes their shared reading of *Antar* – a work by Terrick Hamilton, published in 1819–1820, and subtitled "*a Bedoueen Romance*".[15] A source for his literary study, Shelley's "exceptional" reading of this Eastern "fiction" seems also to have inspired his own Eastern poetry, Medwin ascribing the origins of Shelley's "Lines from the Arabic" to this Oriental "romance". Published soon after his death, and entitled "From the Arabic, an Imitation", Shelley's brief poem highlights Romantic interiority, rather than Orientalist exteriors, its opening lines setting the scene for a lover's lament, addressed to his lost beloved: "My faint spirit was sitting in the light / Of thy looks, my love".[16] Although identified by Medwin as "almost a translation from a translation", and composed while they were "beginning Arabic together", Shelley's Arabic imitation ironically speaks in a familiar voice, its English first-person featuring no references to foreign climes or characters. Poised again on the threshold between native culture and exotic conversion, Shelley's "From the Arabic, an Imitation" reflects his own "Islamite" identity, ambivalently negotiating original composition and deferred imitation, the poem's "I" balancing in a suspended space of "almost", itself a "translation of a translation".

If Arabic offered the primary inspiration for Shelley's minor poem of "Imitation", Arabic will also haunt a major drama produced by Shelley during this very same period. Appearing in the spring of 1822, *Hellas: A Lyrical Drama* would mark the very last poem published by Shelley, printed mere months before his untimely death.[17] Composed while still living in Italy, and still in communication with Medwin, the solidly European title of Shelley's *Hellas* seems to have little to do with their shared Eastern interests. However, inverting his earlier *Revolt of Islam*, which opens by invoking "Islam" but reflects Eurocentric concerns, Shelley's *Hellas* seems solely oriented to Europe, but features deep Islamic investments, recounting the story of Greek resistance to Turkish occupation.[18] It is not Greek heroes, but an Ottoman Sultan and his vizier – "Mahmud" and "Hassan" – who occupy the drama's opening; near the beginning of *Hellas*, Hassan lionizes Muslim conquest, proclaiming to his master Mahmud:

> The lamp of our dominion still rides high;
> One God is God – Mahomet is his prophet.
> Four hundred thousand Moslems from the limits
> Of utmost Asia, irresistibly
> Throng, like full clouds at the Sirocco's cry.[19]

Motivating the "Moslem" army is a spiritual maxim, Shelley's fictional Hassan articulating the authentic basis of the Muslim faith, suggesting the Islamic creed to be "the lamp of our dominion". Paraphrasing the *shahāda* within a single line, Hassan cites "One God is God – Mahomet is his prophet" as the "irresistible" banner of the Ottoman "Throng". As his speech unfolds in this section of *Hellas*, however, Hassan celebrates Muslim victory with ever more vivid and violent detail, his expressions advancing beyond English translation merely, attempting instead Arabic transliteration:

> Samos is drunk with blood; – the Greek has paid
> Brief victory with swift loss and long despair.

> The false Moldavian serfs fled fast and far,
> When the fierce shout of Allah-illa-Allah!
> Rose like the war-cry of the northern wind,
> Which kills the sluggish clouds, and leaves a flock
> Of wild swans struggling with the naked storm
> So were the lost Greeks on the Danube's day![20]

Again conceiving the Muslim creed as a "war-cry", Shelley infuses the heart of his hostile passage with the spiritual core of Islam. Rather than mere British "imitation", however, Shelley seeks to supplement this dramatic scene with actual Arabic, reporting "the fierce shout" that announces "Allah-illa-Allah!" Simulating imperfectly the first half of the Muslim *shahāda* – "*lā ilāha illā 'llāh*" ("there is no god but God") – Shelley's approximation of Arabic is corrupt, even as he voices the corrupt cause of Hassan, who fuses his militant motives with Muslim commitments, glorying in Greek "blood" as well as Islamic belief. Advancing a flawed impression of Muslim piety, as well as a flawed expression of the Muslim creed, Shelley's passage does reflect an attempt to capitalize on his recent language studies; weaving Arabic discourse directly into his British drama, Shelley crosses beyond "translation of translation", and arrives at dubious transliteration, adapting Islam's most essential sounds and significance to serve as the fleeting crux of this most fierce passage.

III

The pejorative portrait of Islam implied in this poetic opening to *Hellas* reflects Shelley's personal sympathies, but also his political purpose. As Jacqueline Mulhallen notes, the "avowed purpose of *Hellas* was to gain sympathy for the struggle for Greek independence" from Ottoman rule; Shelley himself famously insists to his readers in the drama's Preface: "we are all Greeks".[21] Considering this authorial bias, it is unsurprising to find *Hellas* filtering a range of hostile depictions of Muslim characters – a strategy that emerges in the drama's very opening, with Shelley's poem featuring the following introduction:

> SCENE. *A Terrace on the Seraglio.*
> MAHMUD *(sleeping), and Indian slave sitting beside his Couch.*
> *Chorus of Greek Captive Women.*
> We strew these opiate flowers
> On thy restless pillow, –
> They were stript from Orient bowers[22]

Packed into its first words, Shelley's *Hellas* offers a veritable catalogue of Orientalist tropes, his poetic introduction matching precisely our idea of Western essentialism of the East. Opening in a "seraglio", Shelley stresses Muslim "sensualism", mixing together decadent sexuality with intoxication, picturing a harem of "Greek women" attending to a single Muslim male, even as they "strew these opiate flowers". Perhaps more dark in this dramatic debut is Shelley's emphasis upon racial discrimination and female domination; seated "beside" the "couch" of the Sultan "Mahmud" is not only an "Indian slave", but also a faceless female "Chorus", these "Greek" women defined merely through their ethnicity and their "captivity".

This opening is not, of course, promising, if readers hope for a balanced view of the Muslim world – a view which could transcend Shelley's own commitment to the Greek cause. However, amid its Orientalist accents, even while associating Islam with sensuality and aggression, *Hellas* also features subtle hints of Shelley's more earnest interest in Muslim sources. Despite its plot which drives towards the defeat of Turkish forces, Shelley's drama also includes a curious passage that belies its anti-Islamic trends. Near the middle of *Hellas*, Mahmud receives a succession of messengers who ominously predict his army's impending downfall; the third of these messengers relates portents of Turkish overthrow, but also appeals to a surprising proof for his prediction, announcing that:

A Dervise, learned in the Koran, preaches
That it is written how the sins of Islam
Must raise up a destroyer even now.[23]

Consistent with much of his *Hellas*, Shelley links Turkish militarism with Muslim religiosity, suggesting that it is "Islam" and its spiritual "sins" that account for the earthly decline of the Ottomans. Even while offering this critique of "Islam", Shelley's passage nevertheless appeals to Islam as its authority, anticipating the "destruction" of the Sultan and his soldiers in the "preaching" of a Sufi "Dervise". The downfall of Muslim forces in *Hellas* is here revealed by Muslim revelation, with the Turks condemned by their own "Koran". Enthusiastically predicting Ottoman overthrow, Shelley's *Hellas* promotes its own literary prophecy through appealing to Islamic prophecy, anticipating the dénouement of his British drama in words supposedly "written" in Arabic scripture.

It is not the appearance of Muslim prophecy, however, but the appearance of the Muslim Prophet, which provides the most vigorous testimony to Shelley's late Islamic interests. While the published opening of *Hellas* is clearly unsympathetic to Islam, Shelley also drafted an unpublished Prologue to the play, which concerns not worldly politics, but rather the next world, and which presents too an alternate picture of Islam. Granted an afterlife in posthumous editions of Shelley's works beginning in 1862, this aborted Prologue to *Hellas* itself addresses the afterlife, depicting a conversation between spiritual speakers who convene in the Heavens. Opening with a "Herald of Eternity", Shelley sets his celestial scene with the following lines:

PROLOGUE TO HELLAS
Herald of Eternity. It is the day when all the sons of God
Wait in the roofless senate-house, whose floor
Is Chaos, and the immovable abyss
Frozen by His steadfast word to hyaline.[24]

Recalling the beginning to the Book of Job – where "the sons

of God came to present themselves before the LORD" (Job 1:6)
– Shelley too depicts a divine council where differing "sons of
God" assemble on a determined "day".[25] Dedicated primarily
to a dispute between "Christ" and "Satan", Shelley's fragmen-
tary "Prologue" situates these "sons of God" in dramatic debate,
wrangling over the future fate of "Greece". This colloquium in
Heaven is brought to a close with Christ's conclusive rebuke of
Satan:

> *Christ*   Obdurate spirit!
> Thou seest but the Past in the To-come.
> Pride is thy error and thy punishment.
> Boast not thine empire, dream not that thy worlds
> Are more than furnace-sparks or rainbow-drops
> Before the Power that wields and kindles them.
> True greatness asks not space, true excellence
> Lives in the Spirit of all things that live,
> Which lends it to the worlds thou callest thine.[26]

A critique of devilish "Pride", Christ's concluding lines in
Shelley's "Prologue" succeed in silencing Satan, censuring the
"error" of his identifying "true greatness" with earthly "space",
rather than Heavenly "Spirit". However, Christ's closing speech
does not close this "Prologue" completely; instead, Shelley adds
a few final lines, injecting too one final identity into this divine
dialogue. Immediately after Christ's climactic rebuke of Satan,
the Prologue continues on to its fragmentary end with the following verses:

> *Mahomet* . . . Haste thou and fill the waning crescent
> With beams as keen as those which pierced the shadow
> Of Christian night rolled back upon the West,
> When the orient moon of Islam rode in triumph
> From Tmolus to the Acroceraunian snow.
>
> .   .   .   .   .   .
>
>   Wake, thou Word
> Of God, and from the throne of Destiny

Even to the utmost limit of thy way
May Triumph

.   .   .   .

Be thou a curse on them whose creed
Divides and multiplies the most high God.[27]

While it is a "Herald of Eternity" who speaks first in Shelley's Prologue, it is "Mahomet" who speaks last, his final words aptly focused on "the most high God", proclaiming his unity, but also "cursing" those who "Divide and multiply" his divinity. An apt summary of Shelley's own ambivalent relationship with Islam, the Prophet emerges both between and beyond the polarities of *Hellas*' Prologue, with "Mahomet" voicing a final monologue which follows the dialogue between Christ and Satan. Admonishing the Christian "creed", even while seeking to rouse Christ to "Triumph", Shelley's "Mahomet" ambiguously appeals to the "Word / of God", even while heralding his own religion's victory, recounting how "the orient moon of Islam rode in triumph" as the "Christian night rolled back upon the West".[28] A triumphalism that is double in direction, accenting its author's ambivalence, Shelley echoes his earlier appreciation of the Prophet's "greater success", marveling at the "number of his followers", which surpass that of "the Christian religion". Emerging as an ironic "Islamite" in this unfinished sketch to his last published poem, Shelley reserves this fragmentary farewell for the enduring "triumph" of "Mahomet", the Prophet still associated with "success" as he becomes the final successor in this draft "Prologue". Occupying the silence that remains after Christ's own conclusion, Shelley pauses on the last threshold of his poetic life to enter an Islamic afterlife, witnessing to an uncertain Muslim "triumph", filling the celestial spaces above his *Hellas* with the "waning crescent" of his own Islamic interests.

13

"The female followers of Mahomet": Mary Shelley's *Frankenstein*

I

As her last completed novel, Jane Austen's *Persuasion* represents a fit culmination to her career. Published posthumously in 1818, only a few months after her death, *Persuasion* rehearses themes and scenes which have become synonymous with Austen's authorship, recounting a tale of courtship and romance, satirizing societal mores and manners. A novel of familiar domesticity, *Persuasion* does occasionally stray further afield, however, touching on references more foreign. In her eleventh chapter, Austen's female protagonist – Anne Elliot – reflects on her relationship with Captain James Benwick, who is described as:

> evidently a young man of considerable taste in reading, though principally in poetry; and besides the persuasion of having given him at least an evening's indulgence in the discussion of subjects, which his usual companions had probably no concern in, [Anne] had the hope of being of real use to him in some suggestions as to the duty and benefit of struggling against affliction, which had naturally grown out of their conversation. For, though shy, he did not seem reserved; it had rather the appearance of feelings glad to burst their usual restraints; and having talked of poetry, the richness of the present age, and gone through

> a brief comparison of opinion as to the first-rate poets,
> trying to ascertain whether *Marmion* or *The Lady of the
> Lake* were to be preferred, and how ranked the *Giaour*
> and *The Bride of Abydos*; and moreover, how the *Giaour*
> was to be pronounced, he showed himself so intimately
> acquainted with all the tenderest songs of the one poet,
> and all the impassioned descriptions of hopeless agony of
> the other.[1]

Characteristic of Austen's artistry is the inward psychology of
this passage, her heroine pondering the "intimate" details of personal qualities and character. However, this interior moment of
literary fiction also reaches outward to literary history, alluding
to the "richness of the present age", not only the tame and "tender" poetry of Sir Walter Scott's *The Lady of the Lake*, but also
the more "impassioned" and "agonized" productions of Lord
Byron. Naming both his "*Giaour* and *The Bride of Abydos*",
Persuasion here intersects Byron's *Turkish Tales*, Austen alluding
to these Eastern poems to heighten the romance of her English
novel. Debating the relative "ranking" of Byron's verses, Austen's
characters debate too issues of Byronic "pronunciation", discuss-
ing how best to voice the very title of his first *Turkish Tale*. In
considering "how the *Giaour* was to be pronounced", Benwick
offers a surprising signal of how "intimately acquainted" he is
with British poetry, this piece of Middle Eastern diction proving his familiarity with Romantic trends.[2] Bridging distinct literatures and languages, this vignette from *Persuasion* also bridges
genders, witnessing a moment of Islamic literary interest which
features women at its core, Byron's Orientalism meriting notice
from both Jane Austen – the author – and Anne Elliot – her
character.

Although Orientalism is frequently understood as the domain
of men, associated especially with "the Western male gaze",
this fleeting reference in Austen's *Persuasion* hints at a feminine
investment in the Romantic East which is often overlooked.[3] It
is not the leading lady of Austen's romantic fiction who best
exemplifies such a legacy, however, but rather the leading female

fictionist of British Romanticism – Mary Shelley – author of the era's most iconic novel, *Frankenstein*. Daughter of revolutionary thinkers William Godwin and Mary Wollstonecraft, Mary would become wife to Romanticism's revolutionary poet, Percy Bysshe Shelley, participating not only in her husband's artistic life, but also in his Islamic engagements. Introducing his *Revolt of Islam*, for example, Percy Shelley offers a prefatory poem which seeks not to explain this "Islamic" epic, but rather to celebrate his wife, Mary. Immortalizing his beloved as "his queen, his friend, his twin" – and most memorably as a "Child of love and light" – Percy Shelley's dedication positions Mary and her personal life at the very opening to his *Revolt of Islam*, inadvertently wedding his darling wife with this Orientalist Romance.[4] However, if 1818 finds Mary's identity surfacing at the opening to her husband's poem entitled by the Muslim faith, this same year will also mark Mary's own rise to literary fame, publishing her most celebrated work of fiction which also features critical Islamic intersections.

Mary Shelley's *Frankenstein* has proved to be one of Romanticism's most enduring classics, read across continents and centuries, endlessly adapted and imitated. First conceived during an 1816 vacation on Lake Geneva, in company with both Percy Shelley and Lord Byron, Frankenstein arose from personal and literary exchanges; Mary introduces her own novel as "the only [tale] which has been completed" from the several stories traded between these celebrated friends in 1816.[5] Finally appearing in January 1818, *Frankenstein* inaugurates a year that witnesses Jane Austen's allusion to the *Turkish Tales* in her posthumous *Persuasion*, as well as Percy Shelley's own "Islamic" *Revolt*. And while *Frankenstein* presents itself as a contemporary retelling of classical myth – its full title reading *Frankenstein; or The Modern Prometheus* – Mary's novel will nonetheless share with other "rich" Romantic works of this "present age" an interest in the Islamic East – an interest evident in 1818, with the novel's initial publication, and even more so in its revised edition, published in 1831. In the initial pages of this latter edition of her novel, Shelley offers an early

intimation of *Frankenstein*'s ˍOriental engagements; Robert
Walton – the captain who ultimately encounters Victor
Frankenstein and hears his tale – offers a brief catalogue of his
ship's crew in the novel's epistolary opening, concluding the
portrait of his ship's "master" with the following: "he is wholly
uneducated: he is as silent as a Turk, and a kind of ignorant
carelessness attends him, which, while it renders his conduct
the more astonishing, detracts from the interest and sympathy
which otherwise he would command."[6] Coloring his character
with Orientalist conventions, Captain Walton not only describes
his "friend" as "silent as a Turk", but also envelops this essen-
tializing trait with a host of unflattering attributes, from "uneducated", to "ignorant", to "carelessness". As the first gesture to
an Eastern identity in Shelley's 1831 *Frankenstein*, this Turkish
"silence" seems an unpromising start, hinting at a pejorative,
and perhaps peripheral, role for Islam in this Romantic novel.
However, as with much of *Frankenstein*, such initial impressions prove misleading. Despite this unfavorable opening, the
Muslim East will prove a consistent object of "interest and sympathy" in Shelley's novel, relegated not to mere passing references, but serving as a pivotal catalyst in the novel's plot and its
protagonists' development.[7]

II

It is *Frankenstein*'s fourth chapter that features the frightful
discovery which propels the tragic action of the entire novel:
namely, Victor Frankenstein's solving the secret of "animation",
allowing him to bring life from the dead. However, it is precisely
the scene which witnesses this central discovery that also features one of *Frankenstein*'s most explicit gestures to the Islamic
East. Recalling his dramatic moment of scientific breakthrough,
Frankenstein frames his wondrous "experience" through a conspicuously "Arabian" simile:

The astonishment which I had at first experienced on this
discovery soon gave place to delight and rapture. After so
much time spent in painful labour, to arrive at once at the
summit of my desires, was the most gratifying consum-
mation of my toils. But this discovery was so great and
overwhelming, that all the steps by which I had been pro-
gressively led to it were obliterated, and I beheld only the
result. What had been the study and desire of the wisest
men since the creation of the world was now within my
grasp. Not that, like a magic scene, it all opened upon me
at once: the information I had obtained was of a nature
rather to direct my endeavours so soon as I should point
them towards the object of my search than to exhibit that
object already accomplished. I was like the Arabian who
had been buried with the dead, and found a passage to life
aided only by one glimmering, and seemingly ineffectual,
light.[8]

Confessing his crowning achievement, Frankenstein here attains
"the summit of my desires", surpassing in his scientific advance
all the "wisest men since the creation of the world". This "raptur-
ous" climax to Frankenstein's efforts is itself capped, however,
with a rather surprising climax. Culminating not with loud exul-
tation, but with a literary allusion, Frankenstein's narration ends
by likening himself to "the Arabian", who, like Frankenstein,
"had been buried with the dead and found a passage to life".
Referencing an episode from the classic collection of Arabic tales,
A Thousand and One Nights – an episode which recounts the
"escape" of Sinbad from his own wife's tomb, where he had been
"interred alive" – Mary Shelley reaches eastward to characterize
her own European protagonist.[9] It is the critical moment which
Shelley selects for this cross-cultural reference, however, that
heightens its significance. Presenting her novel's central motif to
Romantic readers, Shelley appeals to an "Arabian" romance to
help communicate the "passage to life" that will motivate the plot
of *Frankenstein*, and which will mould the character of Victor
Frankenstein. Gesturing not only abstractly across continents

and cultures, Frankenstein finds his own personal experience anticipated by an Arabic precedent, translating his very identity through an Eastern lens; "I", Frankenstein insists, "was like the Arabian."

Exemplifying its theme of "animation" with an "Arabian" allusion, *Frankenstein* not only imbues the catalyst of its dramatic action with an Eastern color, but also suggests the Eastern directions the novel will subsequently pursue. Punctuating the most pivotal moments of *Frankenstein* are allusions to the Muslim East, with Shelley appealing to Islamic referents as a means of propelling her narrative's progress. Animated to life in Chapter 5, the novel's Monster immediately flees the scene, leaving Frankenstein bereft, and leaving *Frankenstein* without its grotesque character. However, Shelley's story receives new momentum with the arrival of Clerval, Frankenstein's childhood friend. The most Romantic of Shelley's protagonists, Clerval arrives as a confidant for Frankenstein, joining him at the University of Ingolstadt; however, Clerval serves not merely as a familiar comfort, but also shifts Frankenstein's attention towards more foreign interests, as Frankenstein himself recalls:

> Clerval had never sympathized in my tastes for natural science; and his literary pursuits differed wholly from those which had occupied me. He came to the university with the design of making himself complete master of the oriental languages, and thus he should open a field for the plan of life he had marked out for himself. Resolved to pursue no inglorious career, he turned his eyes toward the East, as affording scope for his spirit of enterprise. The Persian, Arabic, and Sanscrit languages engaged his attention, and I was easily induced to enter on the same studies. Idleness had ever been irksome to me, and now that I wished to fly from reflection, and hated my former studies, I felt great relief in being the fellow-pupil with my friend, and found not only instruction but consolation in the works of the orientalists. I did not, like him, attempt a critical knowledge of their dialects, for I did not

contemplate making any other use of them than temporary amusement. I read merely to understand their meaning, and they well repaid my labours. Their melancholy
is soothing, and their joy elevating, to a degree I never
experienced in studying the authors of any other country.
When you read their writings, life appears to consist in
a warm sun and a garden of roses, – in the smiles and
frowns of a fair enemy, and the fire that consumes your
own heart. How different from the manly and heroical
poetry of Greece and Rome![10]

Opening with a juxtaposition between himself and Clerval, pitting "natural scientist" versus "literary" aspirant, Frankenstein
concludes this passage also with a juxtaposition, pitting classical
versus Oriental, "Greece and Rome" versus "the East". At the
personal heart of this passage, however, is the "relief" experienced by Frankenstein as he opens himself to "oriental" languages and literatures, following Clerval as "he turned his eyes
toward the East". Blending together the Indic and the Islamic
– with "Sanscrit" added to "Persian and Arabic" – the Eastern
horizons traced by Frankenstein are hazy in their broad scope.[11]
What is clear, however, is that Islamic culture plays a primary
role in relieving Shelley's protagonist from his recent trauma
and terror, not only "soothed" by the "melancholy" of Muslim
sources, but also "elevated" by their "joy". Perhaps most interesting is that this vignette of Eastern study seems an inverse echo
of Frankenstein's monstrous "discovery", which was also infused
with Oriental allusion. Both immediately before, and immediately after, his tragic creation, Frankenstein's intellectual pursuits
are framed through "Arabian" precedents, with the East envel-
oping his Monster's animation.

Buoyed up by his best friend's arrival, Chapter 6 finds
Frankenstein enjoying his final moments of light-hearted companionship before discovering the death and destruction insti-
gated by his Monster. In the concluding sentences of the chapter,
Frankenstein again emphasizes the Eastern "resources" which
help him to suppress his anxiety and alarm:

[Clerval] rejoiced in my gaiety, and sincerely sympathi-
sed in my feelings: he exerted himself to amuse me, while
he expressed the sensations that filled his soul. The
resources of his mind on this occasion were truly astonishing: his conversation was full of imagination; and
very often, in imitation of the Persian and Arabic writers, he invented tales of wonderful fancy and passion. At
other times he repeated my favourite poems, or drew me
out into arguments, which he supported with great
ingenuity.

We returned to our college on a Sunday afternoon: the
peasants were dancing, and every one we met appeared
gay and happy. My own spirits were high, and I bounded
along with feelings of unbridled joy and hilarity.[12]

This chapter conclusion – with its "unbridled joy and hilarity"
– seems ironically ominous; as careful readers will doubtlessly
anticipate, Frankenstein's good mood is much too good to last,
doomed to be crushed by the consequences of his hideous creation.
Indeed, immediately after the above passage, Chapter 7 will open
by revealing the death of Frankenstein's younger brother, who is
murdered by his Monster. On the precipice of this impending cata-
clysm, however, Shelley infuses this ending to Chapter 6 with an
Eastern atmosphere, with "Persian and Arabic" sustaining the "gay
and happy" exchange between Frankenstein and Clerval. Rather
than a collaborative study of these Eastern languages, however,
the friends now trade "tales" which are "invented" from Muslim
models, Clerval fashioning stories for Frankenstein "in imitation
of the Persian and Arabic writers". Recalling her own literary environs and exchanges – keeping company with Percy Shelley and
Byron, both of whom also author "tales of wonderful fancy and
passion" based upon "Persian and Arabic writers" – Mary Shelley
infuses this portentous moment of "hilarity" with an eerie echo of
her own "imaginative" friends, the East forming a pivotal bridge
between chapters and moods in *Frankenstein*, but also between the
author's own actual world and her world of fiction.

III

Conceived amid literary conversations on Lake Geneva during the summer of 1816, it is perhaps unsurprising that scholarly readers of Shelley's *Frankenstein* have frequently noted the novel's indebtedness to other Romantic works. A top candidate for such influence has been Percy Bysshe Shelley's own *Alastor* (1816) – a poetic narrative that traverses "Arabie / And Persia, and the wild Carmanian waste", Eastern climes which seem to echo into the Oriental yearnings of *Frankenstein*'s Clerval. Perhaps more relevant, however, is the Eastern femininity shared between *Alastor* and *Frankenstein*, with both Percy Shelley's poem and Mary Shelley's novel prominently featuring an "Arab maiden", as Joseph Lew has emphasized.[13] In *Frankenstein*, this female foreigner – "Safie" – makes only a brief appearance, emerging in the novel's middle chapters merely. Minor in scope, Safie nevertheless holds major significance for Shelley's fiction, altering the direction of *Frankenstein* and sustaining its drama. In Chapter 11, after fleeing his creator, Victor Frankenstein, the Monster takes up residence in a "hovel" adjacent to a family's quiet cottage. Introduced to kinship and compassion, the Monster listens intently to this family's domestic interactions, appreciating for the first time human language, as well as humane relations. This unusual apprenticeship is advanced by the sudden "appearance" in Chapter 13 of a stranger – Safie – who is greeted affectionately by the family's son – Felix De Lacey – as the Monster himself recalls: "[Safie] appeared affected by different feelings; wiping a few tears from her lovely eyes, she held out her hand to Felix, who kissed it rapturously and called her, as well as I could distinguish, his sweet Arabian." Observing closely Safie's assimilation into the rhythms of the De Lacey family, the Monster soon also adds:

> My days were spent in close attention, that I might more
> speedily master the language; and I may boast that I
> improved more rapidly than the Arabian, who under-
> stood very little and conversed in broken accents, whilst I

comprehended and could imitate almost every word that
was spoken.[14]

Although buried in the rough backwoods of Europe, the Monster
surprisingly witnesses the arrival of a "sweet Arabian" at the
country cottage. Implausibly intensifying the Oriental investments
of her novel, Shelley's *Frankenstein* no longer merely features a
male character who romantically yearns for the East – Clerval
– but introduces a female character who actually hails from the
East – Safie. Perhaps most striking in this introduction, however,
is the intimacy exhibited between *Frankenstein*'s French son and
its Middle Eastern maiden – between Felix De Lacey and Safie
– an intimacy which the voyeuristic Monster finds infectious,
immediately developing his own sympathies with Safie. Impressed
by this scene's emotions, but also its expressions, the Monster
begins to acquire language through witnessing Safie's own falter-
ing progress, with "the Arabian" serving as the Monster's unconscious mentor, as well as a mirror for his linguistic strangeness.
Measuring his own efforts to "imitate almost every word that was
spoken", Safie serves as a surrogate foreigner for the Monster,
indexing his language acquisition in her "broken accents".[15]

Establishing a hidden "Arabian" apprenticeship for her
Monster, Shelley sketches a "scene of instruction" which is
explicitly Eastern, her Monster acquiring not only language,
but also literary culture, from Safie's study. "While I improved
in speech, I also learned the science of letters, as it was taught to
the stranger", the Monster recalls later in Chapter 13, remarking that "The book from which Felix instructed Safie was
Volney's 'Ruins of Empires'", a "work" which "he had chosen . . . because the declamatory style was framed in imitation
of the eastern authors". "While I listened to the instructions
which Felix bestowed upon the Arabian", the Monster adds
further, "the strange system of human society was explained to
me".[16] Indebted to "the Arabian" for his opportunity to receive
"instruction", the content of the Monster's instruction is also
"Eastern", overhearing Safie's learning from a "book" whose
"style" is fashioned in "imitation of the eastern authors".

Benefitting from Safie's own status as "stranger", it is Safie who ironically allows the Monster to grasp "the strange system of human society", this foreigner from Arabia assisting the Monster as he familiarizes himself with European environs. Reinforcing the parallel between the Monster and Safie, Shelley also here suggests a parallel too between the Monster and Victor Frankenstein, with both creation and his creator profiting from "Eastern" pedagogy. Several chapters before, it was Frankenstein who had sought "consolation in the works of the orientalists" in the wake of the Monster's traumatic flight. In a stunning parallel, it is the Monster himself who now finds nourishment in Oriental study, easing his own alienation through the arrival of a "sweet Arabian", who is taught the eloquence of "eastern authors".[17]

The appearance of Safie in *Frankenstein*'s Chapter 13 not only heightens the broadly Middle Eastern atmosphere of Shelley's novel, however, but also provides a source for specific Islamic reflection. Although a seemingly secondary character in the story as a whole, Safie's background merits substantive attention, her personal genealogy reported in vivid detail:

> Safie related that her mother was a Christian Arab, seized and made a slave by the Turks; recommended by her beauty, she had won the heart of the father of Safie, who married her. The young girl spoke in high and enthusiastic terms of her mother, who, born in freedom, spurned the bondage to which she was now reduced. She instructed her daughter in the tenets of her religion and taught her to aspire to higher powers of intellect and an independence of spirit forbidden to the female followers of Mahomet. This lady died; but her lessons were indelibly impressed on the mind of Safie, who sickened at the prospect of again returning to Asia and being immured within the walls of a haram, allowed only to occupy herself with infantile amusements, ill suited to the temper of her soul, now accustomed to grand ideas and a noble emulation for virtue.[18]

Daughter of Britain's pioneering feminist, Mary Wollstonecraft, it is tempting to see Mary Shelley's own life mirrored in the strong maternal influence that Safie enjoys, as has been recognized by several critics.[19] Recalling Shelley herself, Safie speaks "in high and enthusiastic terms of her mother" – a mother who "instructed her daughter" and "taught her to aspire to higher powers of intellect" and "independence of spirit". Unlike Shelley's own life, however, the motherly priorities which emerge in *Frankenstein* assume a distinctly Islamic identity, with Safie's maternal feminism defined against her Muslim father, and his Muslim faith. Privileging Christian "freedom" over Turkish "bondage", Safie aspires to an "independence" supposedly "forbidden" to "the female followers of Mahomet", Shelley's novel invoking the Prophet's very name while also indicting patriarchy.

Aptly anticipating her own husband's *Hellas*, Shelley's *Frankenstein* seems here to associate the Muslim East with female captivity, celebrating Safie's escape from the "walls of a haram" which had held her mother in sensual "slavery". However, again like Percy Shelley's dramatic poem, a more nuanced view of Islam is also subtly implied in Mary Shelley's treatment. While preferring her Christian mother over her Muslim father, Safie's story seems designed to elicit Islamic sympathy, situating this "Turkish" man as European victim; continuing to relate the history of Safie's family, the Monster notes that:

> The father of Safie had been the cause of their ruin. He was a Turkish merchant and had inhabited Paris for many years, when, for some reason which I could not learn, he became obnoxious to the government. He was seized and cast into prison the very day that Safie arrived from Constantinople to join him. He was tried and condemned to death. The injustice of his sentence was very flagrant; all Paris was indignant; and it was judged that his religion and wealth rather than the crime alleged against him had been the cause of his condemnation.

> Felix had accidentally been present at the trial; his horror
> and indignation were uncontrollable when he heard the
> decision of the court. He made, at that moment, a sol-
> emn vow to deliver him and then looked around for the
> means. After many fruitless attempts to gain admittance
> to the prison, he found a strongly grated window in an
> unguarded part of the building, which lighted the dun-
> geon of the unfortunate Mahometan, who, loaded with
> chains, waited in despair the execution of the barbarous
> sentence.[20]

Although still censured as the "cause" of his family's "ruin",
Safie's "father" does not truly seem at fault; rather, it is the prejudices of the Parisian "government" which trigger his downfall
and Safie's dispossession, with European "injustice" leading to
Turkish "condemnation". Indeed, Shelley here suggests that it
is not merely the Muslim's "wealth" that makes him a target,
but also his "religion"; again associating Islam with persecu-
tion, *Frankenstein* inverts its prior privileging of Christian over
Muslim, portraying the Muslim male not as a captor, but as a
captive, victimized by Western chauvinism. Referencing "religion" explicitly as "the cause of his condemnation", religion
is also implied more subtly in Shelley's character description;
even while emphasizing his "barbarous sentence", Safie's father
is designated no longer as a "Turk", but as a "Mahometan",
ensuring that the Prophet's very name is associated with his
struggle against "injustice". Balancing Shelley's prior portrait
of the persecuted "female followers of Mahomet", it is now
a "Mahometan" man who stands as the persecuted party,
this lone Muslim in *Frankenstein* ambivalently eliciting readers' sympathy as he suffers European discrimination due to his
Islamic adherence.

Soon after these extended meditations on her family, Safie dis-
appears from Shelley's novel, fleeing with the De Laceys after the
Monster reveals himself to the family at the end of Chapter 15.
And yet, Safie's presence echoes to the very end of *Frankenstein*.
As Joyce Zonana has emphasized, the Monster seeks to

demonstrate the "truth of [his] tale" by presenting as proof a
series of letters between Safie and Felix – letters which are cited
again by Captain Walton very near the story's conclusion, with
these written words by the "sweet Arabian" surfacing to legiti-
mize *Frankenstein* in its final pages.[21] A character of "strange"
correspondence, Safie provides a mirror for the novel's fictional
Monster, but also its actual author, with Safie's letters sustaining the veracity of Shelley's *Frankenstein,* even while allowing
Shelley to explore issues of "Arabian" maternity. And, ironically,
it is this latter concern which also finds a faint, yet poignant, echo
in Shelley's own later life and letters. A decade after composing
her iconic novel, Mary would find herself the lone parent to a
growing son, Percy Jr. – the namesake of his deceased father,
Percy Bysshe Shelley. Seven years old in the summer of 1827,
Percy Jr. and his budding literary pursuits occupy his mother's
attention; writing to her friend, Mary Lamb, on July 22, 1827,
Mary Shelley ends her "affectionate" letter with an update on her
son's developments:

> Percy is quite well – & is reading with great extacy the
> Arabian Nights – I shall return I suppose some one day in
> September – God Bless you
>
> Yours Affectionately
> Mary W. Shelley[22]

In this glimpse of her family's daily life, Mary Shelley assures her
friend of the progress and "reading" of young Percy, while also
projecting a "return" visit "in September". Amid these domestic details, however, a more intriguing element emerges, Mary
highlighting Percy's "great" excitement as he reads, for the first
time, "the Arabian Nights". Recalling his own deceased father,
as well as the fictional Victor Frankenstein, Percy Jr. finds delight
in "Eastern authors", enjoying not merely "consolation" but
"extacy" in this "Arabian" classic. It is not merely the men in
Mary Shelley's life – historical or fantastical, senior or junior
– that seem reflected in this moment of "reading", however, but
rather Mary herself. A single mother, the lone parent respon-

sible for instructing Percy Jr. "to aspire to higher powers of intellect", Mary nevertheless encourages her son to experience his own moment of "ecstatic" discovery in this Middle Eastern classic, allowing yet another Shelley generation to feel "like the Arabian", enlightened by the "one glimmering and seemingly ineffectual light" which still shines through "tales of wonderful fancy and passion" coined by "Persian and Arabic writers".

14

"A strong mixture of the Saracenic with the Gothic": Irving's Islamic Biographies

I

By the summer of 1830, Mary Shelley had been a widow and single mother for more than eight years. Relying on her literary gifts for financial gain, Mary found herself in debt, urgently searching for new sources of income. Writing to John Murray on August 9, 1830, Mary reminded the famed publisher of his promise to allow her to contribute to his "Family Library" series – a series of books targeting domestic British tastes, specializing in popular history and biography. "I am now anxious to that we should agree as soon as possible on the subject", Mary insists at the opening of her August letter, citing her need of "defraying" her "present debt", and "earning" a "further sum".[1] First mentioning a possible "Life of Mme de Staël" – the French proto-feminist, and a biographical subject previously suggested by Murray himself – Mary pivots next to her own ideas for a potential biography:

> As [a biography of Madame de Staël] may not enter into your plans, I have been meditating on other subjects to form a volume of your Library. Two or three have struck me. A Friend suggested the life of Mahomet – as not

having been written for some years and therefore permitting novelty.[2]

Although Murray had proposed that Mary write the "life" of a contemporary European woman, Mary counters with a man of Arabian antiquity, nominating a biography on the Muslim Prophet.

Daughter of feminist pioneer, Mary Wollstonecraft, Mary Shelley's exchange of "Mme de Staël" for "Mahomet" seems surprising; however, the irony of such exchange is heightened by Mary's motives in 1830. Aiming to write for Murray's "Family Library" to remedy her own family's debts, Mary proposes a "subject" that is both foreign and sacred, reaching back to Islamic history to infuse her proposed British biography with "novelty". In 1818, Mary's *Frankenstein* had featured a heroine – Safie – who demonstrates an "independence of spirit" supposedly "forbidden to the female followers of Mahomet"; a dozen years later, Mary seeks to gain her own independence by herself becoming a "female follower of Mahomet", turning away from John Murray's own biographical candidate ("Mme de Staël"), proposing to pursue instead a life of the Prophet of Islam.

Seeking to sustain her small family by making such literary proposals to Murray, Mary Shelley would herself receive romantic proposals during her years as a widow, entertaining offers of marriage from prominent authors and artists in the wake of her renowned husband's death. Fending off most of her suitors, Mary seems to have made an exception with an eligible bachelor from abroad, welcoming the attentions of America's most prominent author, Washington Irving. Celebrated writer of sketches and short stories – most famously, his "The Legend of Sleepy Hollow" and "Rip Van Winkle" (1819–1820) – Irving's distinctly American fame was forged even while he pursued a career across the Atlantic; departing his native home in New York in 1815, Irving would reside in England and Europe for more than a decade and a half, writing his most recognized fiction while in foreign nations.[3] Unfolding a flirtation after they first met in 1824, Mary's friendship with Irving continued through the summer of 1830, hosting Irving at her home during the very period that Mary proposed a "life of Mahomet" to Murray.[4] Moreover, this overlap in Mary's personal life and her publishing prospects – entertaining an American author, even while "meditating" on the Arabian Prophet – was likely not a coincidence. Taking tea with Mary in the summer of 1830, Irving had recently returned from a three-year sojourn in Spain, where he had fallen in love with the country's Islamic past, captivated by Moorish architecture and medieval legends. Arriving back in England in 1829, Irving was eager to share his Andalucian adventures with British friends, enthusiastically relating his residence in the Alhambra, Granada's historic palace; indeed, in 1830, Irving had just begun to write an autobiographical account of his stay in Islamic Spain, which would appear two years later as the 1832 *The Alhambra: A Series of Tales and Sketches*.[5]

In Mary's August letter to Murray, she had indicated that it was "a Friend" who had "suggested" that she attempt "the life of Mahomet" – "a Friend" whose name Mary mysteriously withholds, but which seems to fit Irving well. Indeed, while Mary herself ultimately abandons this biographical "suggestion", Irving will pursue precisely this project, agreeing to write a "life of Mahomet" for John Murray's "Family Library" series – a project that would appear exactly two decades later, published as Irving's two-volume *Life of Mahomet and his Successors* in 1849–1850.[6] If Irving is indeed Mary's anonymous "Friend" who had proposed to her a "life of Mahomet", this would also fit the amicable atmosphere that surrounds his Islamic interests during this formative period in his career. The Moorish travels and tales which inspired Irving's authorship in 1830 were themselves rooted in deep friendship, as the first words of his *The Alhambra* make clear. Prefaced by a "Dedication" to David Wilkie – the Scottish artist who accompanied Irving in his Andalucian journeys – *The Alhambra* features an epistolary introduction, addressed directly to Irving's dear friend:

DEDICATION.
TO DAVID WILKIE, ESQ. R.A.

MY DEAR SIR,
You may remember that, in the rambles we once took
together about some of the old cities of Spain, particularly
Toledo and Seville, we remarked a strong mixture of the
Saracenic with the Gothic, remaining from the time of the
Moors; and were more than once struck with scenes and
incidents in the streets, which reminded us of passages in
the "Arabian Nights." You then urged me to write something that should illustrate those peculiarities; "something
in the Haroun Alrasched style," that should have a dash
of that Arabian spice which pervades every thing in Spain.
I call this to your mind to show you that you are, in some
degree, responsible for the present work; in which I have
given a few "Arabesque" sketches from the life, and tales
founded on popular traditions, which were chiefly struck
off during a residence in one of the most Morisco-Spanish
places in the Peninsula.

I inscribe these pages to you as a memorial of the pleasant
scenes we have witnessed together in that land of adventure, and as a testimonial of an esteem for your worth
which is only exceeded by admiration of your talents.

Your friend and fellow traveller,
THE AUTHOR.[7]

Irving opens his *Alhambra* with an open letter, framing his memoir of Spain as a personal conversation, even while framing Spain
itself as a conversation of cultures. Bridging Islamic East and
Christian West, "the old cities of Spain" are defined by Irving
as "a strong mixture of the Saracenic with the Gothic", fusing
together the Arabian and the European. A cultural blend, Spain's
"mixture" is also a creative catalyst, with Andalucia blurring the
lines not only between East and West, but also between fact and
fiction. Shifting from literal passage to literary passages, Irving's

"rambles" through Spanish "streets" lead him to "Arabian" sentences, recalling that "we were more than once struck with scenes and incidents in the *streets*, which reminded us of *passages* in the 'Arabian Nights'" (emphasis added).

Marrying literary imagination with actual life, this dedication to David Wilkie involves too a compositional marriage, with *The Alhambra* defined as a collaborative work, fusing "together" discrete literary traditions and types. Encouraged by Wilkie to emulate "something in the Haroun Alrasched style", Irving pictures his authorship as a hybrid enterprise, flavoring his American memoir with "a dash of that Arabian spice". A collaboration between multiple cultures, *The Alhambra* arises too from multiple authors, owing its origins not to Irving alone, but also to his friend; it is David Wilkie who "urged me to write", Irving insists, and therefore it is Wilkie who is also "in some degree, responsible for the present work". Recalling Mary Shelley's 1830 letter to Murray – proposing a "life of Mahomet" but only at the "suggestion" of a "Friend" – Irving begins his own "Arabian" writings in 1830 by attributing them to a close companion. And, as in Mary's private letter, Irving's name is also missing from this public letter at the opening to *The Alhambra*, signing this epistolary introduction only as "THE AUTHOR", with Irving aptly identifying himself merely as "your friend and fellow traveller". Proposing to write "Arabesque sketches" that imply a complex series of Romantic relationships, Irving's prefatory letter to Wilkie anticipates too the "strong mixture" of identities and imperatives that follow all his "rambles" through Islamic history, emerging not only in his personal autobiography – the 1832 *Alhambra* – but also embodied in his prophetic biography – the 1849–1850 *Life of Mahomet*.[8]

II

Although Irving's fame is undoubtedly due to his early fiction, his later career would increasingly turn to non-fiction, penning bulky works of biography, lionizing men of national significance and worldly renown. Indeed, Irving's decision to travel to Spain in 1826 was motivated not by Romantic fancy, but by profitable history, hoping to compose a marketable life of Christopher Columbus. Researching in the very land that had launched the famous explorer's 1492 mission to the New World, Irving first settled in Madrid, granting him access to unique resources for his biography of this "founder of America"; however, during this same time, Irving's attention was led further afield, attracted instead by the founder of Islam. Inspired by Spain's Moorish atmosphere and aesthetics, Irving's imagination consistently drifted not to Western destinations, but to Eastern origins. Even while completing his *A History of the Life and Voyages of Christopher Columbus* – first published in 1828 – Irving had already begun to conceive another project, his *Life of Mahomet*.[9]

Despite the delay in its appearance – not published until 1849–1850, after its author had permanently returned to America – Irving's biography of the Muslim Prophet vividly reflects a rich synthesis "of the Saracenic with the Gothic" that characterizes his earlier Spanish sojourn in the late 1820s. Indeed, from the very introduction to Irving's 1849–1850 *Life of Mahomet*, readers sense the same "mixture" of cultural identities and compositional approaches that are highlighted at the opening of his 1832 *Alhambra*. Offering a general introduction to Arabia in his biography's Chapter 1, Irving's second chapter turns to his specific subject, introducing "Mahomet" himself. It is the transition between these initial two chapters, however, that best exemplifies the "strong mixture" of style and significance which haunts Irving's authorship, dramatizing diverse perspectives in close succession; reproduced below is the very conclusion to Irving's Chapter 1 and the very opening to his Chapter 2 as they appeared in the 1850 *Life of Mahomet*:

> The time at length arrived when its discordant tribes were
> to be united in one creed, and animated by one common
> cause; when a mighty genius was to arise, who should
> bring together these scattered limbs, animate them with his

own enthusiastic and daring spirit, and lead them forth, a giant of the desert, to shake and overturn the empires of the earth.

CHAPTER II
Birth and Parentage of Mahomet – His infancy and childhood

Mahomet, the great founder of the faith of Islam, was born in Mecca, in April, in the year 569 of the Christian era. He was of the valiant and illustrious tribe of Koreish, of which there were two branches, descended from two brothers, Haschem and Abd Schems. Haschem, the progenitor of Mahomet, was a great benefactor of Mecca.[10]

Concluding Chapter 1 with dramatic suspense, hinting at the advent of a "mighty genius", Irving reserves the Prophet's actual introduction for the opening to his Chapter 2, where the Prophet's "birth and parentage" are finally announced. If sensible in its narrative progress, the narrative style of this chapter transition seems somewhat disjointed, with the soaring rhetoric at the end of Chapter 1 brought down to earth suddenly in the plain facts offered at the beginning of Chapter 2. Moving from mythic vision to historical grounding, Irving shifts between opposing approaches to the Prophet's story in immediate sequence, transitioning from epic expectations to mundane circumstances – from the life of a Promethean hero, to the life of a human personality. Recalling the fusing of the literary and the literal in his *Alhambra*, Irving's "passage" between *Mahomet*'s Chapters 1 and 2 serves to merge spiritual promise with concrete place, traveling between the Prophet's divine potential and his detailed origins.

Featuring a "strong mixture" of styles in his introduction to the Prophet of Islam, Irving also introduces Islam itself as a "strong mixture", describing the religion's advent as a synthetic event. Associating the Prophet's mission with progress

from the "discordant" to the concordant, Irving acknowledges
the "tribal" diversity which precedes Islamic unity, with the
Prophet successfully integrating his "scattered" peoples into
a single unit, who now espouse "one creed" and "one common cause". Recalling the Romantic writings of his own dear
"Friend" – Mary Shelley – Irving seems to echo language that
first surfaces in *Frankenstein*, picturing the Prophet's mission as
a process of bodily "animation". At the end of Chapter 1, Irving's
"Mahomet" emerges as a hero who endows "scattered limbs"
with new life, a solitary "genius" who is uniquely able to "ani-
mate" these separate members through "his own enthusiastic
and daring spirit". It is not only Mary Shelley, but also
Percy Bysshe Shelley, that seems to haunt Irving's first prophetic portrait, with a revolutionary role attributed to Islam
as well. Pictured not only as "a giant of the desert" – a living Ozymandias – Irving's "Mahomet" emerges too as a figure
of Islamic "Revolt", a Prophet who is endowed with political
potential, promising "to shake and overturn the empires of the
earth". Offering a picture with mixed priorities, Irving seems
to draw on a pastiche of literary precedents in his introduction of Islam, sewing together a "scattered" range of previous
accounts, his American biography itself "animating" a range of
Romantic forbears.[11]

Vacillating between vivid imagination and unvarnished biography, Irving's shift between Chapters 1 and 2 anticipates the
entirety of his *Mahomet*, which regularly punctuates its plain
account of the Prophet's life with miraculous moments, revel-
ing in scenes of wondrous transition and travel. Emerging first
at the end of his first chapter, Irving's synthetic approach to
the Prophet's own birth anticipates his approach to the birth of
Islam itself. After addressing Muḥammad's youth and early man-
hood, Irving reaches the initial revelations of his new religion,
with Chapter 6 of *Mahomet* detailing the commencement of the
Qur'ān's communication to the Prophet:

> It was in the fortieth year of his age, when this famous
> revelation took place. Accounts are given of it by Moslem

writers as if received from his own lips, and it is alluded to in certain passages of the Koran. He was passing, as was his wont, the month of Ramadhan in the cavern of Mount Hara, endeavoring by fasting, prayer, and solitary meditation, to elevate his thoughts to the contemplation of divine truth. It was on the night called by Arabs Al Kader, or the Divine Decree; a night in which, according to the Koran, angels descend to earth, and Gabriel brings down the decrees of God. During that night there is peace on earth, and a holy quiet reigns over all nature until the rising of the morn.

As Mahomet, in the silent watches of the night, lay wrapped in his mantle, he heard a voice calling upon him; uncovering his head, a flood of light broke upon him of such intolerable splendor that he swooned away. On regaining his senses, he beheld an angel in a human form, which, approaching from a distance, displayed a silken cloth covered with written characters. "Read!" said the angel.

"I know not how to read!" replied Mahomet.

"Read!" repeated the angel, "in the name of the Lord, who has created all things; who created man from a clot of blood. Read in the name of the Most High, who taught man the use of the pen; who sheds on his soul the ray of knowledge, and teaches him what before he knew not."

Upon this Mahomet instantly felt his understanding illumined with celestial light, and read what was written on the cloth, which contained the decrees of God, as afterwards promulgated in the Koran. When he had finished the perusal, the heavenly messenger announced, "Oh Mahomet, of a verity thou art the prophet of God! and I am his angel Gabriel."[12]

Again approaching his Islamic subject with an artistic sensibility, Irving uncovers a range of sensory experiences implied in this spiritual event. Set in the "silent watches of the night", Irving establishes a dark scene of "holy quiet", whose nocturnal "peace" is dramatically interrupted by "a voice" as well as "a flood of light", which possesses "intolerable splendor". A moment of tense transition – from silence to sound, from dark to light – the dynamism of Irving's scene is amplified too by various verbs of motion and movement. Beginning with the Prophet's "passing" of time in "the cavern of Mount Hara", Irving turns to spatial passages, emphasizing the up and down of vertical travel; while "Mahomet" seeks to "*elevate* his thought" upward, a reciprocal movement downward occurs, with the "descent" of the angel Gabriel "to earth". Commissioned to "bring down" the "decrees of God", the Prophet witnesses Gabriel's "approaching from a distance", with Irving offering his readers a kinetic impression of the Qur'ān's first revelation. Reflecting Irving's own interests in travel and transition, witnessed first at the opening to his *Alhambra*, this pivotal scene from *Mahomet* also reflects Irving's concerns with intimate companionship. As highlighted in Irving's vivid account, the first revelation of "the Koran" coincides with unexpected camaraderie, the Prophet's "solitary meditation" broken up by the surprising presence of another "human form". And recalling Irving's appeal to David Wilkie as he composes his own "Arabesque" *Alhambra*, his *Mahomet*'s critical moment of companionship is also grounded in a literary collaboration, with Gabriel and the Prophet joined "together" by "written" words, giving and receiving a "silken cloth covered with" Arabic "characters". Rather than collaborative authorship, however, Irving finds Islam opening with a collaborative readership, the religion initiated through an act of miraculous literacy, with the Prophet accruing the capacity to "read what was written on the cloth".

Unknown to Irving's own audience, however, this initial moment of Islamic literacy in *Mahomet* involves not only the participation of the Arabian Prophet, but also the participation of *Mahomet*'s American author. The quotation of the Qur'ān provided in Irving's scene – opening "in the name of the

Lord" and continuing until "teaches him what before he knew not" – represents Irving's very own translation of the Muslim scripture. Rather than merely transcribe former English renditions, such as George Sale's *Koran* – the version quoted so frequently by the British Romantics, and by Irving himself – Irving instead elects to render and recreate this first of the Qur'ān's revelations (96:1–5), fashioning his own American version from previous European renditions. Offering a personal paraphrase of the Qur'ān, Irving adds unique extensions and explications to this sacred source, inserting expressions such as "who sheds on his soul the ray of knowledge" – a phrase which is entirely absent from the Qur'ān's Arabic original. Seeking to clarify the meaning of "the Koran" for his own readers, Irving not only translates the scripture's initial imperative – "Read!" – but also audaciously obeys this same imperative, dynamically *rereading* and revising the Qur'ān for his Western audience.[13] Situating the Muslim scripture in the midst of a complex series of dynamic passages, Irving's account of Islamic origins features literary collaborations that unfold both within and without his American text, with the Qur'ān's transmission between Gabriel and Mahomet ironically mirrored in Irving's own "reading" of "the Koran", transmitting this revised text to his American readers.

III

Gabriel's "descent to earth" in Chapter 6 marks a decisive moment in Irving's *Mahomet*, accounting for the origins of Islam; however, this moment also reaches forward to an inverse journey, anticipating the Prophet's own ascent from earth, detailed in *Mahomet*'s Chapter 12. Known traditionally as the "*Mi'rāj*", Muḥammad's journey to the heavens is an episode from the Prophet's life that unsurprisingly attracts Irving's especial notice. Involving familiar themes of interest for the American – transition and travel, epiphany and encounter – the Prophet's celestial flight, lifted from Mecca to Jerusalem, and then up to God's Throne, merits a full chapter in *Mahomet*, occupying the entirety of Irving's Chapter 12. It is, however, the climax of this chapter that best clarifies Irving's particular interest in the "*Miʿrāj*". Once again accompanied by Gabriel, the Prophet's heavenly journey reaches a final apex beyond which his angelic guide is unable to advance; halting briefly on this high threshold, Irving's narrative subsequently follows the Prophet into the "divine presence", where his encounter with God is again offered in rich and sensuous detail:

> Gabriel could go no further. Mahomet now traversed, quicker than thought, an immense space; passing through two regions of dazzling light, and one of profound darkness. Emerging from this utter gloom, he was filled with awe and terror at finding himself in the presence of Allah, and but two bow-shots from his throne. The face of the Deity was covered with twenty thousand veils, for it would have annihilated man to look upon its glory. He put forth his hands, and placed one upon the breast and the other upon the shoulder of Mahomet, who felt a freezing chill penetrate to his heart and to the very marrow of his bones. It was followed by a feeling of ecstatic bliss, while a sweetness and fragrance prevailed around, which none can understand, but those who have been in the divine presence.[14]

Inverting the trajectory of Chapter 6, Irving opens this scene in Chapter 12 not with Gabriel's arrival, but with his departure; no longer "descending" to meet the Prophet, Gabriel is unable to ascend any further, now leaving "Mahomet" to "traverse" the heavens alone. However, it is echoes of Chapter 6 that seem more insistent here, with Chapter 12 again involving dizzying shifts between dual senses. Traveling first through "two" contrasting "regions" – "dazzling light" and "profound darkness" – the Prophet finally arrives "two bow-shots" from God's "throne", where he experiences both "terror" and "bliss", both "freezing

chill" and soft "sweetness".[15] It is perhaps Irving's concern with
personal companionship, however, that seems most resonant in
this epiphany; in reaching its climax, the Prophet's voyage culminates with an intimate encounter. Recalling Gabriel's own appearance "in human form", the Prophet now confronts "Allah" – a
moment which Irving colors with anthropomorphic familiarity,
picturing God as he stretches forth his "hand", literally touching
the human "heart". Concluding in a divine embrace that penetrates the Prophet's "breast", Irving ends this transcendent journey with tender pathos and personality, stressing a sentimental
climax to this spiritual experience, terminating in both "feeling"
and "fragrance".

Recounting this experience of God's proximity, Irving does,
however, subtly leave room for a divine distance in the Prophet's
epiphany, insisting that the Deity's countenance remains unavoid-
ably hidden from "Mahomet". Even while standing "in the
divine presence", the Prophet is yet protected from the "face of
the Deity" by a myriad of intermediaries, his countenance still
"covered with twenty thousand veils". Deferring the Prophet's
direct and full confrontation with "Allah", Irving unconsciously
anticipates his own partial engagement with "Mahomet" himself; while Irving's own heart will be touched by his story, the
Prophet will remain a "veiled" and mysterious riddle for the
American. Spanning hundreds of pages, and stretching to thirty-
nine chapters, Irving's *Life of Mahomet* still concludes with a
quandary, puzzled by the ultimate meaning of the Prophet's mission. Journeying with his biographic "subject" to the end of his
life, Irving dedicates his final chapter to the "person and character
of Mahomet" – a final chapter that itself concludes with persistent questions. Although defending the Prophet from accusations
of "imposture", and emphasizing too his "ardent, persevering
piety", Irving's final sentence yet asserts that:

> we find no other satisfactory mode of solving the enigma
> of his character and conduct, than by supposing that the
> ray of mental hallucination which flashed upon his enthu-
> siastic spirit during his religious ecstasies in the midnight

cavern of Mount Hara, continued more or less to bewilder
him with a species of monomania to the end of his career,
and that he died in the delusive belief of his mission as a
prophet.[16]

Accounting for Islamic origins once again through an imaginative lens, Irving ends his final paragraph by asserting the religion's enduring "enigma". Refusing to credit Islam's external
reality – relegating its revelation to mere "mental hallucination"
– Irving yet continues to be intrigued by the religion's interiority,
attracted by its original moment of epiphany and "ecstasy". And
although apparently dismissive, this conclusion is also remark-
ably open and tentative, with Irving still merely "supposing";
even while returning to the piercing "ray" that first "flashed
upon" the Prophet's "enthusiastic spirit", Irving yet finds himself "veiled" from certainty, suspending his own judgment with
phrases such as "more or less".

This "enigmatic" mixture of fact and fiction which infuses
Irving's Muslim biography – stretching from the Prophet's
mythic beginnings, to Irving's final "supposing" at the end of his
Life – is itself anticipated in Irving's own Muslim autobiography:
his 1832 *Alhambra*. Returning to *The Alhambra* after surveying
Irving's *Life of Mahomet*, the transitions and travels that punctuate the Prophet's *Life* as envisioned by the American seem to
have parallels in his own life experiences. At the conclusion to
the fourth chapter of *The Alhambra*, Irving summarizes his initial
impressions of this Palace of Granada, and its resident "household", including his kindly "handmaid", Dolores. Marveling at
his introduction to the Alhambra's concrete walls and its lively
occupants, Irving finds himself spiritually transported, nostalgically recalling his own boyhood in America, as well as projecting
himself forward, joining the Arabian Prophet in "Paradise":

> These are simple details of simple pleasures; it is the nature
> of the place alone that gives them interest and importance.
> I tread haunted ground, and am surrounded by romantic
> associations. From earliest boyhood, when, on the banks of

the Hudson, I first pored over the pages of an old Spanish story about the wars of Granada, that city has ever been a subject of my waking dreams, and often have I trod in fancy the romantic halls of the Alhambra. Behold for once a day dream realized; yet I can scarce credit my senses, or believe that I do indeed inhabit the palace of Boabdil, and look down from its balconies upon chivalric Granada. As I loiter through the oriental chambers, and hear the murmur of fountains and the song of the nightingale: as I inhale the odor of the rose and feel the influence of the balmy climate, I am almost tempted to fancy myself in the Paradise of Mahomet, and that the plump little Dolores is one of the bright eyed Houris, destined to administer to the happiness of true believers.[17]

A cascade of imaginative travels and transfers unfolds in this fanciful passage, with Irving proceeding vertically west – moving back to American shores – but also horizontally up – ascending forward to the celestial heights. Echoing his portrait of Mahomet's own "traversal of time and space", Irving's tour of the Moorish Palace allows him to traverse hemispheric space and biographic time, returning him to his youth on the "banks of the Hudson", with his entrance into the actual Alhambra predicted imaginatively in America, where he boyishly "pored over the pages" of popular histories on "Granada". Removing back to New York, even as he enters this Old World Palace, Irving's passage concludes with his moving through a yet more "immense space", offering very deliberate echoes of the Prophet's own *Mi'rāj*. At the climax of this "romantic" passage, Irving is rendered not only transatlantically, but also inter-religiously, ascending to Islam's celestial heavens. Ending his journey by finding himself in the Prophet's own "Paradise", Irving's experience in the Alhambra allows him not only to move across geographic seas, but also beyond spiritual horizons, juxtaposing his boyhood in America with an Islamic afterlife.

Characteristically, however, Irving's passage not only covers distances of culture and religion, but also insists on a tentative deferral, with his imaginative account always teetering on the edge of collapse, uneasily balancing authentic belief and ironic "hallucination". Ending his Islamic experience with romantic innuendo – transforming his innocent handmaid, Dolores, into "one of the bright eyed Houris" – Irving again associates Islam with intimate encounter, attaining in this apocalyptic vision yet another dear "friend and fellow traveller". Yet, this conjugal companionship is a mere tease, with Irving always distancing himself from his own Islamic imaginings; refusing to "credit his senses", Irving offers a string of Romantic vacillations, insisting that "I am almost tempted to fancy myself" in the Muslim "Paradise". Reflecting his interest in the Prophet's own heart-touching encounter with the "veiled" Deity, Irving's parallel journey to the Islamic heavens always remains on the threshold of realization, its imaginative act always deferred or partially denied. Still the solitary boy of "waking dreams", Irving himself will never marry, destined to remain until his death the eligible bachelor that had so interested Mary Shelley. However, in the Islamic inscriptions of his own biography, Irving does allow himself glimpses – provisional and playful – of conjugal companionship, with the Prophet's own "Paradise" offering an opposite polarity to his bookish youth on the Hudson, his boyhood home in America consummated in this fleeting vision of married bliss in the Muslim heavens.

15

"Twenty thousand copies of the Koran": Poe's Muslim Medium

I

In 1827, Irving spent his first full year in Spain, pursuing with "patience and assiduity" his *The Life and Voyages of Columbus*; by the autumn, however, Irving's biographic interests had begun the shift from America to Arabia. On November 16, 1827, the first mention of "Mahomet" surfaces in Irving's journals, and on the following day, November 17, Irving notes: "all the morng writing at Mahomet".[1] Marking his first foray into Muslim historiography, Irving's literary appeal to Islam in 1827 also coincided with the initial efforts of another American author, whose own literary debut featured Islamic concerns. Originating closer to home – arising not from the Andalucian deserts, but from the streets of Boston – 1827 witnessed the first publication of America's newest Romantic poet; only forty pages in length, and limited to a run of fifty copies, this inaugural publication comprised a small collection of poems, announced to its American audience with a sparse frontispiece:

TAMERLANE
AND
OTHER POEMS.

BY A BOSTONIAN.

> Young heads are giddy and young hearts are warm,
> And make mistakes for manhood to reform. – Cowper

Boston: Calvin F. S. Thomas . . . Printer.
1827.[2]

Curious in its cursory details, this terse title page teases its readers with its few intriguing facts. Borrowing a quotation from the proto-Romantic poet "[William] Cowper" (1731–1800), this poetry collection offers a preemptive apology, pithily characterizing itself as a product of "giddy" and "warm" youth, prone to regrettable "mistakes". In stark contrast to this prominent British quotation is the collection's own American anonymity, withholding the identity of its author, attributing itself merely to "A Bostonian". Perhaps most striking, however, is the Eastern identity that appears in the title page's very first word. Before its familiar English quotation (from "Cowper"), and before its familiar New England locality ("Boston"), this frontispiece features a foreign name, "Tamerlane": the storied Muslim conqueror of fourteenth-century central Asia, *Timur Lang*.

Submerged beneath this mysterious frontispiece in 1827 – hidden behind *Tamerlane*'s anonymous façade – is the American author whose name will become synonymous with exotic mystery: Edgar Allan Poe. Although known primarily for his Gothic tales of psychological terror, it is this collection of Oriental poetry that launches Poe's publishing career, his *Tamerlane and other Poems* appearing in print more than five years before his first short story. Born in Boston in 1809, Poe's initial publication aptly appears in his own hometown even while he is a "giddy" youth, only eighteen years old in 1827.[3] However, the transatlantic milieu, and eastern title, of Poe's *Tamerlane* also hint at the international experiences and ambitions which he has accrued at this early age. Orphaned while still a toddler, Poe was taken by his foster family to Britain in 1815, living and studying abroad for several of his most formative years. Returning to America in 1820, Poe settled in Richmond, eventually entering the nearby University of Virginia as an undergraduate in February 1826. Drawn to the exotic and the aesthetic, Poe studied not law at the university, but rather languages; finding a temporary home at Virginia's faculty of Ancient and Modern Languages, Poe chose a field that exposed him to the classical tongues, if not "Oriental literature" as well.[4] However, Poe's academic career would be cut short; having "accumulated very large gambling debts, and other debts" at the University of Virginia, Poe would leave by the end of 1826, launching his life of literary aspiration, publishing his "Bostonian" *Tamerlane* the very next year.[5]

Aptly reflecting Poe's personal history – recalling his itinerancy and exotic interests up to 1827 – *Tamerlane and other Poems* has nevertheless been largely forgotten in literary history, overshadowed by the popular tales produced later in the American's career. For Poe, however, *Tamerlane* would sustain his literary interest through his earliest career, meriting republication just two years later in a revised and expanded edition. Appearing again in 1829 – the very year that witnessed Irving's residence at the Alhambra – Poe features a couple of fresh names on the frontispiece of his reissued collection, his revised title page introducing this new edition as:

AL AARAAF,
TAMERLANE,
AND
MINOR POEMS.

BY EDGAR A. POE[6]

Printed on this title page, for the first time, is the name of one of America's most beloved authors; previously labeled as the anonymous "Bostonian" in 1827, "Edgar A. Poe" is now proudly announced as creator of this 1829 collection. However, this revised title page not only clarifies its author's American identity, but also newly hints at an Arabic identity as well. Displacing "Tamerlane" as the lead poem in Poe's collection is another fresh name on his title page: "Al Aaraaf" – a word which is not only Arabic in etymology, but which is borrowed from Arabic scripture. The first poem of Poe's revised collection, "Al Aaraaf" shares its very title with the Qur'ān's own seventh sura – *al-A'rāf* – as mentioned in Chapter 8 above.[7] On the same page that he first reveals his American name in print, Poe also quotes from Islamic revelation, confessing his own authorship even while gesturing to a Qur'ānic precedent for his poetic efforts.

Invoking an Arabic term previously referenced by his British predecessors – including Southey, whose *Thalaba* also alludes to "Al-Araf" – Poe situates his American poetry within a broader tradition of Romantic appeal to Islam. However, Poe also recognizes that such a borrowing would be confusing to his Bostonian readers; again following the British Romantics, Poe elects to provide explanatory footnotes to his poetry, explaining exotic allusions such as "Al Aaraaf". In 1829, Poe's American audience finds this Arabic term parsed by the following annotation, which is appended to his "Al Aaraaf": "With the Arabians there is a medium between Heaven and Hell, where men suffer no punishment, but yet do not attain that tranquil and even happiness which they suppose to be characteristic of heavenly enjoyment."[8] Without specifically mentioning the Muslim scripture – citing instead "the Arabians" as the source for his "Al Aaraaf" – Poe covertly explains a key term from the Qur'ān. A state of otherworldly suspension, Poe defines "Al Aaraaf" as "a medium between Heaven and Hell", a limbo that hovers between "punishment" and "happiness". An apt title for his own literary art, which is consistently concerned with the wonders of the afterlife, Poe's explanation of "Al Aaraaf" also aptly mediates between ancient "Arabians" and his modern American readers, reaching back to the Eastern sacred in order to enliven his Western secular verse. Charting a limbo of culture, religion, and history in his own earliest poetic efforts, Poe's prominent appeal to "Al Aaraaf" as he begins his career in the late 1820s will anticipate too the spiritual suspension that characterizes so much of his later writings, with Islamic allusions echoing ambivalently to the end of his literary life.

II

Infusing the titles and paratexts of his early poetry with Qur'ānic content – announcing "Al Aaraaf" on his frontispiece, and explaining this term in his footnote – the body of Poe's poems will also feature *lexica* specific to Islam; however, unlike "Al Aaraaf", many of these allusions are presented without apology, offered to Poe's American audience without explanation. Relegated to second place in his 1829 collection, Poe's "Tamerlane" is a poem of romantic regret, recounting the lengthy confession of its primary protagonist – Tamerlane himself – who lays on his deathbed, and reflects on the terrible consequences of his quest for worldly dominion. Lamenting the loss of his beloved, Tamerlane concludes this confession by envisioning his own imminent demise, personifying "Death" as it advances towards him:

> Death who comes for me
> From regions of the blest afar,
> Where there is nothing to deceive,
> Hath left his iron gate ajar,
> And rays of truth you cannot see
> Are flashing thro' Eternity – –
> I do believe that Eblis hath
> A snare in every human path –[9]

Concluding this climactic passage is a couplet that transitions from luminous "Eternity" to "human" temptation, from the "regions of the blest afar" to the earthly "snare" – a simple shift which is enriched, however, by an unusual religious reference. Identifying the tempter who lays "a snare in every human path", Poe's penultimate line invokes a name that is again Arabic in its origins: "Eblis". An imperfect transliteration of "*Iblīs*" – the Qur'ān's own term for the Devil (e.g. Q. 2:34) – Poe's borrowing helps to imbue his English verses with an Islamic veracity, allowing his dark hero – Tamerlane, the Muslim conqueror – to invoke the demonic with Muslim conventions, gesturing to "Eblis", rather than, for instance, "Satan". Although a sensible literary strategy,

Poe's reference yet demands from his audience a surprising level of Islamic literacy, this Arabic term confronting his American readers without auxiliary qualification or explanation.

Infusing his poetry with such Qur'ānic color in 1829, Poe's allusive reach will extend further two years later, featuring an Islamic identity as the very topic and title of his 1831 poem "Israfel". Published in Poe's third poetry collection – his succinctly entitled *Poems, by E. A. Poe* – "Israfel" bears a name that is uniquely Muslim, alluding to *Isrāfīl*, the angel charged with blowing the trumpet at the end of time, announcing the "Day of Judgment".[10] Unlike "Eblis", which receives a mere passing reference in Poe's 1829 "Tamerlane", "Israfel" becomes the principal focus for Poe's 1831 poem; however, Poe also explains the Islamic origins of his "Israfel" within the poem itself. Reproduced below is the beginning of "Israfel" – its title, epigraph and first stanza – as well as the poem's concluding two stanzas, stanzas 7 and 8:

ISRAFEL

And the angel Israfel, whose heart-strings are a lute, and
who has the sweetest voice of all God's creatures.

– KORAN

I
In Heaven a spirit doth dwell
"Whose heart-strings are a lute;"
None sing so wildly well
As the angel Israfel,
And the giddy stars (so legends tell)
Ceasing their hymns, attend the spell
Of his voice, all mute.

VII
Yes, Heaven is thine; but this
Is a world of sweets and sours:
Our flowers are merely – flowers,
And the shadow of thy bliss
Is the sunshine of ours.

VIII
If I could dwell
Where Israfel
Hath dwelt, and he where I,
He might not sing so wildly well
  A mortal melody,
While a bolder note than this might swell
From my lyre within the sky.[11]

Celebrating the "sweetest voice" of his angelic character, Poe's "Israfel" deepens his debt to Islamic traditions, this poem proudly admitting its Qur'ānic origins. Supplying readers with a specific citation, confessing his cross-cultural borrowing, Poe interposes a quotation between his poem's title and its first line, with the "KORAN" mediating between "ISRAFEL" and "In Heaven a spirit doth dwell". In the poem's first stanza, however, Poe's audience also discovers his Qur'ānic subtitle echoing into his second line, with the phrase "Whose heart-strings are a lute" surfacing twice, occurring initially in the quotation from the "KORAN", and again in Poe's poetry, his second English verse ("Whose heart-strings are a lute") reading as a verbatim borrowing from the Muslim scripture.

Poe's epigram citation of the "KORAN" seems an honest admission of Islamic influence; however, this candid confession is itself entirely misleading. Derived not from the Qur'ān itself – which never explicitly names "Israfel" – Poe's reference is instead paraphrased from George Sale, whose Preface to his 1734 *Koran* translation does indeed characterize "Israfîl" as possessing "the most melodious voice of all God's creatures".[12] A scholarly source previously invoked by Southey and Byron, George Sale provides a portrait of "Israfîl" that Poe repurposes for his own poetry, adapting academic prose to fit his own artistry. Playfully inspiring his audience's confusion, Poe's critical appeal to the "KORAN" encourages us to believe that we are reading the very language of Islamic revelation as we read Poe's poetry. Again infusing a Qur'ānic "limbo" into his creative writing, Poe poises the "KORAN" between the poetic head and poetic body of his own "Israfel", offering a deceptive clarification which links his Islamic title to his American text.

Beyond its false attribution, "Israfel" also seems to offer a fitting culmination to Poe's Qur'ānic gestures in his early poetry, serving to round off an unseen world which is distinctly Islamic in identity and topography. Occupying all levels of the spiritual realm for Poe are Muslim personalities and places; in Hell below, he invokes "Eblis", in Heaven above, "Israfel", and in between is Poe's "Al Aaraaf". Expressing the exotic wonders of the next world through exotic references, Poe conveys his American readers across a threshold of culture, even while conveying them also across the threshold of life and death, traversing "here" and "hereafter", as they traverse too a transatlantic "medium" between Occident and Orient. It is, however, the polemical purpose that emerges at the conclusion of Poe's "Israfel" that best explains the persistent role played by Islamic references in his literary efforts, echoing from early poetry to later prose. While Poe's eight-stanza "Israfel" opens by celebrating its Islamic archangel, praising his superlative voice – "the sweetest" of "all God's creatures" – Poe's poem ultimately turns towards a lyric contest, resisting the angel's artistic ascendance. In the final stanza of the poem, Poe's speaker suggests that his own human potential may even surpass Israfel's talents. "If I could dwell / Where Israfel / Hath dwelt, and he where I", Poe suggests enviously, "He would not sing one half as well". An ironic end to his Islamic poem, Poe implies that his speaker's poetic inferiority is due merely to earthly confinement, residing in this ambivalent "world of sweets and sours"; if, however, it was Poe's speaker who "dwelt" in heaven – rather than "Israfel" – it would be "a stormier note than this" which would resound "From my lyre within the sky." Articulating a Promethean ambition so often associated with Romantic poetry, Poe's imagined struggle for aesthetic superiority with an Islamic angel hints at the darker implications of his religious reach eastward – implications which seem especially significant as it "has become customary" in Poe criticism "to identify Poe with his angel [Israfel]", as Thomas Mabbott notes.[13] Selecting a sacred and "sweet" subject for his celestial poem, Poe's "Israfel" also dramatizes a shadier side to his allusive ambition, reflecting not only the American's appropriation of Islam, but also his attempts to overcome his Islamic referents. Revising the "KORAN" for his own purposes in his opening epigram, Poe concludes his poem by seeking to revise his own relationship with the Islamic heavens. Ironically paralleling Irving's own romantic ascent to the "Paradise of Mahomet" published in the 1832 *Alhambra*, Poe launches an aesthetic ascent in the 1831 "Israfel", reaching upward to occupy a superior poetic place, striving to "dwell where Israfel / Hath dwelt" so he might grasp there the Muslim "lyre within the sky."

III

Just a year after the 1831 appearance of "Israfel", Poe would publish his first short story. Appearing anonymously in the *Philadelphia Saturday Courier*, Poe's 1832 "Metzengerstein" begins a decade of periodical publications, his fiction surfacing in the pages of journals such as the *Southern Literary Messenger* and *Burton's Gentlemen's Magazine*, which will feature such future classics as "The Fall of the House of Usher" (1839).[14] By 1840, Poe had produced enough material to merit a book-length collection of tales. Shifting in genre from his initial collection of poetry, published in 1827, Poe's first volume of fiction in 1840 nevertheless recalls *Tamerlane and other Poems* by sporting an exotic title, published as his *Tales of the Grotesque and Arabesque*.[15] Twinning two terms that accent the monstrous and the mysterious, the outrageous and the intricate, Poe's first book of fiction twins also East and West, his American *"Tales"* advertised as *"Arabesque"*. Often identified by his critical readers as a "master of the Gothic horror tale", Poe instead introduces his own fiction with a term that seems more "Oriental" than European, his invocation of the *"Arabesque"* recalling Islamic art and architecture, aspiring to imitate the dizzying complexity of Eastern design in his Western fictions.[16]

Echoing Irving's own ambitions in his *Alhambra* – which celebrated Spain's "strong mixture" of "Saracenic and Gothic", while aspiring to inscribe "Arabesque sketches" – Poe's allusion to the *Arabesque* anticipates the Islamic interests that inform his later career as literary critic and creative writer. As suggested by the 1831 "Israfel", it is Poe's concern with artistic superiority that sustains his attraction to Islam, fascinated in particular by the Qur'ān – a book which uniquely claims to be divine in origin, and flawless in composition. Perhaps less prominently than his early poetry, Poe's Qur'ānic allusions yet persist through his mature fiction, exploring issues of textual production and literary precedence. For instance, just four years before his untimely death in 1849, Poe published his short story "The Thousand-and-Second Tale of Scheherazade" in February 1845 – a satiric sequel to the Arabic classic *A Thousand and One Nights*.[17] Recalling the "*Arabesque*" label borne by his first fiction collection, Poe's later story includes a fantastic series of Eastern vignettes, one of which concerns a wondrous "conjuror" who "fashioned for himself a mighty thing that was neither man nor beast". Demonstrating the superlative "might" of this grotesque "creature", Poe's story characterizes this "thing" as possessing:

> fingers that it employed with such incredible speed and
> dexterity that it would have had no trouble in writing out
> twenty thousand copies of the Koran in an hour; and this
> with so exquisite a precision, that in all copies there should
> not be found one to vary from another by the breadth of
> the finest hair.[18]

Seeking an ideal image of miraculous "dexterity", Poe is able to find no better spectacle than a fantastic feat of Islamic inscription, marveling at the magically quick replication and reproduction of the Muslim scripture. Producing "twenty thousand copies of the Koran", Poe wonders at these fantastic "fingers", which are capable of such transcription in "an hour". However, it is not the pace, but the "precision", of this incredible act which seems most essential in Poe's whimsical account. Despite being produced with "incredible speed", these scriptural "copies" are nevertheless "exquisite", marred by neither variance nor error – a textual perfection which is essential to the Qur'ān, whose content is indeed traditionally understood as not varying "by the breadth of the finest hair". Inventing a marvelous episode in his own fiction writing, Poe alludes to an act of writing that surpasses all fiction, his own creative vignette formed from the Qur'ān's inscribed perfection.

A sacred text which resists mundane categories of literary creativity and critique, the Qur'ān ironically becomes a topic not only for Poe's creative writing, but also his non-fiction criticism. Even while preparing his "The Thousand-and-Second Tale of Scheherazade" for its 1845 publication, Poe would again invoke the integrity of the Arabic scripture in his editorial efforts, referencing the Qur'ān in his 1844 "Marginalia". A haphazard series of bookish reflections, published in the *United States Magazine and Democratic Review*, Poe's "Marginalia" dedicates a brief entry to commenting on a recent edition of the Portuguese poet, Luís Vaz de Camões; marveling at the lack of *errata* found in the book under his review, Poe's entry asserts: "Here is an edition, which so far as microscopical excellence and absolute accuracy of typography are concerned, might well be prefaced with the phrase of the Koran – 'There is no error in this book.'"[19] Playful and parenthetical, Poe not only names "the Koran" in his brief entry, but also provides a citation from the scripture. Loosely quoting the celebrated opening to its second chapter – "That is the Book, wherein is no doubt" (Q. 2:1) – Poe recalls for his reader the Qur'ān's awareness of its own textual integrity, citing the scripture's assertion simply as "There is no error in this book". And although very brief, Poe's editorial entry offers American readers a remarkable complement and contrast to previous citations of "the Koran" that echo throughout his prose and poetry. No longer serving merely as an inspiration for Poe's literary creation, the Qur'ān here stands as a benchmark for his literary criticism, a standard for evaluating "typographic" stability. Evoking the Qur'ān's inimitable claim – its self-referential testimony that it contains "no error" – Poe posits the Muslim scripture as a bibliographic model, light-heartedly recognizing its exceptional status through juxtaposing this sacred text with a modern edition of secular verse. While "copies of the Koran" had been endowed with "so exquisite a precision" in his fantastic "Thousand-and-Second Tale of Scheherazade", Poe now borrows the Qur'ān's textual perfection to contextualize an actual book, applying its sacred miracle to secular manufacturing.

In appealing to the actual language of the Qur'ān, Poe's entry also seems to reach back to his earliest poetry, recalling the scripture's citation in the titles and texts of his youthful verses. However, unlike the 1831 "Israfel" – which features a false epigram quotation from the "KORAN" – the Muslim scripture now merits a more accurate place and paraphrase in Poe's 1844 "Marginalia", seeming to repent for his youthful "mistake". Correctly identifying his citation as deriving from the Qur'ān's "preface" – recognizing this "phrase of the Koran" to be original to its opening – Poe reflects his own interest in the Qur'ān's bibliographic precision; even while lauding the Qur'ān as a textual model, Poe himself more closely approaches textual honesty, quoting and contextualizing the Qur'ān with better accuracy. However, perhaps the most intriguing element in Poe's 1844 citation is the fresh forum in which the Qur'ān now appears. Published in the pages of an American periodical, written in an entry with a conversational style, Poe's "Koran" no longer appears as an exotic import, but rather as a domesticated element of his critical lexicon – a source which is invoked as familiar to both American author and his American audience, a quotable commonplace appropriate for passing reference within Poe's informal "Marginalia".[20] Situated between poetry and prose, between false quotation and inscribed precision, between the underworld and heavenly heights, the Muslim Sacred now also intervenes between Poe's informal reflections and his ideals of formal perfection, mapping a limbo of Islamic allusion which pervades his diverse and dark *corpus*, continually suspended in a literary "medium" which balances ironic humor and vital earnestness.

16

"Unveiled Allah pours the flood of truth": Emerson's Islamic Civics

I

The Romantic careers of Washington Irving and Edgar Allan Poe were each impacted by extended stays in England, both authors arriving separately in 1815 to spend formative years abroad. It would be nearly two decades later, however, that England would host perhaps the most celebrated moment in transatlantic Romanticism. On the late morning of August 5, 1833, Samuel Taylor Coleridge was still in bed, at home in his Highgate apartments, near London. Now less than a year away from death, the aged and ailing poet was interrupted just before noon this summer morning by the arrival of a young Bostonian. Sending up a note to request an audience with Coleridge, the American was asked to return after one o'clock, at which time the British poet would rise and prepare to greet this unknown youth, who gave his name as Ralph Waldo Emerson.[1]

Subsequently recognized as "the father of American literature", Emerson's 1833 visit to Coleridge precedes all the philosophy and poetry which sparked his celebrity, his trek to Highgate coming well before he published his landmark *Nature* (1836), or his iconic essay "Self-Reliance" (1841).[2] However, viewed retrospectively, August 5, 1833 appears a critical pivot point in literary history, this encounter between Coleridge and Emerson embodying Romanticism's progress, moving forward in time and westward in space. Spanning Atlantic nations and literary ages, the unproven Emerson first meets his famous predecessor even as Coleridge approaches his death in 1834, with the beginnings of New England Romanticism rising from the fatal decline of England's Romantic pioneer. Embodying polarities of nation and age, a religious gulf is also suggested in this August 5 meeting. By 1833, the elder Coleridge had become a champion of traditional and Trinitarian Christianity, fiercely defending his native Anglicanism; conversely, the young Emerson who arrives in England was a Unitarian in both creed and culture, having recently served for three years as a minister at a Unitarian church in Boston. It is this religious difference between Coleridge and Emerson, rather than their Romantic overlaps, which motivated much of their afternoon discussion on August 5. Spouting a "declamation on the folly and ignorance of Unitarianism", Coleridge dedicated his time with Emerson to critiquing his guest's religion; as Emerson later recalled, Coleridge felt entitled to offer such an inhospitable reception as he "knew all about Unitarianism perfectly well, because he had once been a Unitarian".[3] An American echo of Coleridge's own youthful commitments, Emerson arrives to Highgate as both a budding Romantic as well as a religious Unitarian, offering a transatlantic mirror of inversion and resemblance for the aging British poet.

Hidden beneath its overt contrasts and continuities, this 1833 encounter between Coleridge and Emerson would also offer a more covert reflection between the two Romantics – a covert reflection centered in the Qur'ān. Unknown to Coleridge, it would not be his Highgate apartments that Emerson first visited during the week leading up to their August 5 meeting, but rather a London bookshop on Chancery Lane. Stopping at the popular store owned by Edward Lumley – bookseller and publisher – Emerson purchased several items, including the following acquisition, recorded in his pocket diary:

30 [July 1833]

                                                   Lumley Chancery Lane

Alcoran   2/6[4]

A simple and silent transaction, Emerson tersely notes his purchase of the "Alcoran", recording merely its price – two shillings
sixpence ("2/6") – without adding further comment. Coinciding
closely with his visit to Coleridge, separated by just six days in
the summer of 1833, Emerson's buying of the Qur'ān contrasts
sharply with his upcoming meeting, this quiet Islamic acquisition
seeming unconnected with his famous Romantic encounter. And
yet, this July 30 purchase itself offers another American echo
of Coleridge's British biography. As a young Unitarian himself,
Coleridge had journeyed abroad to Germany in 1798, returning
to England the following year, immediately to begin a poem on
the Muslim Prophet; for the young Emerson, his own journeys
abroad lead him to Coleridge's door, but only after acquiring a
copy of the Muslim scripture. Purchasing the Qur'ān in London,
even while meeting Britain's aging poet, Emerson unconsciously
extends an Islamic inheritance which punctuates European and
British Romanticism – an Islamic inheritance which emerges
publicly as Emerson returns to the New World to begin his
own American career, writing philosophic prose and innovative
poetry.

Published nearly a decade after meeting Coleridge, one of
Emerson's first major poems would appear in an 1842 edition
of the *Dial* – the magazine of New England Transcendentalism.
From its first lines, this early poem seems to exhibit Emerson's
Romantic influences, suggesting his reading of poets such as
Coleridge and Byron; however, it is this poem's very first word
that also implies a very different influence on the American:

> SAADI.
>
> TREES in groves,
> Kine in droves,
> In ocean sport the finny herds,
> Wedgelike cleave the air the birds,
> To northern lakes fly wind-borne ducks,
> Browse the mountain sheep in flocks,
> Men consort in camp and town,
> But the poet dwells alone.[5]

Climbing up a catalogue of Nature – progressing from *flora* ("Trees"), to *fauna* ("Kine"), to humanity ("Men") – Emerson's first lines recall his forebears in both England and Europe, accenting an "organic naturalism" characteristic of Romantic poetry.[6] Contrasting different kinds of communities, Emerson opens with pastoral "herds" and "flocks", which lead to an urban "camp and town", mirroring human society in the organizations of the natural world. It is the conclusion of this first stanza of Emerson's early poem, however, which perhaps seems most Romantic, emphasizing not only human uniqueness, but specifically poetic solitude; insisting upon artistic "loneliness", Emerson's irregular lines identify his ideal bard as an irregular outsider, reserving his final line of the above for the solitary words: "But the poet dwells alone". These elements of Emerson's poem would all be expected from America's preeminent Romantic; somewhat more unexpected, however, is this poem's title, "Saadi" – the name of a celebrated Persian poet and predecessor of Ḥāfiẓ, a paragon of Islamic spiritual verse. Visiting Coleridge in the early 1830s – discovering the aged British "poet" as he himself "dwells alone" in Highgate – Emerson launches his own poetic career in the early 1840s by echoing a Romantic allegiance to the East, reaching to medieval Persian poetry as a precedent for his own American verses. Recalling most urgently not the efforts of the aged Coleridge, it is the late poetry of Goethe that seems most evident in Emerson's poetic beginnings, with the American commencing where the German poet had concluded his own career, domesticating a Sufi poet for Western readerships.

II

Although invoking a Muslim name in his poem's title, the setting and scenery which Emerson establishes at the opening to "Saadi" seem entirely innocent of Orientalist trappings, presenting topics and topography that would be entirely familiar to American

readers. Anticipating the 1842 poem that unfolds after this initial stanza – and also the poetic career Emerson pursues after
1842 – the introduction to "Saadi" marries Islamic identity with
New England expression, invoking an Eastern icon in its title,
even while reflecting American ideas in its text. Stretching to
184 lines, Emerson's "Saadi" will recruit vocabulary unmistakably evocative of the Muslim East, appealing to God as "Allah",
while establishing "Persia" as the poem's setting. However, the
concerns that surface through the poem seem as much targeted
to modern America as they are borrowed from medieval Persia.
Consider, for example the following passage from "Saadi", in
which the poem's title character – the Persian poet himself – is
commanded by his Muse to:

> Let the great world bustle on
> With war and trade, with camp and town;
> A thousand men shall dig and eat;
> At forge and furnace thousands sweat;
> And thousands sail the purple sea;
> And give or take the stroke of war;
> Or crowd the market and bazaar;
> Oft shall war end, and peace return,
> And cities rise where cities burn,
> Ere one man my hill shall climb,
> Who can turn the golden rhyme;
> Let them manage how they may,
> Heed thou only Saadi's lay.
> Seek the living among the dead,
> Man in man is imprisoned.[7]

Beyond Saadi's own name, and perhaps Emerson's passing allusion to the "bazaar", there is very little to suggest these verses
are grounded in Muslim Persia. Rather, the principal concern of
Emerson's passage seems reflective of his own American place
and time. Penned exactly two decades before the Civil War,
Emerson gestures to the fraught position of the Romantic artist as he contemplates "war and trade"; jostled by societal strife

and unbridled industry, the poet confronts both "forge and fur-
nace" as they ignite incessantly in America. Reflecting the sick-
ening cycles of national conflict that will soon engulf his own
nation, Emerson prophetically predicts that "cities rise where cities burn", concluding his passage by obliquely gesturing to the
critical problem that plagues the Republic in the 1840s: namely
the "imprisonment" of "Man" by "man". Speaking to a Yankee
audience increasingly outraged at "America's peculiar institution" – slavery – Emerson pictures poetry itself as a vehicle of
inward escape, turning from the prospects of the "stroke of war",
with "Saadi's lay" recommended as a remedy for the miseries of
human "imprisonment".

Recruiting a medieval poet of the East to refract problems of
the modern West, it is the conclusion of "Saadi" which offers
the most overtly Islamic material in Emerson's poem, relying on
Muslim nomenclature while promoting a mystic awakening in
American readers. Still speaking to Saadi, the Muse closes the
poem by commanding its poet to:

> Open innumerable doors
> The heaven where unveiled Allah pours,
> The flood of truth, the flood of good,
> The Seraph's and the Cherub's food,
> Those doors are men; the Pariah hind
> Admits thee to the perfect Mind.
> Seek not beyond thy cottage wall
> Redeemer that can yield thee all.
> While thou sittest at thy door
> On the desart's yellow floor,
> Listening to the gray-haired crones,
> Foolish gossips, ancient drones,
> Saadi! see, they rise in stature
> To the height of mighty Nature,
> And the secret stands revealed
> Fraudulent Time in vain concealed,
> That blessed gods in servile masks
> Plied for thee thy household tasks.[8]

Again isolating sacred art from the secular "bustle", these final lines of "Saadi" refigure the solitary task of the poet as an act of divine communion, encountering God even while sitting solidly within "thy cottage wall". Distinct from the pastoral naturalism of its American opening, "Saadi" closes with celestial abstraction and Islamic accents; speaking directly to his titular subject, Emerson ends with an esoteric imperative, directing Saadi to seek "The heaven where unveiled Allah pours / The flood of truth, the flood of good". In an aptly Sufi climax to "Saadi", Emerson offers a final picture of his poet as he gnostically ascends to "Allah", admitted "to the perfect Mind", where the "secret stands revealed". However, despite its mystic direction and Muslim diction, Emerson's conclusion to "Saadi" also succeeds in returning to more domestic American concerns. In his pantheistic last lines, Emerson privileges the most plain and private – "household tasks" – ending "Saadi" by envisioning a redeemed form of "service". Associating housework with divine beneficence, rather than human compulsion, the concluding couplet of "Saadi" finds "servile masks" worn not by domestic slaves, but rather by celestial "gods", endowing "household tasks" with a sense of "blessed" grace, rather than mortal bondage.

Marrying American aesthetics with Sufi mysticism, Emerson launches his poetic career by appealing to a Muslim surrogate for his own authorial identity, mirroring his personal aspirations and national anxieties in "Saadi's lay".[9] An oblique meditation on artistic liberty, "Saadi" also anticipates Emerson's overt activism in the years leading up to the looming Civil War, with the ancient Persian poet supporting his modern advocacy for African-American liberty. Rising to authorial celebrity during precisely these years, Emerson's efforts through the later 1840s and early 1850s also allow him to join the swelling ranks of American abolitionists, recruiting his literary gifts for the anti-slavery cause. A decade after penning "Saadi", Emerson will target this tragic issue dividing the nation, first delivering his "Fugitive Slave Law Address" to his fellow "Citizens of Concord" on May 3, 1851. Speaking again on the "Fugitive

Slave Law" three years later for a New York audience, Emerson pens a new "Address" that offers a critique of American slavery, but which also includes a surprising appeal to Persia's own seminal poet. At the heart of Emerson's 1854 "Fugitive Slave Law Address", his abolitionist arguments take a spiritual turn, invoking divine assistance, even while protesting human slavery:

> [To make a man] feel that he is to owe all to himself, is the way to make him strong and rich. And here the optimist must find, if anywhere, the benefit of slavery. We have many teachers. We are in this world for nothing else than culture: to be instructed in nature, in realities; in the laws of moral and intelligent nature; and surely our education is not conducted by toys and luxuries, – but by austere and rugged masters, – by poverty, solitude, passions, war, slavery – to know that paradise is under the shadow of swords; that divine sentiments, which are always soliciting us, are breathed into us from on high, and are a counterbalance to a universe of suffering and crime, – that self-reliance, the height and perfection of man, is reliance on God. The insight of the religious sentiment will disclose to him unexpected aids in the nature of things. The Persian Saadi said, "Beware of hurting the orphan. When the orphan sets a-crying the throne of the Almighty is rocked from side to side."[10]

A difficult passage due to its dense style and dialectical approach, Emerson paradoxically begins with "the benefit of slavery", an evil institution which Emerson yet finds to be "instructive", serving as one of the "austere and rugged masters" which directs our attention to "divine sentiments". This pedagogic process leads to the climax of Emerson's paragraph, clarifying the concept which is most often identified with Emerson himself – namely "self-reliance" – defined here not as muscular individualism, but as "reliance on God", appealing to the divine which resides within every individual. This paradox of "self-reliance" is followed by a piece of poetry, Emerson appealing not to his own verses, however, but to the verses of another: "Saadi" himself. Referencing this "Persian" poet, Emerson ends the above selection with a translated line from Saadi's *Gulistan* – *The Rose Garden* – "Beware of hurting the orphan. When the orphan sets a-crying the throne of the Almighty is rocked from side to side".[11]

Lifting up the lowliest – describing the humble "orphan" as having access to "the Almighty" – Emerson recalls his 1842 "Saadi", appealing again to an Islamic precedent while linking the most "servile" to the most sacred. However, inverting and amplifying his earlier poem, Emerson no longer implicitly critiques domestic politics under the name of the Persian poet; instead, the Persian poet is here recruited within an explicitly political work of Emerson's prose, his Sufi poetry helping to express abolitionist "sentiments", offering an Islamic foil to American problems of "poverty, solitude, passions, war, slavery". This passage from Emerson's "Address" also surpasses his earlier "Saadi" in not only overtly appealing to this Islamic mystic, but also in covertly appealing to the Islamic Prophet. Describing the diverse "education" engendered by "slavery", Emerson includes in this list a striking maxim, namely: "to know that paradise is under the shadow of swords". This bellicose lesson fits well Emerson's American "Address", anticipating the zealous cause of the U.S. Civil War. However, what Emerson does not acknowledge is that this American line is itself an Arabian quotation; citing none other than the Prophet himself, Emerson here paraphrases a famous *ḥadīth* first spoken by Muḥammad, asserting that: "Surely, the gates of Paradise are under the shadows of the swords".[12] Prophesying the coming conflict between North and South, Emerson traces a transmission that passes between East and West, appealing to Islamic prophecy as a means of emboldening his own American audience. Quoting openly from Saadi's wisdom, Emerson also retreats even further back to Muslim antiquity, secretly recruiting the Prophet's own promise of "Paradise" in order to propel his compatriots to take up their "swords".

III

In his "Fugitive Slave Law Address", Emerson cites Persian poetry in his polemical prose, critiquing the nation's social problems with a Sufi allusion. However, even while he was fashioning his first "Address", Emerson would publish poetry which also claims Persian origins, and yet critiques American "slavery". In 1851, the same year that Emerson delivered his Concord "Fugitive Slave Law Address", he also made a literary contribution to the *Liberty Bell* – a Boston gift-book, published annually by the city's Female Anti-Slavery Society. Featured alongside a scattered assortment of articles, essays, and verses, the 1851 *Liberty Bell* also included Emerson's "The Phoenix", a five-stanza poem that reads in full:

> My bosom's Phoenix has assured
> His nest in the sky-vault's cope,
> In the body's eye immured,
> He is weary of life's hope.
>
> Round and round this heap of ashes
> Now flies the bird amain,
> But in that odorous niche of heaven
> Nestles the bird again.
>
> Once flies he upward, he will perch
> On Tuba's golden bough;
> His home is on that fruited arch
> Which cools the blest below.
>
> If over this world of ours
> His wings my Phoenix spread,
> How gracious falls on land and sea
> The soul-refreshing shade!
>
> Either world inhabits he,
> Sees oft below him planets roll;
> His body is all of air compact,
> Of Allah's love, his soul.[13]

Seeking to support the political aims of the American journal, Emerson's poetic contribution seems ideal for the *Liberty Bell*, utilizing symbols and settings that complement the magazine's abolitionist aims. Dramatizing a spiritual struggle for freedom, Emerson's poem recruits images of "flight" and "escape", allegorically picturing the "soul" as a "bird" which flees its captivity, soaring up "over this world of ours". Contextualized within the pages of the *Liberty Bell* specifically, "The Phoenix" seems a plea on behalf of American slaves, envisioning both their current plight and their potential release, hoping for the day in which these "immured" spirits may spread their "wings" to glide effortlessly away.

If the general themes of "The Phoenix" seem to suit the American *Liberty Bell*, its specific terminology makes this poem a somewhat more surprising choice for a magazine dedicated to domestic social politics. While much of the poetry and prose printed in the *Liberty Bell*'s 1851 edition reflect Christian piety, Bostonian readers may have been startled to discover an Islamic spirituality implied in Emerson's contribution. Punctuating the poem's finale, for instance, is God's name in Arabic, with "The Phoenix" describing the "soul" as composed entirely of "Allah's love". This climactic Islamic allusion is, moreover, not the poem's first; retreating back to its third stanza, "The Phoenix" pictures the soul as it soars "upward" where "he will perch / On Tuba's golden bough". Confronting readers of the 1851 *Liberty Bell* with an alien reference, Emerson's "Tuba's golden bough" is, however, recognizable to those familiar with Islamic sources. Traditionally understood in scripture as a "Tree of Paradise", the Arabic term "Ṭūbā" is invoked in the Qur'ān, occurring in the 29th verse of its 13th chapter, which promises "Ṭūbā" to "those who believe and do righteous deeds".[14] Consistent with the avian allegory that unfolds through "The Phoenix", Emerson's third stanza borrows an arborous image from the Qur'ān; a religious reward for the righteous, the symbol of the "Tuba" supports well the liberating strategy of "The Phoenix", picturing the bird of the soul as it flees confinement to settle on the "bough" of this celestial tree.

It is striking to find a Qur'ānic allusion printed in the American pages of the *Liberty Bell*; however, more striking is what this allusion implies: namely, that "The Phoenix" is not an American original, but rather an American translation, comprising Emerson's rendition of a Persian *ghazal*, authored by none other than Muḥammad Shamsuddīn Ḥāfiẓ. Opening his poetic career with "Saadi" in 1842, Emerson implicitly recalls the end of Goethe's own career, whose *West-östlicher Divan* is built from Persian models (see Chapter 6). In the decade which follows Emerson's "Saadi", however, the American will continue to follow Goethe's lead, turning his attention increasingly towards Ḥāfiẓ. Discovering Joseph Hammer's edition of Ḥāfiẓ in the spring of 1846 – the very same edition which inspired Goethe – Emerson dedicates his next decades to translating hundreds of the *Divan*'s verses from Hammer's German. Completing a complex arc of literary transmission – from Persian origins, through a European mediator, to its American destination – Emerson's "Phoenix" embodies the complex, westward flight of Sufi poetry. However, this "translation of a translation" also signals Emerson's indebtedness to his Romantic forebears. Recalling trends of Islamic interest that were first expressed in Goethe's earliest efforts, Emerson appeals to Muslim models not only for artistic inspiration, but also for political purposes; a half century after Islamic precedents were recruited by European and British poets to critique Napoleonic wars, Islamic precedents now anticipate the U.S. Civil War, retaining a political resonance even while shifting their national theater, advancing from Europe at the end of the eighteenth century to America at the middle of the nineteenth.[15]

If consistent with his Continental predecessors, Emerson's translation of Ḥāfiẓ in the pages of the *Liberty Bell* also implies countless ironies. Acclaimed as the prophet of American "Self-Reliance", Emerson here relies on another's voice, and another's verses, to promote his political activities; rather than submit original American poetry, Emerson elects to contribute Persian poetry for this most American of causes, recruiting ideas that are original to the fourteenth-century East in order to critique issues that plague the West's modern frontier. Emerson's use of a Sufi poem for his anti-slavery activities too seems curious. Conventionally associated with contemplative retreat – with spiritual withdrawal from worldly affairs – it is Sufism that aids Emerson as he anticipates the most bloody war in his nation's history. And while the protest against American slavery seems very physical in its concerns – debating the rights and liberty of the human body – Emerson's "Phoenix" seems entirely metaphysical in focus, accenting a "liberty" of soul, dramatizing an interior quest to escape confinement that is centred in "my bosom". Rather than seeking to overcome the divides of race and class – the central crises of American slavery – the Sufi "Phoenix" seems more interested in overcoming the divide between this world and the next, aspiring to progress from here to the hereafter.

Translating Ḥāfiẓ in the pages of the *Liberty Bell*, and quoting Saadi in his "Fugitive Slave Law Address", Emerson's appeal to Sufi poetry in the early 1850s reaches forward to the Civil War which begins in 1861; however, Emerson's Sufi interests will also echo throughout the war's duration, resounding even in the final days of this "nation-defining struggle".[16] During the carnage of the Civil War's final months, a new edition would arrive on Boston book shelves: Francis Gladwin's translation of *The Rose Garden* – Saʿdī's classic manual of spiritual verse, his *Gulistan*.[17] This initial American edition of Saʿdī would also come equipped with a definitively American endorsement, featuring an introduction authored by Emerson himself. Recognized as the leading American apologist for Persian poetry by the 1860s, Emerson was invited by *The Gulistan*'s Boston publishers to pen a Preface, tasked with recommending "Saadi" to U.S. readers. Praising the poet's virtues, Emerson seeks to define "Saadi" for his new American audience through a number of analogies, characterizing *The Gulistan*'s author in the following passage:

> Saadi, though he has not the lyric flights of Hafiz, has wit, practical sense, and just moral sentiments. He has

the instinct to teach, and from every occurrence must draw the moral, like Franklin. He is the poet of friendship, love, self-devotion, and serenity. There is a uniform force in his page, and, conspicuously, a tone of cheerfulness, which has almost made his name a synonyme for this grace. The word *Saadi* means *fortunate*. In him the trait is no result of levity, much less of convivial habit, but first of a happy nature, to which victory is habitual, easily shedding mishaps, with sensibility to pleasure, and with resources against pain. But it also results from the habitual perception of the beneficent laws that control the world. He inspires in the reader a good hope. What a contrast between the cynical tone of Byron and the benevolent wisdom of Saadi![18]

Defining the term "Saadi" for his American audience – parsing this Persian name as "*fortunate*" – Emerson also contextualizes Sa'dī through a range of contrasts and comparisons, juxtaposing the Sufi poet with figures from both East and West, medieval and modern. Opening with a distinction between "Saadi" and "Hafiz", Emerson associates the former with the "moral" and "practical", and the latter with "lyric flights" – a distinction that aptly recalls Emerson's own "flighty" appeal to Ḥāfiẓ's "Phoenix". After this intra-national contrast between Persian poets, Emerson next offers an international comparison; celebrating his "instinct to teach", "Saadi" is likened by Emerson to "[Benjamin] Franklin", this patriarch of Persian poetry mirrored in an American "Founding Father". Bridging East and West, Emerson's pairing of Sa'dī and Franklin also crosses the critical bridge from poetics to politics. Implying a distinctly *national* significance for "Saadi" at a time of national crisis, Emerson presents him as a Persian "Franklin", offering U.S. readers an opportunity to commune with their own country's "moral" past, even as they read poetry authored by a medieval Muslim.

It is the climactic comparison offered in Emerson's passage, however, that seems a fitting climax to his late Romantic engagement with Islam, indexing a parallel between these two contending commitments, while hinting too at the limits of their mutual appeal. Returning to a contrast more poetic than political, Emerson ends by identifying Sa'dī's virtues through a disparity, juxtaposed not with a fellow Persian poet, but rather with a British Romantic: "Byron". Writing at the very end of Romanticism's reach, Emerson again fuses Romantic and Islamic artistry; however, Emerson sees these two traditions not in tandem – not paired together in the "West-East" merger of Goethe's *Divan*, for instance – but instead privileges the Islamic *over* the Romantic, raising "Saadi" over "Byron". Lauding the former's "wisdom", while deprecating the latter's "tone", Emerson finds Sa'dī's "beneficence" prevailing over Byron's "cynicism", preferring the Sufi capacity to "inspire". Completing a circular progress of Western appropriation, Emerson here offers his own Romantic critique of Romanticism through an Islamic lens; in a startling instance of internal appraisal, America's preeminent Romantic criticizes the "tone" of Britain's preeminent Romantic through appealing to a Sufi source. While Islam serves as a primary influence for Emerson, helping to shape his early Romanticism, Islam here offers a catalyst for his later Romantic self-consciousness, helping to reveal this tradition's transatlantic continuities, as well as cracks.

Exhibiting the lateness of Emerson's own authorship – his Preface to *The Gulistan* was penned a full half-century after Byron's first *Turkish Tale* – Emerson's critique seems solidly grounded in the 1860s, reflecting not only his nation's darkest days, but also the dying days of Romanticism. A turning point in literary history, the Civil War is traditionally understood as the terminus of American Romanticism, a fitting time for Emerson to reject his Byronic predecessor.[19] However, while it is the horrors of American carnage that help exhaust Romanticism, Emerson yet finds a cause for "good hope" in 1865, with Sa'dī offering a revitalizing resource, providing a model for the "shedding" of American "mishaps". Reflecting his own traumatic times, Emerson flees the nostalgic darkness of Byron, living in a nation where brooding "cynicism" now seems empty, and Sufi "happiness" seems a healthy remedy. Beginning his career by famously visiting

Coleridge at Highgate in 1833, it is Emerson's unknown acquisition of the "Alcoran" in 1833 which perhaps better anticipates this moment three decades later, Emerson seeking to evade negative rhetoric on "folly and ignorance", searching instead for an affirmative poetics of "friendship, love, self-devotion, and serenity". Published during the final months of America's moral crisis – as well as the final days of Romanticism – Emerson finds a "moral" and civic model in Muslim poetry, Sa'dī's artistry offering a Sufi cure for national and personal ills, this Persian poet embodying not only "resources against pain", but also offering a restorative "sensibility to pleasure".

Epilogue

Romantic Requiem:
The Islamic Interment of
Yūsuf bin Ḥāmir

Seven years before writing his "Preface" to Saʻdī's *Gulistan,*
Emerson had offered his American audience a more general overview of Islamic verse, publishing an essay in April
1858 simply entitled "Persian Poetry". Appearing in the *Atlantic
Monthly* – destined to become the "most prestigious of American
literary magazines" – Emerson's essay introduces his readers to a
range of Sufi poets, supplying ample selections from their poetry,
translating not only Saʻdī and Ḥāfiẓ, but also Niẓāmī, ʻAṭṭār and
Jāmī.[1] Celebrating Persian poetry as containing "the formulas
which supersede all histories", Emerson accents the transcendent
and superlative qualities of Sufi verse: "That for which mainly
books exist", Emerson asserts sharply in his essay's introduction
"is communicated in these rich extracts".[2] The very beginning of
Emerson's "Persian Poetry" is focused not on the Islamic East,
however, nor on the American West, but rather on a European
intermediary; in the first simple sentence of his essay, Emerson
announces: "To Baron von Hammer Purgstall, who died in
Vienna in 1856, we owe our best knowledge of the Persians."[3]
Rather than medieval Sufi poets, it is a modern Austrian scholar
who receives initial mention in Emerson's essay, this American
meditation on Muslim mystics commencing with a European
Catholic. Observing the recent death of "Hammer Purgstall",
Emerson ironically begins his "Persian Poetry" with a definitive

conclusion, his essay starting with the very end of a Viennese life. And although memorializing a singular man – an aristocratic "Baron" – Emerson nevertheless speaks collectively; it is a plural and democratic "*we*" who "owe" a debt to the departed, with Emerson framing his dedication to the Austrian dead as a communal obligation.

These polarities of Emerson's American memorial, published in the *Atlantic Monthly*, offer a transatlantic perspective on Hammer-Purgstall – a perspective anticipated in the public attention triggered at home in Austria two years earlier. The death of Joseph von Hammer-Purgstall in Vienna on November 23, 1856 was regarded as an event of national significance, marked by a "ceremonial funeral . . . in St. Stephan's Cathedral", the prime ecclesiastical seat of the capital city.[4] Blending Austrian nationalism and Christian piety, this prominent funeral would find its own contrary opposite, however, in Hammer-Purgstall's quiet granite grave, tucked away on the outskirts of Weidling, a village ten miles north of Vienna. Situated at the heart of this small town's secluded cemetery is a stone memorial dedicated to Hammer-Purgstall – a memorial distinguished by neither its size nor its style, but by its unusual scripts. Unlike the neighboring rows of Catholic graves, adorned with crosses and angels, Hammer-Purgstall's grave is instead adorned with texts written in ten different languages, his monument's many sides covered with quotations from both West and East. Featured on its broad base is a broad catalogue of European tongues – German, English, Italian, French, Spanish, Latin, Greek – filtering quotations from poets such as Dante and Shakespeare, Calderón and Horace. However, it is the upper portions of Hammer-Purgstall's grave – the tablets erected at eye level – which are most likely to engage and intrigue the visitor, engraved exclusively in Middle Eastern languages, traced in fluid lines of Turkish, Persian and Arabic (Figures 4 and 5).[5]

Confronting this curious memorial, the visitor discovers that the lone text on this monument dedicated specifically to Hammer-Purgstall himself is composed entirely in Arabic, the Austrian's own epitaph inscribed solely in the liturgical language of Islam (Figure 6):

Figure 4 Profile of Hammer-Purgstall Grave, Weidling Cemetery, Austria. Author's photo.

Figure 5 Hammer-Purgstall Grave, oblique view. Author's photo.

Figure 6 Hammer-Purgstall Grave, upper façade, featuring Arabic epitaph. Author's photo.

هو الحی
المرحوم و المغفور
المحتاج الی رحمة
ربه العفو الغفور
مترجم الالسنة الثلاثة
يوسف بن حامر
لروحه ذكر جميل

[He (God) is the Living!
the deceased, the departed,
the one needful of the mercy
of his Lord, the Pardoning, the Forgiving,
the translator of the three languages,
Yūsuf bin Ḥāmir
to his spirit be a beautiful remembrance!]

Although speaking a foreign tongue, this self-commemoration seems distinctly familiar, its Arabic memorial to the dead recalling other insignias adopted by the Austrian during his lifetime, echoing the embossing stamp hidden inside Hammer's book covers, as well as the plaque proudly displayed outside his imposing Schloss (see Chapter 4). Offering a final signature on his own sepulcher, Hammer's last Arabic autograph, however, seems his most definitive, not only designating his ultimate resting place, but also offering a name that reaches new Eastern limits. Characterized as "the translator of the three languages" ("مترجم الالسنة الثلاثة"), Hammer also translates his own name, not only inscribing "Joseph Hammer" in Arabic, but also adding a filial marker to his family, self-identifying as "يوسف بن حامر" – i.e. *Yūsuf bin Ḥāmir* (emphasis added). Subtly revising his paternal line with this slight insertion, Hammer bequeaths back to generations past a new Arabic genealogy, framing himself as the European "son" ("bin") of Eastern fathers. Remarkable for its new Arabian addition, Hammer's name is remarkable also for omitting all aristocratic privilege; despite his legitimate claim to class prominence, Hammer suppresses all sense of status in his personal memorial, mentioning neither his identity as "Baron", nor his "Purgstall" name and estate. First honored by a distinguished funeral in Vienna's opulent St. Stephan's, Hammer subsequently shifts to a rural Austrian interment, where he leaves behind all Western rank and title, assuming a persona both foreign and humble, becoming an Eastern "departed" who pleas for "the mercy of his Lord" ("رحمة ربه").[6]

Paring down his national identity, Hammer's grave is also surprising for yet another omission: its lack of all markers that suggest a Christian commitment. Unlike the adjacent graves in this Catholic cemetery, Hammer's monument displays neither icon nor emblem, refusing to confess a Christian identity in its design or diction. Instead, Hammer's own epitaph seems Islamically invested, not only speaking in the language most sacred to Islam, but in phrases that evoke Islamic scripture. Especially conspicuous is Hammer's appeal to the Almighty, invoking God as العفو الغفور" ("the Pardoning, the Forgiving") – two words which form a recurrent refrain throughout the Muslim scripture, this Qur'ānic phrase finding a fresh home in Weidling's Catholic cemetery.[7] Amplifying the interreligious and intimate flavor of his grave's façade is what lies beneath Hammer's own epitaph: namely, a plaque commemorating his beloved Caroline, his wife's memorial inscribed in German immediately below Hammer's own Arabic marker. Recalling the *Prayerbook* dedicated to Caroline at her 1844 death, Hammer's grave too features a frontispiece that fuses languages and genders, its dual façade performing a shared act of remembrance that reflects a marriage of religious legacies, marrying identities of Catholic and Jewish paternity under a banner of Muslim idioms.

It is not the front, but the back, of Hammer's grave, however, that most clearly confesses his interreligious allegiance. Pointing away from human personality and particularity, the reverse panel of Hammer's monument is also written entirely in Arabic, but emphasizes divine presence, opening with sacred quotation, rather than specific memorial (Figure 7):

هو الباقي
كل نفس ذائقة الموت
انا لله وانا اليه راجعون

[He is the Everlasting
Every soul shall taste of death
Surely we belong to God, and to Him we return]

Shifting from individual life to universal source, the back of Hammer's headstone is inscribed with Qur'ānic quotations

Figure 7 Hammer-Purgstall Grave, reverse façade, featuring Islamic phraseology. Author's photo.

that vacillate between divine endurance and human ephemerality, first denominating God as "the Everlasting", then citing Q. 3:185 ("Every soul shall taste of death"), followed by Q. 2:156 ("Surely we belong to God, and to Him we return").[8] Implying an Islamic character, these quotations also ironically envision an end to all cultural and religious difference, accenting the ubiquity of "death", as well as Allāh's transcendent abiding. Mapping the divide between mortality and immortality, the reverse of Hammer's grave no longer spans mere national identities – East and West – but rather embraces existential horizons, reaching from temporal to eternal, from terrestrial to celestial. Performing yet another fusion of polarities, this opposite end of Hammer-Purgstall's monument allows his grave to stretch from the death of an actual man to an "Everlasting" Deity; while the mourner confronts a singular bereavement in the grave's Arabic façade, its Arabic reverse transports the mourner back to divine "belonging",

accenting God's universal permanence, and his ultimate possession, in the face of our own particular transience.

An Islamic memorial to a Romantic life, Hammer's grave
offers a powerful, final reminder of the intersections between
Islam and Romanticism which have formed our own focus, with
the diverse lives covered in the present study also culminating in
this single marker of European passing. Engraved in its elegant
style and form, Hammer's grave seems a fit expression of the
artistic appeal that Islam has exercised on his Romantic contemporaries, with the "sublimity" of Muslim scripture endowing an
aesthetic "beauty" even to the "remembrance" of death itself.
From Byronic passion to Emersonian prophecy, from Goethean
"Eternity" to Poe's "Israfel", Hammer's grave recalls a Romantic
trend of appealing to Qur'ānic eloquence as a means of expressing the most personal and most poignant of passages, the transition from life to death. Perhaps more obvious in Hammer's grave
is not its artistic sublimity, however, but its cultural synthesis,
with the Romantic urge to imaginatively merge opposites itself
mirrored forcefully in this final tribute. Marrying together margins of nation, class, and gender, the Islamic core of Hammer's
memorial suggests a "unifying" of tribal difference (*à la* Herder
and Irving), as well as a bond between masculine and feminine
(*à la* Novalis and Mary Shelley). A tribute to a life of translation, this memorial too embodies Romanticism's investment in
Islamic rendition, with "the translator of the three languages"
personifying a Western impulse to convey Muslim sources into
new tongues and traditions, accenting the literal and literary renditions that have unfolded from J. W. Goethe, to Percy Bysshe
Shelley, to R. W. Emerson.

Offering future European generations a memorial that reaches
back to ancient Muslim traditions, Hammer's grave also expresses,
more simply, an imperative to "remember" – an imperative so
often associated with Romanticism, a movement ambivalently
poised between nostalgic poetry and visionary prophecy, negotiating past commitments and spiritual potential. Recalling each
of the figures in this study, it is both a personal and a communal
story that seems revised and retold in Hammer's self-inscription,

with the Qur'ān's engraved curves and elevated content implying not Hammer alone, but involving also his successors and descendants, commanding them and us to endow "his spirit" with a "beautiful remembrance". Featuring imperatives to remember that are equally Romantic and Islamic, this final monument perhaps most obviously recalls the first of this study's monuments, returning our attention to the Goethe-Hafiz Memorial. Echoing this initial granite marker, Hammer's own granite grave too fuses opposites, concretely unifying religion, culture, and language. Overlapping in function, these memorials also overlap in form; while the Goethe-Hafiz Memorial is constructed through confronting seats and is adorned with distinct languages, Hammer's grave too offers juxtaposed faces that are marked with alternate languages, its base and headstones situating diverse tongues in amicable opposition. Recalling the opening of the present study, Hammer's memorial returns us not merely to our beginning, however, but to a beginning *before* our beginning; enshrined most insistently in this final memorial is Joseph Hammer and the Qur'ān, the two sources which served as the formative influences for the two figures with which our study began: Goethe and Ḥāfiẓ, the former inspired by Hammer's scholarship, and the latter acquiring his very name from Qur'ānic commitment. Yet, if Hammer's grave offers an anterior beginning to our study, pointing back beyond its opening, this same grave too seems to offer a new beginning, pointing forward, its multiple languages surpassing the starker dualities with which we started. Although both memorials – Weimar and Weidling – stand as present-day reminders of past relationships, the Goethe-Hafiz Memorial enacts a linguistic distance and a spatial divide, its opposite chairs suggesting dueling identities of literatures and languages, staging a seated encounter between Orient and Occident. Alternately, Hammer's grave offers visitors not two, but ten, languages, positing not a dialectic between East and West, but a religious and linguistic multiplicity that seems to gesture to a more inclusive globalism. Most prominently inscribed with Islamic expression, Hammer's grave also encompasses literary selections that originate from multiple eras and areas, reaching forward from the terminus of

Romanticism in the mid-nineteenth century to touch the cultural complexities that will infuse the twentieth and twenty-first. A Muslim memorial which yet embraces a multifaceted modernity, Hammer's grave itself transcends dichotomies of East and West, serving as a prophetic vessel for an authentic "World Literature". Concluding our Romantic study with Hammer's own Islamic end, we find ultimately a new birth in his death marker, his grave offering a signal of a burgeoning global genesis where languages surpass their specific histories, this Arabic imperative to "remember" Hammer's own "spirit" unfolding a more universal memory, opening a world of Romantic futures that yet remain indebted to Islamic origins.

Notes

Introduction Weimar, 2000: Memorializing Goethe's Ḥāfiẓ

1. The *Goethe-Hafis Denkmal* formed the focus of my 2005 "The Genesis of *Weltliteratur*"; Chapter 1 expands the discussion first featured in this article, and reproduces this article's images of the *Denkmal*. The Weimar memorial has been treated by numerous previous studies, and is regularly invoked at the opening of such studies; see, for example, the most recent collection by the pre-eminent expert on Goethe and Islam – Katharina Mommsen – whose 2012 "*Orient und Okzident sind nicht mehr zu trennen*" ("Orient and Occident are no more to be separated") quotes verses in its very title which are also reproduced on the *Denkmal*, and which features a foreword by Jochen Golz which mentions the memorial (p. 7).
2. For "*divan*" as a pun implying both "poetry collection" and "furniture" see Mommsen, "*Orient und Okzident sind nicht mehr zu trennen*", p. 38.
3. Critical debates regarding Ḥāfiẓ's piety, as evidenced by his poetry, are protracted; for the poet's reputed unorthodoxy, and even accusations of his "heresy", see Ridgeon, *Sufi Castigator: Ahmad Kasravi and the Iranian Mystical Tradition*, p. 146.
4. For Goethe's fraught association and affinity with Romanticism, as well as his own "anti-Romantic polemics", see Nicholls, *Goethe's Concept of the Daemonic*, p. 116.
5. These lines appear on p. 108 of the first edition of Goethe's *Divan* (1819).
6. The "*ergeben*" ("to yield, to surrender") of Goethe's first line recalls the etymology of "*Islām*", which literally means "submission [to God]".
7. While Said's 1978 *Orientalism* continues to impact contemporary criticism of Western literary engagements with Islam, recent studies

have increasingly challenged his approach; see, for instance, Wai Chee Dimock's 2006 *Through Other Continents: American Literature across Deep Time* which embraces a "paradigm" that is the "obverse of Edward Said's *Orientalism*" (p. 28), and Humberto Garcia's 2012 *Islam and the English Enlightenment, 1670–1840*, which is interested in "sympathetic literary and cultural representations" (p. xi). For the most comprehensive critique of Said and his *Orientalism*, see Daniel M. Varisco's 2007 *Reading Orientalism: Said and the Unsaid*.

8. Although interest in Romantic readings of Islam stretches back to the first decades of the last century – for instance, Arthur Christy's influential *The Orient in American Transcendentalism* (1932) – several treatments appeared even while the present study neared completion; in addition to Mommsen (2012) and Garcia (2012) above cited, see also the 2013 edited collection *Coleridge, Romanticism and the Orient: Cultural Negotiations*.

9. These "criteria" of Romanticism are quoted from the opening to McFarland's "Involute and Symbol in the Romantic Imagination" (p. 29). For the vexed history of "Romanticism" and its terminology, see Perry, "Romanticism: The Brief History of a Concept", pp. 3–11. The concept of "Romanticism" has been labelled "amorphous and multifarious" by Fusso, "The Romantic Tradition", p. 171.

10. Karoline von Günderrode authored *Mahomed, der Prophet von Mekka*, a dramatic poem which recalls Goethe's own efforts to stage the Muslim Prophet (see Chapter 3 of Hilger, *Women Write Back: Strategies of Response and the Dynamics of European Literary Culture, 1790–1805*). William Blake produced subversive and sympathetic paintings of the Prophet, as well as integrating "Mahomet" into his poetic prophecies (see Whitehead, "'A wise tale of the Mahometans'", pp. 27–47). Friend of Byron, Thomas Moore authored the period's most commercially successful poem grounded in the Muslim East, his 1817 *Lalla Rookh* (see Meagher, "Thomas Moore, Ireland, and Islam", pp. 233–248). Author of the 1851 *Moby-Dick*, Herman Melville includes regular allusions to Islam in his fiction and poetry (see Marr, *The Cultural Roots of American Islamicism*, pp. 219ff., and Einboden, *Nineteenth-Century U.S. Literature in Middle Eastern Languages*, pp. 99ff.).

1 Weimar, 1800: Dramatizing Goethe's "Mahomet"

1. This quotation is from Hilger, *Women Write Back*, p. 100. Hilger here also cites Voltaire's 1740 letter to the King of Prussia, where

Voltaire acknowledges that "I know that Mahomet did not exactly plot the kind of treason that is the topic of this tragedy".

2. For the performance context of Voltaire's *Mahomet* see Carlson, *Voltaire and the Theatre of the Eighteenth Century*, pp. 54–56, who also notes Voltaire's withdrawal of the play after its initial performances, prompted, in part, by "widespread protest against the play, not only from the Turkish ambassador, as might be expected, but from religious leaders and other critics who insisted that the notorious sceptic Voltaire was attacking Christianity under the guise of an alien fanaticism" (p. 55).

3. For Goethe and Schiller's pursuit of "the ennoblement of the German stage" during "the last year of the eighteenth century", see Düntzer, *Life of Goethe*, II, p. 181. For this quotation from Carlson, see his *Goethe and the Weimar Theatre*, p. 139.

4. See Hilger, *Women Write Back*, p. 102. Such stylistic innovations in Goethe's rendition of Voltaire's *Mahomet*, and Goethe's revision of his original's content, is also addressed by Solbrig, "The Theater, Theory and Politics", p. 31.

5. For previous recognition of Goethe's revision of Voltaire's title see Hilger, *Women Write Back*, p. 102.

6. The origins of Goethe's fragmentary play, *Mahomet*, composed in the early 1770s, is addressed by Mommsen, *Goethe und die Arabische Welt* ("Goethe and the Arab World"), pp. 194ff. See also Goethe's own autobiography, where he recalls that "I had shortly before read with great interest, and studied, the life of the Eastern Prophet, and was therefore tolerably prepared when the thought occurred to me . . . of taking the life of Mahomet [as my subject]" (Goethe, *The Autobiography*, II, p. 266).

7. This is Goethe's own description of the opening to his aborted *Mahomet*; see Goethe, *The Autobiography*, II, p. 266. Goethe also confesses here that "I composed this hymn with great delight: it is now lost, but might easily be restored for the purpose of a cantata, and would commend itself to the musical composer by the variety of its expression" (p. 267).

8. This passage is quoted and treated by Mommsen, *Goethe und der Islam* ("Goethe and Islam"), p. 59. The stylized English translation here provided – crafted by William P. Andrews – is one of the first and only offered for Goethe's lines; see Andrews, "Goethe's Key to *Faust*", p. 546.

9. This issue of the *Goettinger Musenalmanach* ("Göttingen Muses' Almanac") – an almanac for 1774 – was published in 1773; see Düntzer, *Life of Goethe*, I, p. 208. For the title "*Mahomets-Gesang*" ("Song to Mahomet") – including its dash

and significance – see Goethe, *Gedichte, 1756–1799* ("Poems, 1756–1799"), p. 915.

10. This description of "*Mahomets-Gesang*" as arising from a dialogue sung "at the highest point of [the Prophet's] success" is Goethe's own; see *The Autobiography*, II, p. 268.

11. Nicholls, *Goethe's Concept of the Daemonic*, p. 134.

12. For "*Mahomets-Gesang*" as the lead poem in Goethe's *Die Erste Weimarer Gedichtsammlung* ("The First Weimar Poetry Collection"), see Goethe, *Gedichte, 1756–1799*, pp. 193 and 915.

13. This translation of "*Mahomets-Gesang*" is John Whaley's; see Goethe, *Selected Poems*, p. 7.

14. Reflected in Whaley's translation are the irregular line lengths, rhymes, and stanzas of Goethe's German original; see Goethe, *Gedichte, 1756–1799*, pp. 193ff.

15. This phrase – "desert and harems" – is derived from John Esposito's characterization of Western stereotypes of "Arabs"; see Esposito, *The Islamic Threat*, p. 3.

16. Quinn, *The Sum of All Heresies* (p. 86), notes that Goethe's poem "contained no references to Islam", and "never mentioned [the Prophet] by name".

17. Goethe, *Selected Poems*, p. 7.

18. Boyle, *Goethe: The Poetry of Desire*, p. 201.

19. Goethe, *Selected Poems*, pp. 7 and 9.

20. For Goethe's likening the Prophet to a "swelling estuary", see Boyle, *Goethe: The Poetry of Desire*, p. 201; as Boyle also implies here, the "ocean" to which the Prophet leads his "brothers" assumes a paternal character (portrayed as "Father Ocean", in Boyle's words).

21. Goethe, *Selected Poems*, p. 9.

22. Schiller and Goethe, *Correspondence between Schiller and Goethe*, II, p. 296.

23. See, for example, Schiller's October 15, 1799 letter which recommends that *Mahomet*'s translation be attempted, supplying too notes on the project; here, Schiller also recognizes the need to overwrite "the Alexandrine rhythm" of the French original, retaining only Voltaire's "subject-matter" for the German stage (Schiller and Goethe, *Correspondence between Schiller and Goethe*, II, pp. 278–279).

24. Guthrie, *Schiller the Dramatist*, p. 115.

25. This is E. P. Arnold-Forster's translation as included in Schiller, *The Poems of Schiller*, p. 351.

26. For the importance of Schiller's poem to his own dramatic efforts at this time – with its lines able to "equally well stand in the

prologue to Schiller's own [*Wallenstein*] trilogy" – see Guthrie, *Schiller the Dramatist*, p. 115.

27. For these circumstances of *Mahomet*'s production, including Duke Karl August's investment in the project, see Carlson, *Goethe and the Weimar Theatre*, pp. 137–138.

28. Napoleon's Qur'ānic reverie is quoted in multiple sources; this specific iteration of his recollection is from Mostyn, *Egypt's Belle Epoque*, p. 17. Also see Cole, *Napoleon's Egypt: Invading the Middle East*, pp. 130–131 for Napoleon's "use [of] Islamic rhetoric as part of his ruling strategy", and for his departure from Egypt in August (p. 244).

29. For Goethe's contemporaries "often [drawing] a parallel between Mahomet and the new world conqueror, Napoleon", see Richards, *Goethe's Search for the Muse*, p. 64, which also acknowledges the censorship of *Mahomet* in Vienna. Solbrig too has noted that Goethe's *Mahomet* "suffered the same fate [of censorship as Voltaire's original] in Vienna", where the "notorious censor Häglin prohibited the production because he believed he saw allusions to Napoleon in the figure of Mahomet" ("The Theater, Theory and Politics", p. 26). These "parallels" between "Mahomet and Napoleon" in Goethe's play have most recently received notice from Hilger, *Women Write Back*, p. 100.

30. Lewes, *The Life of Goethe*, p. 505. This episode has received regular treatment by Goethe's biographers and critics; see, for example, Brown, *Life of Goethe*, II, pp. 546–547 and Seibt, *Goethe und Napoleon*, p. 223. This 1808 encounter has also previously been invoked as a means of contextualizing Goethe's *Mahomet*. For example, in his 1979 discussion of this rendered play, Richards posits that Goethe himself made a connection between *Mahomet* and Napoleon, which is evidenced "by the fact that [Goethe] discussed the work with Napoleon during his famous interview" (*Goethe's Search for the Muse*, p. 64); in 1990, Solbrig began her own treatment of Goethe's *Mahomet* by recalling his meeting of Napoleon in 1808 ("The Theater, Theory and Politics", p. 21).

2 "Mohammed Came Forward on the Stage": Herder's Islamic History

1. Clark, *Herder: His Life and Thought*, p. 416. Hilger too highlights Herder's rejection of Goethe's *Mahomet*, noting that it was Herder's wife – Karoline – who recorded his reaction; see Hilger, *Women Write Back*, p. 104. Mommsen also notes Karoline

Herder's own critique of *Mahomet*, who accused the play of com-
mitting a "sin against history" (*Goethe und die Arabische Welt*,
p. 233).

2. Goethe himself recalls in his autobiography that "the most important event, one that was to have the weightiest consequences for
me, was my acquaintance with Herder". Yet, he also recognizes
that "It was not long, however, before the repelling pulse of his
nature began to appear, and placed me in no small uneasiness",
adding later that "behave as one might, one could never expect
approval [from Herder]". See Goethe, *The Autobiography*, II,
pp. 8, 10, and 12.

3. Gillies, *Herder*, p. 21. For the "permanent rift" between Herder
and Goethe, with "personal conflicts" added to "political and aesthetic disagreements" in 1794, see Köpke, "Herder's Views on the
Germans and their Future Literature", p. 225.

4. See, for example, Mommsen, "*Orient und Okzident sind nicht
mehr zu trennen*", pp. 105–106.

5. For this quotation from Goethe's 1772 letter, see Goethe, *Early
Letters of Goethe*, p. 92. Following his query "Look, what sort of a
musician is he who keeps looking at his instrument?", and preced-
ing his citation of the Qur'ān, Goethe includes two quotations from
Greek poetry. Goethe's quotation from the Qur'ān adapts Q. 20:25.
In his *The Koran* – which the present study regularly cites for its
English translations from the Qur'ān – Arberry renders this phrase as
"Lord, open my breast". The Arabic term "sura" ("*sūra*") signifies
a "chapter" of the Qur'ān, and will be used throughout. Mommsen
also treats this 1772 letter in her "*Die Bedeutung des Korans für
Goethe*" ("The Significance of the Koran for Goethe"), p. 139.

6. Richards, *Goethe's Search for the Muse*, pp. 56–57 emphasizes
Goethe's hesitancy regarding *Mahomet* and his own rendition of
Voltaire's play, as well as his attempts at "dissociating himself"
from the project. Mommsen too suggests that Goethe harbored res-
ervations regarding the prospects of translating *Mahomet*, yet was
compelled to render the play at the behest of Duke Karl August; see
Goethe und die Arabische Welt, p. 222, as well as Hilger, *Women
Write Back*, p. 104.

7. Beiser, *The German Historicist Tradition*, p. 149.

8. In this chapter, I cite T. O. Churchill's 1800 translation of Herder's
Ideen, i.e. *Outlines of a Philosophy of the History of Man* (for the
passage quoted above, see I, pp. 356–357). Although more than
two centuries old, and somewhat outmoded and idiosyncratic, I
reference Churchill's edition as his is the "only complete English
translation of Herder's seminal work" (Spencer, *Herder's Political*

Thought, p. 70). However, the citation of Churchill's 1800 edition in the present study of Romanticism also has the added benefit of giving a sense of the *Ideen* as it was read by British and American Romantics, who were significantly influenced by precisely this translation; Emerson, for example, read Churchill's edition, and was thereby significantly impacted by Herder's thought (see Menze, "Herder's Reception and Influence in the U.S.A.", pp. 31–32).

9. Beiser, *The German Historicist Tradition*, p. 149.
10. For the German original of this passage, see Herder, *Ideen zur Philosophie der Geschichte der Menschheit* ("Ideas for a Philosophy of the History of Mankind"), p. 300. Rendered as "romantic men" by Churchill, Herder's "*staunende Menschen*" is parsed as "men filled with wonder and amazement" by F. M. Barnard in his *Herder on Social and Political Culture*, p. 300. The association of "solitude" and "sublimity" with Romanticism has recently been highlighted in the very title of Frances Ferguson's 2013 *Solitude and the Sublime: The Romantic Aesthetics of Individuation*.
11. Herder, *Outlines of a Philosophy of the History of Man*, I, p. 357.
12. Herder, *Outlines of a Philosophy of the History of Man*, II, p. 582.
13. Ibid., p. 583.
14. Ibid., pp. 583–584.
15. See Almond, *History of Islam in German Thought*, p. 70, whose chapter on Herder provides the most comprehensive treatment of his ambivalent appeal to Islamic sources, addressing not only the *Ideen*, but also his correspondence and ancillary works.
16. Herder, *Outlines of a Philosophy of the History of Man*, II, p. 584. See Almond, *History of Islam*, p. 58 for an alternate translation of the first lines of this passage; Almond also emphasizes the "tensions" exemplified in the contending adjectives which Herder here applies to "the Koran" – "tensions" which Almond understands to be "between the Romantic and Christian perspectives on the phenomenon of Islam" (p. 58).
17. Herder, *Outlines of a Philosophy of the History of Man*, II, p. 592.
18. Almond, *History of Islam*, p. 66.

3 "In the Footsteps of Mohammed": Friedrich Schlegel and Novalis

1. Herder, *Outlines of a Philosophy of the History of Man*, II, p. 593.

2. I cite Peter Firchow's English translation of the *Athenaeum* from Schlegel, *Lucinde and the Fragments*, p. 254. For Novalis' own response to Schlegel's intimate *Ideen* dedication, see Littlejohns, "Collaboration as Ideology", pp. 52–55.

3. Schlegel, *Lucinde and the Fragments*, p. 256.

4. Germana, "Self-Othering in German Orientalism", p. 85.

5. This selection from Schlegel's October 20, 1798 letter to Novalis is frequently quoted; I cite here the translation offered in Riasanovsky, *The Emergence of Romanticism*, p. 60. For other iterations, see Almond, *History of Islam*, p. 91 and Eichner, *Friedrich Schlegel*, p. 79.

6. O'Brien, *Novalis, Signs of Revolution*, p. 11 notes that "Censorship – official and unofficial . . . – cut short Hardenberg's literary career as effectively as did his terminal illness". O'Brien also adds that "Without Tieck and Schlegel, Hardenberg's writings would almost certainly have persisted as a mere footnote in the history of German Romanticism."

7. Mahoney, *The Critical Fortunes of a Romantic Novel*, p. xi.

8. For "the famous symbol of the blue flower", and an overview of *Heinrich von Ofterdingen*'s narrative shape, see Blackall, *The Novels of the German Romantics*, p. 120.

9. With some exceptions, as noted below, I quote from Palmer Hilty's translation of Novalis' novel, first published in 1964, i.e. *Henry of Ofterdingen: A Novel*; this quotation is from pp. 59–60.

10. Novalis, *Henry of Ofterdingen: A Novel*, p. 60. I correct the typographic error "he confronted the singer" in Hilty's translation to read instead "he comforted the singer". Also, while Hilty provides "the praise of her country and her people" for Novalis' "*dem Lobe ihrer Landsleute und ihres Vaterlandes*", I instead provide "the praise of her countrymen and fatherland", which follows the more literal translation offered in the 1842 *Henry of Ofterdingen: A Romance*, p. 79.

11. Novalis, *Henry of Ofterdingen: A Novel*, p. 61. I alter Hilty's "how splendidly" to "how beautifully" in the above, so as to better capture Novalis' "*wie schön*"; this substitution is also supported by the rendition offered by *Henry of Ofterdingen: A Romance*, p. 81.

12. For previous recognition of this cultural critique, see Hodkinson, *Women and Writing in the Works of Novalis*, p. 211 which asserts that "Heinrich not only offers Zulima space to sing her song; he offers her the means and space to illustrate that there is more to her existence than the identity imposed on her by the crusaders".

13. Hodkinson, *Women and Writing in the Works of Novalis*, p. 186.

14. Novalis, *Henry of Ofterdingen: A Novel*, p. 63.
15. As O'Brien notes, Novalis had "produced a clean draft of part 1" in "April 1800", but had "to abandon part 2 in its early stages" (*Novalis, Signs of Revolution*, p. 14). According to O'Brien, Friedrich Schlegel was instrumental in preventing his fellow *literati* from themselves finishing *Heinrich von Ofterdingen*, allowing for the editorial postscript subsequently appended to the Schlegel and Tieck edition.
16. This English translation from the Novalis postscript is quoted from *Henry of Ofterdingen: A Romance*, p. 223.
17. This extensive postscript on the future development of Novalis' novel was supplied by Tieck; for the German original of this "account" of the novel's "continuation" (i.e. "*Bericht über die Fortsetzung*"), see Novalis, *Heinrich von Ofterdingen, Schriften*, pp. 359ff.

4 "Allāh is the best Keeper": Joseph Hammer's Ḥāfiẓ

1. For Hammer's departure in May 1799, and his journey to Constantinople (Istanbul) lasting "about four weeks", see Solbrig, *Hammer-Purgstall und Goethe*, pp. 49–50.
2. Hammer himself notes the commencement of his Ḥāfiẓ rendition in June 1799; see Solbrig, *Hammer-Purgstall und Goethe*, p. 51. For the Turkish commentaries referenced by Hammer in Istanbul as aids to his rendition of Ḥāfiẓ's Persian, see Mommsen, "*Orient und Okzident sind nicht mehr zu trennen*", pp. 260–261.
3. In addition to Ḥāfiẓ's *ghazals*, Hammer included German renditions of Ḥāfiẓ's "*Kasside*" and "*Rubajat*", in his 1812–1813 edition, for instance. For Hammer's completion of his rendition in 1806, during his second stay in Istanbul, see Solbrig, *Hammer-Purgstall und Goethe*, p. 86.
4. The influence of Hammer's translation on Goethe and Emerson is treated, respectively, in Chapters 5–6, and Chapter 16, below.
5. See Ḥāfiẓ, *Der Diwan von Mohammed Schemsed-Din Hafis* ("The Divan of Muhammad Shamsuddin Hafiz"), I, p. iii.
6. Ibid., p. vii.
7. Ibid.
8. An analysis of Hammer's "Preface" – i.e. his "*Vorrede*" – is provided by Solbrig, *Hammer-Purgstall und Goethe*, pp. 111ff.
9. For previous recognition of Hammer's embossing stamp as a reflection of his interreligious interests, see Einboden, "Stoicism or Sufism?", p. 67.

10. Clive, *Beethoven and his World*, pp. 158–159 treats Joseph Henikstein's role in "founding the Gesellschaft der Musikfreunde", as well as his conversion from Judaism. For Hammer described as a "conservative Catholic", see Stahuljak, *Pornographic Archaeology*, p. 77, as well as Fichtner, *Terror and Toleration*, p. 137. See also Chaghatai, *Hammer-Purgstall and the Muslim India*, p. 10.

11. For the latest appraisal of Hammer-Purgstall's "monumental ten-volume Ottoman history", see Gürpınar, *Ottoman/Turkish Visions of the Nation, 1860–1950*, which labels this "history" as "arguably the equivalent of Gibbon's *Decline and Fall* for Ottoman historiography" (p. 24). Hammer-Purgstall's eclectic program of publication is referenced in Einboden, "Stoicism or Sufism?", p. 66.

12. The history of Schloss Hainfeld, and the Hammers' possession of the palace, is most authoritatively treated in Galter and Haas's 2008 *Joseph von Hammer-Purgstall: Grenzgänger zwischen Orient und Okzident* ("Joseph von Hammer-Purgstall: Border-Crosser between Orient and Occident"); see, in particular, pp. 183ff. for the contribution co-authored by Rupert Wernhart and Annabella Dietz.

13. This dedication is featured on an unpaginated page immediately before the German opening of Hammer-Purgstall, *Zeitwarte des Gebetes in Sieben Tageszeiten*. In my following discussion, I refer to Hammer's collection simply as his *Prayerbook*, taking a cue from this work's subtitle, i.e. *Ein Gebetbuch Arabisch und Deutsch* ("A Prayerbook, Arabic and German").

14. Hammer-Purgstall, *Zeitwarte des Gebetes in Sieben Tageszeiten*, p. 1.

15. This image comprises the first page of the Arabic portion of Hammer-Purgstall's *Zeitwarte des Gebetes in Sieben Tageszeiten*.

16. See Hammer-Purgstall, *Zeitwarte des Gebetes in Sieben Tageszeiten*, p. 56, which forms the last page of its German prayers, and which concludes "*Vollendet am 22. Julius 1844, / dem acht und vierzigsten Geburtstage / Carolinens*" ("Completed on July 22 1844, Caroline's forty-eighth birthday"). This date and dedication is also recorded in Arabic on the final page of Hammer's Arabic prayers. See also Hammer-Purgstall, "*Erinnerungen aus meinem Leben*" ("Recollections from my Life"), p. 348.

17. Hammer-Purgstall, "*Erinnerungen aus meinem Leben*", p. 348.

18. I translate the Qur'ānic phrase "فالله خير حافظا" (Q. 12:64) as "For *Allāh* is the best Keeper", seeking to retain the broadest etymologic significance of "حافظا" ("*ḥāfizan*"); less idiomatic would be a rendition such as Arberry's, which reads instead as "God is the best guardian".

19. See Einboden, "Stoicism or Sufism?", p. 65 for another example of

Hammer citing a date according to the *Hijri* calendar (AH) rather than according to Christian reckoning (AD).

5 "In no other Language": Goethe's Arabic Apprenticeship

1. Goethe, *West-East Divan: The Poems, with "Notes and Essays"*, p. 277.
2. Ibid. Additional key scholars that merit their own sections in Goethe's *Notes and Essays* include Heinrich Friedrich Von Diez and Silvestre de Sacy.
3. Katharina Mommsen remains the leading expert on Goethe's study of Arabic, and Islamic sources more broadly; see Mommsen, *Goethe und die Arabische Welt*, pp. 25–26 for Goethe's earliest linguistic efforts. Goethe's Arabic studies have received some recognition in English scholarship; for example, see N. Berman's acknowledgment of Goethe's "several attempts to learn the Arabic language and script", and Goethe's aspiration to study specifically with the Göttingen professor, Johann David Michaelis (*German Literature on the Middle East*, p. 141).
4. For an overview of such scholars and their scholarship as context for Goethe's efforts, see Nebes, "*Orientalistik im Aufbruch*" ("Orientalism on the Rise"), esp. pp. 68–70 and 72–76. See also Mommsen, *Goethe und die Arabische Welt*, pp. 37–45, 142ff.
5. For the German original of Goethe's quotation, see Bosse, ed., *Meine Schatzkammer Füllt Sich Täglich* ("My Treasure-Room Fills Daily"), I, p. 173. The English translation here provided follows the partial rendition offered by Mommsen, "Goethe and the Arab World", p. 80. Also see, however, the translation included in Zapf, *Alphabet Stories*, p. 38, which offers a stylistic rendition of Goethe's sentence ("In no other language, perhaps, are spirit, word, and script so organically fused together").
6. Such celebrations of Goethe are common; for this particular formulation, see, for instance, Swanwick and Frothingham, eds, *Johann Wolfgang Von Goethe*, p. 5.
7. For this Arabic manuscript, see Bosse, ed., *Meine Schatzkammer Füllt Sich Täglich*, II, p. 607; this manuscript is annotated on p. 610. Paulus also traces additional terms in Arabic and Persian on this same manuscript page, transliterating them into Roman script, with Goethe selectively copying from Paulus' example. Both Paulus and Goethe use black ink in "Bl. 126"; my shade distinction (black/grey) aims to highlight their distinct contributions to this same page. Goethe's Arabic manuscripts have received cursory

mention in several previous studies, including his specific script-
ing of Q. 114; see, for instance, Mommsen, "Goethe and the Arab
World", p. 80. However, unlike my following discussion, Goethe's
Arabic manuscripts rarely receive detailed attention.

8. This translation from the Qur'ān's Chapter 114 is from Arberry,
Koran.

9. The "fragmentary imperative" of Romanticism is emphasized
in the very title of Strathman's 2006 *Romantic Poetry and the
Fragmentary Imperative.*

10. This 1819 title page is reproduced in Goethe, *West-östlicher Divan*,
pp. 4–5, published in 2000. My treatment of the dualities implicit in
the *Divan*'s frontispiece first appeared in Einboden, "The Genesis
of *Weltliteratur*", pp. 242–243.

11. It is Johann Gottfried Kosegarten who assisted Goethe in the formulation of his dual language title page, providing the Arabic design
that occupies its left side; see Unseld, *Goethe and his Publishers*,
p. 200.

6 "Is The Qur'an From Eternity?": Goethe's Divan and The "Book of Books"

1. See my "The Genesis of *Weltliteratur*", p. 242, which first featured
this overview of Goethe's *Divan.*

2. The present chapter cites Goethe's German from his original 1819
West-östlicher Divan; the title page to its first book ("Book of the
Singer"), occurs on p. 1, which features the Persian transliterated
title "*Moganni Nameh*" printed above, and noticeably larger than,
its German title ("*Buch des Sängers*").

3. See, for example, Gray, *Goethe: A Critical Introduction*, which
describes the "Poet" in "*Beiname*" as an identity in whom "we are
very possibly invited to see Goethe himself" (p. 231).

4. This is Martin Bidney's translation quoted from Goethe, *West-East
Divan: The Poems, with "Notes and Essays"*, pp. 18–19. Bidney
renders the poem's title "*Beiname*" as "Sobriquet", rather than
"Surname", which is the title adopted by Edward Dowden (see
Goethe, *West-eastern Divan: In Twelve Books*, p. 21).

5. Goethe, *West-East Divan: The Poems, with "Notes and Essays"*,
p. 192.

6. These two poems originally appeared on pp. 8–9 of Goethe's 1819
West-östlicher Divan, with no intervening text between the stanzas,
except the title "*Talismane*" itself. For the English translation, see

Goethe, *West-East Divan: The Poems, with "Notes and Essays"*, pp. 4–5.

7. These Qur'ānic echoes in Goethe's early *Divan* poems are well recognized; see, for instance, Mommsen, *"Orient und Okzident sind nicht mehr zu trennen"*, pp. 185–205 for the most extended treatment of Goethe's "Talismans", and the complex background to its overt Qur'ānic borrowing. The English translations from the Qur'ān are from Arberry, *Koran*.

8. Goethe, *West-East Divan: The Poems, with "Notes and Essays"*, p. 124; the quotation here reproduced represents the first stanza of the poem, which features a second stanza that forms a celebration of mystic "wine". The German original of *"Ob der Koran von Ewigkeit sei?"* appears on p. 185 of Goethe's 1819 *West-östlicher Divan*.

9. *"Ob der Koran von Ewigkeit sei?"* has been previously treated by Mommsen, *Goethe und der Islam*, p. 313, including the poem's possible "ironic distance" from its Qur'ānic subject.

10. For the German original of these statements in Charlotte Schiller's letter, see Schiller, *Briefe von Schillers Gattin an einem Vertrauten Freund*, pp. 181–182. For Goethe's own manuscripts, which seem to confirm Schiller's report, see Bosse, ed., *Meine Schatzkammer Füllt Sich Täglich*, I, pp. 373–374.

11. See also Mommsen, who treats Schiller's letter, and Goethe's probable recitation of the Qur'ān, in her *Goethe und der Islam*, pp. 223ff.

12. I cite this English version from Edward Dowden's translation, published in Goethe, *West-eastern Divan: In Twelve Books*, p. 75; I modernize, however, Dowden's "Mussulman" to read instead as "Muslim". Bidney's version, which is somewhat more stylized, may be found on p. 63 of Goethe, *West-East Divan: The Poems, with "Notes and Essays"*.

7 "The Flight and Return of Mohammed": S. T. Coleridge and Robert Southey

1. This collaborative poem has recently begun to receive substantive attention, with treatments appearing in print even as the present study was in its final stages of authorship. See, for instance, Tim Fulford's 2013 "Coleridge's Sequel to *Thalaba* and Robert Southey's Prequel to *Christabel*" which appears in *Coleridge, Romanticism and the Orient: Cultural Negotiations* (esp. pp. 57–59), as well as Humberto Garcia's 2012 *Islam and the English Enlightenment*,

1670–1840, which dedicates its fifth chapter to the poem and its contexts.

2. This political context for "The Flight and Return of Mohammed" is highlighted by Garcia, *Islam and the English Enlightenment,* pp. 157–158.

3. See Class, *Coleridge and Kantian Ideas in England, 1796–1817,* pp. 127–128 for Coleridge's sojourn in Germany, including his "matriculat[ion]" at Göttingen's "Georg-August University", and his attending "Johann Gottfried Eichhorn's lectures on Higher Biblical Criticism". While Coleridge's Islamic interests during his time in Germany have not received significant attention, his notebooks attest to such interests. See, for instance, Coleridge's extended transcription of a Muslim sermon in German which quotes from the Qur'ān ("*Ein jeder muss den Tod schmecken*"; i.e. "Everyone must taste death", reproducing the Qur'ān 21:35); see pp. 394–395 of Coleridge's February–May 1799 notebooks as published in Coleridge, *The Notebooks of Samuel Taylor Coleridge,* I:1. For this quotation from the Qur'ān, see also my discussion of Hammer's Weidling grave, in the Epilogue, below.

4. Although a substantive and influential study, Sharafuddin's *Islam and Romantic Orientalism,* for instance, does not include mention of "Flight and Return of Mohammed". Fulford does connect "Flight and Return of Mohammed" to Coleridge's "Kubla Khan", noting their "similarity" and positing their contemporaneous composition, suggesting the possibility of "Kubla Khan" taking "firmer shape in late summer 1799", and being further "developed in autumn 1799" (despite its traditional 1797 dating); see "Coleridge's Sequel to *Thalaba* and Robert Southey's Prequel to *Christabel*", pp. 56 and 64.

5. Coleridge, *The Poetical Works of S. T. Coleridge,* II, p. 68.

6. Garcia, *Islam and the English Enlightenment,* p. 157, labels "The Flight and Return of Mohammed" as a prospective "grand Miltonic epic"; Coleridge's "UTTER the song, O my soul!" is also quoted by Garcia as his book's epigram.

7. Garcia even characterizes "The Flight and Return of Mohammed" as a "Unitarian epic" in the title to Chapter 5 of his *Islam and the English Enlightenment* (p. 157). It should be noted, however, that Coleridge's own commitment to Unitarianism would begin to erode as the eighteenth century turned to the nineteenth, leading ultimately to his embrace of more traditional orthodoxy; for this extended and complex transition, see Wendling, *Coleridge's Progress to Christianity,* esp. pp. 111ff., and my discussion of Coleridge's 1833 encounter with Emerson, below.

8. See Madden, ed., *Robert Southey: The Critical Heritage*, p. 4.
9. Southey's letter is dated July 29, 1799, and is quoted from Southey, *Selections from the Letters of Robert Southey*, p. 77. Southey's letter continues on by accusing the Prophet of making "too free with the wife of Zeid", yet asserting that there "is nothing to shock belief" in the Qur'ān, if one "[a]dmit[s] the inspiration of the writer".
10. I quote Southey's contribution to "The Flight and Return of Mohammed" from Southey, *Poetical Works, 1793–1810*, V, pp. 475–479, although I do not include Southey's redactions (e.g. in his second line above, Southey's "semblant of" was inserted to replace "like unto", which he struck out; see p. 475). It is clear that Southey intended his draft portions to belong to the "second book" of the potential epic; for Southey's contribution, see Fulford, "Coleridge's Sequel to *Thalaba* and Robert Southey's Prequel to *Christabel*", pp. 56ff.
11. Coleridge and Southey's "Outline" for "Mohammed" – transcribed initially by Warren Ober (1958), with emendations offered by A. R. Kidwai (1993) – suggests that the entire poem was plotted to begin with a scene at "The Deathbed of Abu Taleb" in Book 1; however, Book 2 was to open with "Mohamed & Abubekr in the Cavern", which indeed suggests that Southey's lines could have formed the beginning to this second book. The "Outline" has more recently been included as an appendix to Garcia, *Islam and the English Enlightenment*, pp. 233–234.
12. Southey, *Poetical Works, 1793–1810*, V, p. 476.
13. Ibid., p. 477. Southey's depiction of "Mohamed & Abubekr in the Cavern" has Qur'ānic origins, derived ultimately from Q. 9:40, which reads in part: "when the two were in the Cave, when [the Prophet] said to his companion, 'Sorrow not; surely God is with us.' Then God sent down on him His Shechina, and confirmed him with legions you did not see; and He made the word of the unbelievers the lowest; and God's word is the uppermost; God is All-mighty, All-wise" (Arberry, *Koran*).
14. Southey, *Poetical Works, 1793–1810*, V, p. 479.

8 "The all-beholding Prophet's aweful voice": Southey's *Thalaba the Destroyer*

1. Southey, *The Collected Letters of Robert Southey*, II, p. 459.
2. Ibid.

3. Jeffrey's "famous review" and such views of Southey are treated by Madden in his *Southey: The Critical Heritage*, pp. 6ff.

4. For Southey's influence on Coleridge, see Fulford's "Coleridge's Sequel to *Thalaba* and Robert Southey's Prequel to *Christabel*". See also Keane, *Coleridge's Submerged Politics*, p. 196 for *Thalaba*'s broader influence, including on Shelley and his Prometheus. For Southey and Poe, see Chapter 15, below.

5. For Heron as the source of Southey's "Dom Daniel" see Fulford's introduction to *Thalaba the Destroyer* in Southey, *Poetical Works, 1793–1810*, III, p. x. An alternate source was suggested previously by Sharafuddin, *Islam and Romantic Orientalism*, p. 50, namely "Henry Weber's . . . *New Arabian Tales*". The definition of "the Dom Daniel" as a den "under the deepest abysses of the ocean" that serves as "the seminary of the evil magicians" is from a revised edition of Southey's poem issued shortly before his death; see Southey, *The Destroyer; or, the Sorcerers of the Domdaniel*, p. 3.

6. This characterization of *Thalaba* is offered by Southey in his 1838 Preface to his *The Curse of Kehama* (initially published in 1810); see Southey, *Poetical Works, 1793–1810*, IV, pp. 3–4. Southey's Preface is also treated by Javadi, *Persian Literary Influence on English Literature*, pp. 75ff.

7. Thalaba as "a male Joan of Arc" was proposed in a letter penned by Southey in 1805; see Southey, *Poetical Works, 1793–1810*, III, p. vii.

8. Ibid.

9. Ibid., for "the Prophet Houd" (pp. 19–20); "[Mount] Kaf" and the "Simourg" (p. 123); and "the Garden of Irem" (pp. 194–195).

10. For previous treatment of Southey's "tendency to support his fantastic tales with factual footnotes" see Fulford, Lee, and Kitson, *Literature, Science and Exploration in the Romantic Era*, p. 101, as well as Fulford, "Coleridge's Sequel to *Thalaba* and Robert Southey's Prequel to *Christabel*", pp. 61–62, which addresses this point when treating *Thalaba* and its "taking up where *Mohammed* left off" (p. 61); recognition of this "tendency" reaches back to Francis Jeffrey's "famous review" in 1802, as Fulford, Lee, and Kitson here suggest.

11. Southey, *Poetical Works, 1793–1810*, III, p. 108.

12. Ibid., p. 258.

13. For the occurrence of "*Zaqqūm*" in the Qur'ān, see not only Q. 37:62, but also 44:43 and 56:52. As is customary for British Romantics, Southey borrows this quotation from George Sale's English translation of the Qur'ān, adapting Sale slightly (e.g. rather

than Sale's "mixture of filthy and boiling water", Southey provides "mixture of boiling water" merely).

14. Southey, *Poetical Works, 1793–1810*, III, p. 191.

15. "*Al-Aʿrāf*" – literally "the heights", or accordingly to Arberry, "the battlements" – serves as the title of the Qur'ān's seventh sura, and is depicted as a space between heaven and hell (see Q. 7:46–51). See also Poe's allusion to this same Qur'ānic space in Chapter 15 below. Sharafuddin, *Islam and Romantic Orientalism*, pp. 76–78 also treats these pivotal passages near *Thalaba*'s conclusion.

16. Southey, *Poetical Works, 1793–1810*, III, pp. 191–192.

17. For the occurrence of "a mercy to the worlds" in the Qur'ān, see 21:107, a verse which is traditionally understood to be addressed to the Prophet.

18. Southey, *Poetical Works, 1793–1810*, III, p. 192.

19. For occurrences of "*ḥūrī*" in the Qur'ān – the celestial "fair ones" – see, for instance, 55:72 and 56:22.

9 "The Prophet, who could summon the future to his presence": Landor's Eastern Renditions

1. Southey, *The Life and Correspondence of Robert Southey*, II, p. 56.

2. For Southey in Portugal, see Speck, *Robert Southey: Entire Man of Letters*, p. 84. For the production and publication of *Thalaba*, see Southey, *Poetical Works, 1793–1810*, III, p. xx.

3. See Southey's "Review of *Gebir*", p. 29. Southey's admiration for Landor – including his 1799 appraisal of *Gebir* in the *Critical Review* – has been widely recognized. See Sharafuddin, *Islam and Romantic Orientalism*, who dedicates his first chapter to Landor and his *Gebir*, as well as emphasizes Southey's reliance on the poem (pp. 1ff., as well as pp. 43–44).

4. Southey, *The Poetical Works of Robert Southey*, p. 8.

5. See Craig, "Subservient Talents? Robert Southey as a Public Moralist", p. 102: "Landor buoyed Southey's spirit, encouraged him to return to poetry and to finish *Kehama*, even offering to pay for the printing costs if necessary."

6. For early critical recognition of this convoluted transmission, see Williams, "The Sources of Landor's *Gebir*", p. 315. More recently, this genealogy has been treated by Sharafuddin, *Islam and Romantic Orientalism*, pp. 1–2 and Barfoot, "English Romantic Poets and the 'Free-Floating Orient'", p. 75.

7. This quotation from *Gebir*'s introduction is itself highlighted at the opening of Southey's "Review of *Gebir*", p. 29.
8. Landor, *Gebir, Count Julian, and other Poems*, p. 1.
9. For this opening line of *Gebir* as "indebted to some degree to the *Aeneid*" and adopting an "orthodox epic" style, see Nitchie, *Vergil and the English Poets*, p. 208.
10. Sharafuddin, *Islam and Romantic Orientalism*, p. 2 argues that "Landor's Gebir" represents "a name derived from the Arabic 'Jubair', but wrongly thought by Landor to be the etymological source of the name 'Gibraltar', whence his Gebir apparently originates".
11. Landor, *Gebir, Count Julian: and other Poems*, p. vii.
12. For an early summary of this exchange see, Forster, *Walter Savage Landor: A Biography*, I, pp. 126–127; Forster here notes that Landor's "Prose Postscript to Gebir" – written in reaction to an attack on *Gebir* from an 1800 edition of the *Monthly Review* – was "suppressed".
13. Landor, *The Poetical Works of Walter Savage Landor*, III, p. 480. This passage from Landor's "Prose Postscript" is partially quoted, and addressed, by Sharafuddin, *Islam and Romantic Orientalism*, p. 4.
14. Landor, *The Poetical Works of Walter Savage Landor*, III, p. 481.
15. Colvin, *Landor*, p. 36. The Preface to Landor's 1800 *Poems* also casts playful doubt on their "authentic" Eastern origins, with Landor asserting that "Some poems have reached the continent, I believe in number not exceeding nine, represented as translations from the Arabic and Persian. Ignorant of both these languages, I shall not assert their authenticity." See Landor, *The Complete Works of Walter Savage Landor*, III, p. 242.
16. For these tropes interspersed through Landor's "Poems from the Persian", see Landor, *The Complete Works of Walter Savage Landor*, III, pp. 243–246. While Landor's 1800 *Poems from the Arabic and Persian* is often mentioned in previous criticism, it rarely receives detailed attention.
17. Landor's "[Poems] From the Arabic" appear in *The Complete Works of Walter Savage Landor*, III, pp. 245–248; this poem cluster is headed by a note that asserts: "We now take leave of the persian, and shall notice the arabic, poems. All of them, excepting the last, were written by the son of the unfortunate Sheik Daher" (p. 245).
18. Landor muses mischievously in the appended notes to his "Addressed to Rahdi" that "Perhaps this Rahdi might be some private friend, but he possibly might be a more known and exalted character. There was a Rahdi, the twentieth of the Abbasides, and

the twenty-ninth of the successors of Mahomet" (likely a reference to the Khalif ar-Rāḍī bi'llāh, d. 940); see Landor, *The Complete Works of Walter Savage Landor*, III, p. 433.

19. Ibid., p. 248.
20. Barfoot, "English Romantic Poets and the 'Free-Floating Orient'", p. 80. For the "time when the victories of Napoleon were in many minds associated with the hopes of man", see the introduction to Landor, *Gebir, and Count Julian*, p. 7. The Napoleonic context for *Gebir* is addressed by Bainbridge, *Napoleon and English Romanticism*, who resists the tradition of reading *Gebir*'s initial publication as an intentional allegory, asserting that "it is highly unlikely that [Landor] had even heard of Napoleon at the point when he began writing the poem in 1796" (p. 32).
21. As quoted in Barfoot, "English Romantic Poets and the 'Free-Floating Orient'", p. 80. Landor's revision of *Gebir* in light of his "disillusion" with Napoleon has long been recognized; see, for instance, Cavaliero, *Ottomania*, p. 125.
22. This footnote to the revised *Gebir* has received wide attention; see, for instance, Bainbridge, *Napoleon and English Romanticism*, p. 51; Sharafuddin, *Islam and Romantic Orientalism*, pp. 40–41; and Garcia, *Islam and the English Enlightenment*, p. 148.
23. For *Gebir*'s specific reference to a "city" in its opening lines which recalls the Qur'ān's "city of Irem" see Garcia, *Islam and the English Enlightenment*, pp. 149–150; this same Qur'ānic allusion is also the concern of Sharafuddin, *Islam and Romantic Orientalism*, pp. 10–11. Landor's general reliance on George Sale's notes to his *Koran* has been observed by Cavaliero, *Ottomania*, p. 125.
24. Such political implications of Landor's *Gebir*, including its Napoleonic contexts and Qur'ānic allusions, are comprehensively addressed by Garcia's Chapter 4, which is dedicated to Landor's *Gebir* and "Ali Bonaparte in Hermetic Egypt" (*Islam and the English Enlightenment*, pp. 126ff.); for a prior exposition of these ideas, see also Sharafuddin, *Islam and Romantic Orientalism*, pp. 38–41.
25. See Bradshaw, "Landor, Walter Savage, *Imaginary Conversations*", p. 773, for Landor's borrowing of the "formal idea of using prose dialogue" from Southey. Southey also features in two of Landor's *Imaginary Conversations*, one of which even pairs together Landor and Southey.
26. These dialogues between "Mahomet and Sergius", as well as between "Soliman and Mufti", represent dialogues 17 and 14 respectively in Landor's *Dialogues of Sovereigns and Statesmen*. See Landor, *Imaginary Conversations: Dialogues of Sovereigns and Statesmen*,

pp. 211–222, and pp. 182–187.
27. Ibid., pp. 211–222, and 182. Despite their targeting of Islamic identities, Landor's *Imaginary Conversations* – like his *Poems from the Arabic and Persian* – are regularly overlooked in scholarship that exposits Landor's engagement with Muslim sources.
28. Ibid., pp. 183–184.

10 "I Blush as a Good Mussulman": Byron's Turkish *Tales* and Travels

1. This quotation derives from Elwin, *Lord Byron's Wife*, pp. 270–271. The ellipsis which follows "'The East – ah, there it is,'" is in the original; I insert "Edin[burgh Review]" for Lady Byron's "Edinr." for the sake of clarity. "Halnaby" was where the Byrons spent time on their honeymoon. This testimony from Lady Byron receives attention from Cochran, *Byron and Orientalism*, p. 47, and is partially quoted also by Sharafuddin, *Islam and Romantic Orientalism*, p. 224.
2. The *Turkish Tales* are conventionally thought to include *The Giaour* (1813), *The Bride of Abydos* (1813), *The Corsair* (1814), and *The Siege of Corinth* (1816). Byron's Ottoman travels as preface to his *Turkish Tales* have most recently been treated by Cavaliero, *Ottomania*, esp. pp. 82–83.
3. See Byron, *Works of Lord Byron: With his Letters and Journals, and his Life*, I, p. 146; this entry occurs after Byron "enumerat[ed] the various poets, both ancient and modern, of Europe". It is also followed by an entry on "Persia", which mentions "Ferdousi . . . Sadi, and Hafiz". See also Cochran, *Byron and Orientalism*, p. 9 which has previously cited this entry.
4. See Byron, *Works of Lord Byron: With his Letters and Journals, and his Life*, I, p. 217. For Byron's "grandiose plans for the Eastern trip", see Grosskurth, *Byron: The Flawed Angel*, p. 69.
5. For Percy Bysshe Shelley and Byron, see Chapter 12 below. For Byron's impact on Thomas Moore and his 1817 *Lalla Rookh*, see, for example, Sharafuddin, *Islam and Romantic Orientalism*, p. 139.
6. The centrality of the feminine to Byron's *Turkish Tales* and travels reflects his broader career and life; Byron himself famously confessed that "My brain is feminine" (a phrase which is often quoted, serving, for example, as the primary title to a 1990 essay by Jerome McGann). The centrality of an "Oriental heroine" to "each of his 'Turkish Tales'" has been observed by, for example, Kidwai, *'Gorgeous Fabric'*, p. 99.

7. Byron's poem has even been cited by Cannon and Kaye in their *The Persian Contributions to the English Language: An Historical Dictionary*; see p. 86 for the Persian etymology of Byron's "giaour". For this quotation from *The Giaour*, see Byron, *The Poetical Works of Byron*, p. 310. An overview of *The Giaour*'s publication background and plot is provided by Teo, *Desert Passions: Orientalism and Romance Novels*, p. 51.

8. Byron, *The Poetical Works of Byron*, p. 315. Franklin, *Byron's Heroines*, selects the final line of the above to serve as the title for her second chapter; however, this passage's Islamic allusions are not Franklin's primary concern, but rather "Leila" as "passive victim" (pp. 38ff.).

9. For Byron and Persian poetry specifically, see Javadi, *Persian Literary Influence on English Literature*, pp. 82–83. Leila's very name may recall the heroine of Niẓāmī's Persian classic, i.e. *Layla and Majnun*. For the gazelle in Persian poetry, and in *Layla and Majnun* specifically, see Schimmel, *A Two-Colored Brocade: The Imagery of Persian Poetry*, p. 193.

10. For "Houris", see Chapter 8, footnote 19 above. For "Al-Sirat" in the Qur'ān, see its first chapter, where "*aṣ-ṣirāṭ*" is used to signify the believers' "[straight] path" (1:6). However, as implied by Byron's passage, "*ṣirāṭ*" may also signify the "bridge to or over Hell"; see Smith and Haddad, *The Islamic Understanding of Death and Resurrection*, pp. 78–79.

11. Byron, *The Giaour, A Fragment of a Turkish Tale*, p. 26.

12. For this prevalent misconception regarding Muslim teachings, and Lady Montagu's parallel efforts to correct it, see Kidwai, *Orientalism in Lord Byron's 'Turkish Tales'*, p. 52, and Sharafuddin, *Islam and Romantic Orientalism*, p. 220. The irony of Byron's corrective note on the "vulgar error" expressed in his own poetry is heightened by Byron's own inaccuracy in suggesting that "the Koran allots at least a third of Paradise to well-behaved women" – a stipulation not contained in Muslim scripture.

13. For the compositional background to *The Bride of Abydos*, see Mole, "*The Bride of Abydos*: The Regime of Visibility and the Possibility of Resistance", p. 20.

14. See Byron, *Byron's Letters and Journals*, III, pp. 168–169. I have removed the editors' "[sic]" after "Spencer's", as well as "[*vastly*]" before "*fine*".

15. Byron, *Byron's Letters and Journals*, III, pp. 190–191.

16. Ibid., p. 191. This second letter to Murray is dated uncertainly by Byron's editor as "Dec. 3–4, 1813?"; it therefore follows the first letter either later during the same day (December 3), or, at the

latest, the next day (December 4). These letters have received some limited attention from Byron scholars, usually cited, but rarely closely read; see, for instance, Sharafuddin, *Islam and Romantic Orientalism*, pp. 221–222, which also contends that the second letter was sent "the next day".

17. See Gwilliam, "Cosmetic Poetics: Coloring Faces in the Eighteenth Century" who asserts that "The blush is, of course, the prized sign of female sensibility and modesty" (p. 148).

11 "Beautiful beyond all the bells in Christendom": Byron's Aesthetic *Adhān*

1. Byron, *The Poetical Works of Byron*, p. 329; for this passage's placement in an early edition of the poem, see Byron, *The Bride of Abydos*, pp. 28–29.

2. Sharafuddin, *Islam and Romantic Orientalism*, pp. 245–246. Sharafuddin also notes this passage's fusion of its "banquet of the senses" with "religious purity" (p. 246).

3. The opening of the Qur'ān 2:255, as translated by Arberry, reads "His Throne comprises the heavens and earth."

4. See Byron, *The Bride of Abydos*, p. 67. This footnote has not received significant attention in Byron scholarship.

5. Byron, *The Poetical Works of Byron*, p. 333.

6. In a footnote to his poetic passage, Bryon parses "Aden" as "'Jannat al Aden,' the perpetual abode, the Mussulman paradise" (Byron, *The Poetical Works of Byron*, p. 1018). For Qur'ānic occurrence of the term, see, for instance, Q. 9:72.

7. Ibid., p. 335.

8. Sharafuddin, *Islam and Romantic Orientalism*, pp. 237–238, although the primary focus of this discussion is the "distinctiveness of . . . ceremonies" in Byron's verses, rather than their Islamic aurality.

9. Byron, *The Poetical Works of Byron*, p. 387.

10. This passage is less often treated in scholarship on Byron and Islam; an exception is Kidwai, *Orientalism in Lord Byron's 'Turkish Tales'*, p. 140, where it is partially quoted.

11. McGann is cited and contextualized in Rawes, "Byron's Confessional Pilgrimage", p. 121. In his *Desert Passions: Orientalism and Romance Novels*, Teo emphasizes the Islamic elements of Byron's *Pilgrimage* as anticipating, and prompting composition of, his *Turkish Tales* (p. 51).

12. Byron, *The Poetical Works of Byron*, p. 28.

13. For this footnote in the 1832 edition of *Childe Harold's Pilgrimage*, see Byron, *Works of Lord Byron: With his Letters and Journals, and his Life*, VIII, p. 91. Hobhouse's own memoir of his time in Albania with Byron was published in 1813, and appears to be the source for this footnote in later editions of *Childe Harold's Pilgrimage*; see Hobhouse, *A Journey Through Albania and Other Provinces of Turkey in Europe*, I, pp. 98–99. For a critical account of Byron and Hobhouse's arrival in Tepelene, Albania, on October 19, 1809, see Franklin, *Byron*, p. 6.
14. Byron, *The Poetical Works of Byron*, p. 317. For this passage, see Sharafuddin, *Islam and Romantic Orientalism*, p. 240, which cites these verses as a means of highlighting "the density and distinctiveness of Hassan's religious environment".
15. For the occurrence of this footnote in an 1813 edition of *The Giaour*, see Byron, *The Giaour, A Fragment of a Turkish Tale*, p. 40, where the footnote is situated directly below the passage which cites "Alla Hu", synthesizing on the same page Byron's fictional authorship and his factual experience.

12 "The orient moon of Islam rode in triumph": Percy Bysshe Shelley as "Islamite"

1. Medwin, *Conversations of Lord Byron*, pp. 79–80.
2. Medwin reunited with Shelley in the fall of 1820 in Pisa; see Bieri, *Percy Bysshe Shelley: A Biography*, pp. 210–211, and White, *Shelley*, II, pp. 227–228.
3. See also Holmes, *Shelley: The Pursuit*, p. 689, who links Byron's "Islamite" epithet for Shelley to "the doctrines of atheism and free love in *The Revolt of Islam*".
4. Cavaliero, *Ottomania*, p. 98.
5. Shelley, *The Complete Poetry of Percy Bysshe Shelley*, III, p. 131.
6. As Haddad emphasizes, "Shelley's preface" establishes that *The Revolt of Islam* is meant "to communicate the lessons of the French Revolution" (*Orientalist Poetics*, p. 13).
7. Donovan, "Epic Experiments", p. 267. Also see Appendix C of Shelley, *The Complete Poetry of Percy Bysshe Shelley*, III, which catalogues the revisions that transformed *Laon and Cythna* into *The Revolt of Islam* (pp. 1077ff.).
8. Shelley, *The Complete Works*, VI, p. 255.
9. Medwin, *The Life of Percy Bysshe Shelley*, I, pp. 366–367. See also Ernest J. Lovell's introduction to *Conversations of Lord Byron* for

Medwin's service in India as "an officer in His Majesty's 24th Light Dragoons" (p. vii).

10. For Shelley and Medwin at Syon House Academy, see Medwin, *Conversations of Lord Byron*, p. vii.
11. In addition to his *The Life of Percy Bysshe Shelley*, Medwin also published in 1824 his controversial *Conversations of Lord Byron*; see Medwin, *Conversations of Lord Byron*, p. vii.
12. Shelley, *The Letters of Percy Bysshe Shelley*, II, p. 245.
13. Ibid., p. 243. White also notes in the fall of 1820 that "[Shelley] and Medwin planned to begin at once the study of Arabic together" and that "[b]y the middle of November the studies had begun" (*Shelley*, II, p. 229).
14. Medwin, *The Life of Percy Bysshe Shelley*, II, p. 178.
15. See, however, Shelley, *The Faust Draft Notebook*, p. lxxviii which questions Medwin's dating of Shelley's reading of *Antar*, and p. xliii for Shelley and Medwin's study of Arabic as a foreground to "From the Arabic, an Imitation", with Murray "conjecture[ing]" that "the general inspiration [for 'From the Arabic, an Imitation'] was provided by Shelley's taking up the study of Arabic with Medwin".
16. For the manuscript version of these lines, see Shelley, *The Faust Draft Notebook*, p. 308.
17. Although not published until the spring of 1822, as Bieri notes, Shelley had sent *Hellas* in for "*immediate* publication" in November 1821, and was angered by its delayed appearance (*Percy Bysshe Shelley: A Biography*, p. 265).
18. Haddad labels Shelley's *Hellas* as an "orientalist longer poem", and emphasizes its "linkage of Islam with tyranny and violence" (*Orientalist Poetics*, p. 18).
19. Shelley, *The Complete Works of Percy Bysshe Shelley*, III, p. 28.
20. Ibid.
21. Mulhallen, *The Theatre of Shelley*, p. 178. See also Haddad, *Orientalist Poetics*, p. 19, as well as White, *Shelley*, II, p. 328 for Shelley's prefatory assertion, and the historical circumstances surrounding his *Hellas*.
22. Shelley, *The Complete Works of Percy Bysshe Shelley*, III, p. 19.
23. Ibid., p. 37.
24. Ibid., p. 11. For the initial appearance of the "Prologue" in Richard Garnett's 1862 *Relics of Shelley*, see Shelley, *The Complete Poetry of Percy Bysshe Shelley*, I, p. xxvi.
25. For the background to Shelley's "Prologue to *Hellas*", see Bieri, who suggests that Shelley's "long fragment" – which involved

"Christ, Satan, and Mahomet" – was "abandon[ed]" by Shelley before he elected to "tur[n] to Aeschylus's *Persians* for his poem's structure" (*Percy Bysshe Shelley: A Biography*, p. 265). See Shelley, *The Faust Draft Notebook*, p. xlv for previous recognition of the "decisive influence" exercised by the Book of Job on Shelley's "Prologue" draft. Job 1:6 is quoted from the King James Version.

26. Shelley, *The Complete Works of Percy Bysshe Shelley*, III, pp. 15–16.
27. Ibid., p. 16.
28. The ambiguous nature of Shelley's "*Mahomet*" declaring "the orient moon of Islam rode in triumph" in *Hellas'* fragmentary "Prologue" is also amplified by the fact that a near identical sentiment is voiced by Mahmud in *Hellas'* published text (i.e. "When the orient moon of Islam roll'd in triumph / From Caucasus to White Ceraunia!"); see Shelley, *The Complete Works of Percy Bysshe Shelley*, III, p. 28.

13 "The female followers of Mahomet": Mary Shelley's Frankenstein

1. Austen, *Northanger Abbey and Persuasion*, III, pp. 237–238. Although 1818 is the recorded date of publication for Austen's novel, *Persuasion* was printed in December 1817, and available by "the end" of the month; see Fergus, "The Professional Woman Writer", p. 15.
2. This episode has most recently been highlighted by Murphy, *Jane Austen the Reader*, who notes that "Byron and Scott" are "the only two authors whose merits are explicitly discussed by [*Persuasion*'s] characters" (p. 158).
3. The "Western male gaze" is quoted from Varisco, *Reading Orientalism*, p. 165.
4. This description of Percy's dedication to Mary is provided by Seymour, *Mary Shelley*, pp. 188–189.
5. Shelley, *Frankenstein; or the Modern Prometheus*, ed. M. K. Joseph, p. 14. For the complex circumstances, and relationships, which serve as context for *Frankenstein*'s genesis, see Seymour, *Mary Shelley*, pp. 146ff.
6. Shelley, *Frankenstein; or the Modern Prometheus*, p. 21. For differences between Shelley's 1818 and 1831 texts, see James Rieger's introduction to Shelley, *Frankenstein, or the Modern Prometheus: The 1818 Text*; Rieger here highlights the prevalence of the 1831 revised edition, from which I quote above (p. xxiii).

7. Mary Shelley's Islamic interests have most recently been treated by Garcia, *Islam and the English Enlightenment*, which concentrates on her *The Last Man*, rather than *Frankenstein*, citing the scholarly need "to move beyond" Shelley's most celebrated novel (p. 190).

8. Shelley, *Frankenstein, or the Modern Prometheus: The 1818 Text*, pp. 47–48. Shelley, *Frankenstein; or the Modern Prometheus*, ed. M. K. Joseph, pp. 52–53.

9. This reference to *A Thousand and One Nights* – otherwise known as *The Arabian Nights* – is widely recognized; see, for example, Small, *Mary Shelley's Frankenstein: Tracing the Myth*, p. 116, and more recently, Lew, "The Deceptive Other", p. 256.

10. Shelley, *Frankenstein; or the Modern Prometheus*, p. 69.

11. Clerval, *Frankenstein*'s "orientalist", has even been likened to "Schlegel" by Joseph Lew, who also notes that Clerval "maternally nurses" Victor Frankenstein with his "domesticating" Eastern interests; Lew highlights too that Clerval studies "Hebrew", rather than "Sanscrit", in addition to "Persian" and "Arabic", in the 1818 *Frankenstein*, with Shelley initially restricting his philological interests to the Middle East (Lew, "The Deceptive Other", pp. 262 and 264).

12. Shelley, *Frankenstein; or the Modern Prometheus*, pp. 70–71.

13. For "Arabie / And Persia, and the wild Carmanian waste" in *Alastor*, see *The Complete Poetry of Percy Bysshe Shelley*, III, p. 13. *Alastor*'s influence on *Frankenstein* has been addressed, for instance, by Bonca, *Shelley's Mirrors of Love*, pp. 50–51. See also Lew, "The Deceptive Other", p. 276.

14. Shelley, *Frankenstein; or the Modern Prometheus*, pp. 117 and 118.

15. McLane designates this complex relationship of language instruction involving Felix, Safie, and the Monster as a "covert triangulated pedagogical scene" (*Romanticism and the Human Sciences*, pp. 14–15).

16. Shelley, *Frankenstein; or the Modern Prometheus*, pp. 119–120.

17. Kahf, *Western Representations of the Muslim Woman*, p. 167 discusses the parallel between these mutual strangers – Safie and the Monster – but ultimately accents the relationship's asymmetry. For this parallel, also see Lew, "The Deceptive Other", p. 275.

18. Shelley, *Frankenstein; or the Modern Prometheus*, pp. 119–120.

19. An overview of such an approach to precisely this *Frankenstein* passage is provided by Zonana, "'They Will Prove the Truth of My Tale'", p. 173.

20. Shelley, *Frankenstein; or the Modern Prometheus*, pp. 122–123.

21. It is Zonana's "'They Will Prove the Truth of My Tale'" which has emphasized the centrality of Safie's letters, her epistles "serv[ing] as

the best evidence for the truth of the monster's and Frankenstein's tales" (p. 181).

22. Shelley, *The Letters of Mary Wollstonecraft Shelley*, I, p. 555. The irony of Percy Jr.'s "great extacy" is heightened too by Mary's own documented reading of "the Arabian Nights" in the years before authoring *Frankenstein*; see Zonana, "'They Will Prove the Truth of My Tale'", p. 184. Mary Shelley's reference to "the Arabian Nights" in a letter to Mary Lamb, in particular, seems especially significant, in light of the latter's Islamic interests, as exhibited in her short story "Margaret Green: or, The Young Mahometan", published first in 1809; see Straight, "Women, Religion, and Insanity in Mary Lamb's 'Margaret Green: or, The Young Mahometan'".

14 "A strong mixture of the Saracenic with the Gothic": Irving's Islamic Biographies

1. For Mary as a "single mother, always needing money", see Cahill, *Desiring Italy*, p. 35. For Mary's letter, see Shelley, *The Letters of Mary Wollstonecraft Shelley*, II, p. 113; the "present debt" cited by Mary is "towards you [i.e. John Murray himself]". For John Murray's "Family Library" as targeting the "common reader", seeking to "publish across class lines", see Feltes, *Modes of Production of Victorian Novels*, p. 10.

2. Shelley, *The Letters of Mary Wollstonecraft Shelley*, II, p. 113.

3. For Irving's 1815 departure for England, see Chapter 6 of Jones, *Washington Irving*. Due to his straddle between national identities – American, British, and European – Irving has become a favorite of transatlantic literary studies; see, for instance, Giles, *Transatlantic Insurrections*, pp. 142ff, as well as Dimock, "Hemispheric Islam", esp. pp. 44–48, which represents one of the most recent treatments of Irving's Islamic engagements.

4. For the early relationship between Shelley and Irving, meeting in 1824, and their flirtation through 1825, see Seymour, *Mary Shelley*, p. 351 and pp. 370–371. Shelley even deferred another of her suitors – John Payne – by declaring facetiously to him in an 1825 letter "as yet I am still faithful to W.I.!" (see Shelley, *The Letters of Mary Wollstonecraft Shelley*, I, p. 486).

5. For Mary's hosting Irving for "tea" on "25 March 1830", in company with her father and several other friends, see Shelley, *The Journals of Mary Shelley*, II, p. 604. Published in Philadelphia, Irving's two-volume 1832 American edition was entitled *The*

> *Alhambra: A Series of Tales and Sketches of the Moors and Spaniards.*

6. Published as the two-volume *Mahomet and his Successors* in 1849–1850, Irving's biography subsequently appeared under titles including *Life of Mahomet and his Successors*, as well as *Life of Mahomet* (the latter, designating Irving's biography of the Prophet solely). The following chapter will adopt the latter title for clarity. Although Irving's prophetic biography was initially intended for John Murray's publication, this arrangement fell through, leading to a two-decade delay in its appearance. For the most thorough treatment of Irving's authorship of *Life of Mahomet* and the circumstances of its publication, see the "Historical Note" which is appended to Feltskog and Pochmann's critical edition of *Mahomet and his Successors* (1970), pp. 517ff., and especially pp. 525ff. for John Murray's involvement.

7. Irving, *The Alhambra*, I, pp. iii–iv.

8. For previous recognition of Irving's traversal of "passages – both physical and verbal" in his *The Alhambra*, see Einboden, *Nineteenth-Century U.S. Literature in Middle Eastern Languages*, pp. 47–48.

9. These contexts for Irving's *Life of Mahomet*, as well as Columbus as Irving's original target for his Spanish sojourn, are addressed in Irving, *Mahomet and his Successors*, p. 522. During this early period, Irving conceived of his prophetic biography as "The Legendary Life of Mahomet".

10. Irving, *Mahomet and his Successors*, pp. 14–15.

11. The British Romantics, in particular, impacted both Irving's art and life; in addition to Mary Shelley, for instance, Irving formed a lasting friendship with Thomas Moore, another Romantic author deeply implicated in Orientalism, whose *Lalla Rookh* (1817) proved immensely popular. For Moore and Irving, see, for example, Jones, *Washington Irving*, pp. 267ff.

12. Irving, *Mahomet and his Successors*, pp. 31–32.

13. For previous recognition of Irving's own stylized renditions of Qur'ān, "editing and blending previous European renditions", see Einboden, "The Early American Qur'an", p. 5; this essay also addresses Irving's attempts to learn Arabic (pp. 5–6). For Irving's own quotation from Sale's *Koran*, see the "Editorial Appendix" to Irving, *Mahomet and his Successors*, p. 619. Arberry's rendition of these same verses from the Qur'ān read: "Recite: In the Name of thy Lord who created, created Man of a blood-clot. Recite: And thy Lord is the Most Generous, who taught by the Pen, taught Man that he knew not." It is worthwhile to note that Irving's account leading

up to these quoted verses also includes Qur'ānic paraphrase, with his "During that night there is peace on earth, and a holy quiet reigns over all nature until the rising of the morn" recalling sura 97.

14. Irving, *Mahomet and his Successors*, pp. 68–69.
15. Seemingly idiomatic, the "two bow-shots" here named as the Prophet's proximity to God is a Qur'ānic allusion, recalling Q. 53:9.
16. Irving, *Mahomet and his Successors*, p. 200.
17. Irving, *The Alhambra*, I, pp. 81–82.

15 "Twenty Thousand Copies Of The Koran": Poe's Muslim Medium

1. This initial occurrence of "Mahomet" in Irving's journal is high-lighted in the "Historical Note" appended to Irving, *Mahomet and his Successors*, which recognizes that "On November 16, 1827, there appears Irving's first terse journal entry 'Mahomet,' followed, next day, by 'all the morng writing at Mahomet,' and, on November 18, 'all day writing legend of Mahomet.' Similar entries run through November 20" (p. 522). My discussion of Poe and Emerson in chapters 15 and 16 feature, and expand on, research which first appeared in the *Journal of Qur'anic Studies*, published as my 2009 "The Early American Qur'an: Islamic Scripture and US Canon" (11.2; pp. 1–19).
2. This frontispiece is reproduced in Quinn, *Edgar Allan Poe: A Critical Biography*, pp. 120–121.
3. Quinn, *Edgar Allan Poe*, p. 119 notes that *Tamerlane* "was published, probably in the early summer of 1827", but also admits that "Little is known of the circumstances of the publication."
4. Quinn speculates that "Poe was more interested in his modern language study than in his work in ancient languages", although his evidence is weak, relying merely on "library cards" whose patterns "may have been accidental" (ibid., p. 99). For Jefferson's frustrated hopes for Hebrew to be taught at the University of Virginia during the very time that Poe attended, and the inability to secure a scholar of "Oriental literature", see Hayes, *The Road to Monticello: The Life and Mind of Thomas Jefferson*, p. 623.
5. For this quotation, see Silverman, *Edgar A. Poe: Mournful and Never-Ending Remembrance*, p. 32.
6. Poe's frontispiece is reproduced in Quinn, *Edgar Allan Poe*, p. 155.

7. For *al-A'rāf* see footnote 15 of Chapter 8 above.

8. Poe, *Collected Works of Edgar Allan Poe*, I, pp. 111–112. Poe's practice of "gloss[ing] his texts with learned prefaces and footnotes in the manner of Robert Southey and Thomas Moore" has been emphasized by Luedtke, *Nathaniel Hawthorne and the Romance of the Orient*, p. 64.

9. Poe, *Collected Works of Edgar Allan Poe*, I, p. 60. This conclusion, alluding to "Eblis", was added to "Tamerlane" when the poem was republished in 1829.

10. For this portrait of *Isrāfīl*, see Leaman, ed., *The Qur'an: An Encyclopedia*, p. 316.

11. This version of "Israfel" is quoted from Poe, *Collected Works of Edgar Allan Poe*, I, pp. 173–175, which reproduces the final iteration of Poe's poem, set in 1845; for clarity, I insert stanza numbers which are not included in the 1845 text. When first published – in 1829 – the epigraph of "Israfel" read more simply as "And the angel Israfel who has the sweetest voice of all God's creatures – KORAN" (Poe, *Collected Works of Edgar Allan Poe*, I, p. 173).

12. In his commentary to *Collected Works of Edgar Allan Poe*, Thomas Mabbott suggests Poe's dependence on Thomas Moore as the source for his adapted quotation from George Sale (see I, pp. 172 and 177).

13. Mabbott cites, for instance, Hervey Allen's biography of Poe, which is simply entitled *Israfel: The Life and Times of Edgar Allan Poe* (Poe, *Collected Works of Edgar Allan Poe*, I, p. 173).

14. For Poe's initial publication of a fictional tale in the *Philadelphia Saturday Courier* "five days before his twenty-third birthday", see Anderson, *Pictures of Ascent in the Fiction of Edgar Allan Poe*, p. 17.

15. Poe's frontispiece is reproduced in Quinn, *Edgar Allan Poe*, p. 288.

16. For Poe as "master of the Gothic horror tale", see Fisher, "Poe and the Gothic Tradition", p. 72. Poe's appeal to the "Arabesque" has recently been of primary concern to Jacob Rama Berman, treated in his 2012 *American Arabesque: Arabs, Islam and the 19th-Century Imaginary*; for this term as invoked by both Poe and Irving, and its distinct meaning in their respective usages, see pp. 23 and 236.

17. See Poe, *Collected Works of Edgar Allan Poe*, III, p. 1151 for the appearance of "The Thousand-and-Second Tale of Scheherazade" in February 1845, a tale which was "probably written very late in 1844", according to Mabbott. Malini Schueller has emphasized the importance of "the Near East" to Poe's fiction, asserting that "Out

of twenty-five tales in his collection *Tales of the Grotesque and Arabesque*, only five do not have references to the Near East" (*U.S. Orientalisms*, p. 110).

18. Poe, *Collected Works of Edgar Allan Poe*, III, pp. 1166–1167.

19. For Poe's 1844 analogy referencing the "Koran", see Poe, "Marginalia", p. 585. The edition which Poe likens to the Qur'ān is named by him as "Camöens – Genoa – 1798"; however, Monteiro, *The Presence of Camões*, p. 41, notes the absence of such an edition of Camões in 1798, positing instead Poe's reference to a later edition (1817).

20. See Einboden, "The Early American Qur'an", pp. 9 and 18.

16 "Unveiled Allah Pours The Flood of Truth": Emerson's Islamic Civics

1. Emerson himself provides an account of his visit to Coleridge in his *English Traits* (1850); see Emerson, *The Collected Works of Ralph Waldo Emerson*, V, pp. 5–6. For previous treatment of this celebrated meeting between Emerson and Coleridge, as well as the tensions and polarities involved, see Einboden, "Emerson's Exegesis", p. 158.

2. For Emerson's traditional portrait as "the father of American literature", as well as challenges to this portrait, see Zwarg, *Feminist Conversations: Fuller, Emerson, and the Play of Reading*, p. 22.

3. Emerson, *The Collected Works of Ralph Waldo Emerson*, V, p. 5.

4. Emerson, *The Journals and Miscellaneous Notebooks*, I, p. 171. Emerson also purchased other works on July 30, recording items such as "Plutarch's Morals" and "Mackintosh" before "Alcoran". This discussion of Emerson's 1833 journal entry first appeared in Einboden, "The Early American Qur'an", p. 1.

5. Emerson, "Saadi", p. 265. Published between 1840 and 1844, under the editorships of Margaret Fuller, and subsequently, of Emerson himself, the *Dial* featured several of Emerson's earliest poems including "Silence" (October 1840), "The Sphinx" (January 1841), "Grace" (January 1842), as well as "Saadi" in October 1842. One of his first published poems, Emerson's "Saadi" is exceptional in its length, as well as the resonance it will enjoy throughout Emerson's career; however, the poem has been regularly overlooked in Emerson criticism, even in scholarship that addresses Emerson's Orientalism. See, for example, the mere passing mention given

to "Saadi" in Carpenter, *Emerson and Asia* (pp. 170 and 174), and Yohannan, "The Influence of Persian Poetry upon Emerson's Work" (p. 31).

6. For the phrase "organic naturalism", and its "roots in the German Romantic movement", see Richards, *The Tragic Sense of Life*, p. 126.

7. Emerson, "Saadi", p. 267.

8. Ibid., pp. 268–269.

9. While Saadi is the first published Muslim surrogate for Emerson's poetic authorship, Emerson had also begun to invoke the name "Osman" as early as 1840 in his private journals, inventing this Eastern identity to serve as "a sublimed self, a sort of ideal man", as first suggested by the editors of Emerson, *The Journals of Ralph Waldo Emerson*, V, p. 433.

10. Emerson, *The Later Lectures of Ralph Waldo Emerson*, I, p. 334. For the most comprehensive treatment of Emerson's antislavery activism, see Gougeon, *Virtue's Hero: Emerson, Antislavery, and Reform*, which addresses the 1851 and 1854 iterations of Emerson's "Fugitive Slave Law Address" on pp. 160ff. and pp. 192ff. respectively.

11. Emerson's source for this citation was likely a quotation "From the Gulistan of Saadi" that appeared in the January 1844 issue of the *Dial*, which begins: "Take heed that the orphan weep not: for the Throne of the Almighty is shaken to and fro, when the orphan sets a-crying" (p. 404).

12. This is correctly noted by the editors of *The Later Lectures of Ralph Waldo Emerson*, I, p. 334, who also recognize that this same *ḥadīth* serves as an epigram to an early Emerson essay ("Heroism"); see also Einboden, "The Early American Qur'an", p. 10 for a discussion of this epigram.

13. Emerson, "The Phoenix", pp. 78–79. Gougeon, *Virtue's Hero: Emerson, Antislavery, and Reform*, describes the circumstances surrounding Emerson's 1851 submission of poetry to the *Liberty Bell*, noting that "Emerson was moved to send along no fewer than five poems", which were "all 'translations from the Persian,' providing an interesting insight into Emerson's understanding at this time of the relationship of art to reform, and his own function as a scholar/poet in a time of social crisis" (p. 144). Although Gougeon provides close readings of Emerson's "translations from the Persian", their Islamic origins are not his primary concern.

14. Emerson parses "Tuba" as "The Tree of Life" in a footnote which he includes to his translated poems in the *Liberty Bell*; see Emerson,

"The Phoenix", p. 78. This English rendition from Q. 29:13 is Arberry's, who renders "*Ṭūbā*" simply as "blessedness".

15. Purchasing Hammer-Purgstall's *Der Diwan von Mohammed Schemsed-Din Hafis* in April 1846, Emerson began a landmark campaign of translation, ultimately rendering more than two thousand lines of Persian poetry; see my *Ralph Waldo Emerson, Persian Poetry and the German Critical Tradition* (unpublished PhD thesis, University of Cambridge, 2005), esp. chapters 5 and 6. Emerson's engagement with Persian poetry has recently gained notice from prominent early Americanists; for example, Dimock, *Through Other Continents: American Literature across Deep Time*, pp. 44ff. Such contemporary studies customarily cite John D. Yohannan's 1943 article "Emerson's Translations of Persian Poetry from German Sources", however, which significantly underestimated Emerson's Persian poetry translations as amounting to "something like seven hundred lines" (p. 407).

16. For this label applied to the American Civil War, see Hollinger, *After Cloven Tongues of Fire*, p. 172.

17. Francis Gladwin's translation of Saʿdī's *Gulistan* was published as *The Gulistan or Rose Garden* by Boston publishers Ticknor and Fields in 1865. Emerson's "Preface" to this American edition appears as pp. iii–xv, and is dated "February, 1864" (p. xv).

18. Emerson, "Preface", pp. vii–viii.

19. See Blankenship, *American Literature as an Expression of the National Mind* for the "opening of the Civil War" as the time traditionally "fixed as the terminal date" of American Romanticism (p. 198).

Epilogue Romantic Requiem: The Islamic Interment of Yūsuf bin Ḥāmir

1. For this characterization of the *Atlantic Monthly*, see Singley, ed., *A Historical Guide to Edith Wharton*, p. 24.

2. Emerson, "Persian Poetry", p. 724.

3. Ibid.

4. For notice of Hammer-Purgstall's "ceremonial funeral . . . in St. Stephan's Cathedral", see Daviau, ed., *Major Figures of Nineteenth-Century Austrian Literature*, p. 299.

5. The Hammer-Purgstall grave has been treated in Ludwig, "*Das Hammer-Purgstall-Grabmal auf dem Weidlinger Friedhof*" ("The Hammer-Purgstall Tomb in the Weidling Cemetery"), pp. 43–49 and Einboden, "Stoicism or Sufism?", pp. 66–67. The following

discussion is based on my own visit to Hammer-Purgstall's Weidling grave in 2007, during which the photos here included were taken.

6. Hammer-Purgstall's self-designed inscriptions for the grave were printed in a brief pamphlet in 1844, i.e. his *Inschriften des Grabmals der Freiinn Hammer-Purgstall zu Weidling am Bach* ("Inscriptions of the Tomb of Baroness Hammer-Purgstall at Weidling am Bach").

7. For these precise terms occurring together in Muslim scripture, see Q. 4:43 and 4:99.

8. These English translations from the Qur'ān are Arberry's. The phrase "Every soul shall taste of death" occurs not only in Q. 3:185, but also 21:35 and 29:57. "The Everlasting" ("*al-bāqī*") is traditionally understood to be one of Allāh's ninety-nine divine names. These Arabic quotations from the Qur'ān on the reverse of Hammer's grave are followed by lines of Arabic poetry which reiterate the same themes of human mortality and God's eternity.

Bibliography

Allen, H. *Israfel: The Life and Times of Edgar Allan Poe*. New York, Farrar & Rinehart, 1934

Almond, I. *History of Islam in German Thought from Leibniz to Nietzsche*. New York, Routledge, 2010

Anderson, D. *Pictures of Ascent in the Fiction of Edgar Allan Poe*. New York, Palgrave Macmillan, 2009

Andrews, W. "Goethe's Key to *Faust*", *Atlantic Monthly*, vol. 67, 1891, pp. 538–546

Arberry, A. J. *The Koran Interpreted*. London, Allen & Unwin, 1955

Austen, J. *Northanger Abbey and Persuasion*. London, John Murray, 1818

Bainbridge, S. *Napoleon and English Romanticism*. Cambridge, Cambridge University Press, 1995

Barfoot, C. C. "English Romantic Poets and the 'Free-Floating Orient'", in Barfoot, C. C. and D' Haen, T. (eds) *Oriental Prospects: Western Literature and the Lure of the East*. Amsterdam, Rodopi, 1998

Barnard, F. M., ed. and trans. *Herder on Social and Political Culture*. Cambridge, Cambridge University Press, 1969

Beiser, F. *The German Historicist Tradition*. Oxford, Oxford University Press, 2011

Berman, J. *American Arabesque: Arabs, Islam and the 19th-Century Imaginary*. New York, NYU Press, 2012

Berman, N. *German Literature on the Middle East: Discourses and Practices, 1000–1989*. Ann Arbor, University of Michigan Press, 2011

Bieri, J. *Percy Bysshe Shelley: A Biography: Exile of Unfulfilled Renown, 1816–1822*. Newark, University of Delaware Press, 2005

Blackall, E. A. *The Novels of the German Romantics.* Ithaca, Cornell University Press, 1983

Blankenship, R. *American Literature as an Expression of the National Mind.* New York, Cooper Square Publishers, 1973

Bonca, T. C. *Shelley's Mirrors of Love: Narcissism, Sacrifice, and Sorority.* Albany, SUNY Press, 1999

Bosse, A., ed. *Meine Schatzkammer Füllt Sich Täglich: Die Nachlassstücke Zu Goethes "West-östlichem Divan": Dokumentation, Kommentar,* 2 vols. Göttingen, Wallstein, 1999

Boyle, N. *Goethe: The Poet and the Age. Volume 1, The Poetry of Desire.* Oxford, Oxford University Press, 1991

Bradshaw, M. "Landor, Walter Savage, *Imaginary Conversations*", in Burwick, F., Goslee, N. M., and Hoeveler, D. L. (eds) *The Encyclopedia of Romantic Literature,* vol. 2. Malden, Wiley-Blackwell, 2012

Brown, P. *Life of Goethe,* 2 vols. London, John Murray, 1920

Byron, G. *The Bride of Abydos: A Turkish Tale.* London, T. Davison, Whitefriars, for John Murray, 1813

—— *Byron's Letters and Journals,* ed. L. A. Marchand. Cambridge, Belknap Press of Harvard University Press, 1973–1982

—— *The Giaour, A Fragment of a Turkish Tale,* 5th edition. London, T. Davison, Whitefriars, for John Murray, 1813

—— *The Poetical Works of Byron,* ed. R. F. Gleckner. Boston, Houghton Mifflin, 1975

—— *Works of Lord Byron: With his Letters and Journals, and his Life,* 17 vols, ed. T. Moore. London, John Murray, 1832–1833

Cahill, S. N. *Desiring Italy: Women Writers Celebrate the Passions of a Country and Culture.* New York, Fawcett Columbia, 1997

Cannon, G. H. and Kaye, A. S. *The Persian Contributions to the English Language: An Historical Dictionary.* Wiesbaden, Harrassowitz, 2001

Carlson, M. A. *Goethe and the Weimar Theatre.* Ithaca, Cornell University Press, 1978

—— *Voltaire and the Theatre of the Eighteenth Century.* Westport, Greenwood Press, 1998

Carpenter, F. *Emerson and Asia.* New York, Haskell House, 1930

Cavaliero, R. *Ottomania: The Romantics and the Myth of the Islamic Orient.* London, I. B. Tauris, 2010

Chaghatai, M. I. *Hammer-Purgstall and the Muslim India.* Lahore, Iqbal Academy, 1998

Christy, A. *The Orient in American Transcendentalism: A Study of Emerson, Thoreau, and Alcott*. New York, Columbia University Press, 1932

Clark, R. T. *Herder: His Life and Thought*. Berkeley, University of California, 1955

Class, M. *Coleridge and Kantian Ideas in England, 1796–1817: Coleridge's Responses to German Philosophy*. London, Bloomsbury, 2012

Clive, H. P. *Beethoven and His World: A Biographical Dictionary*. New York, Oxford University Press, 2001

Cochran, P. *Byron and Orientalism*. Newcastle, Cambridge Scholars Press, 2006

Cole, J. R. *Napoleon's Egypt: Invading the Middle East*. New York, Palgrave Macmillan, 2007

Coleridge, S. T. *The Notebooks of Samuel Taylor Coleridge*, 5 vols., ed. Kathleen Coburn. Princeton, Princeton University Press, 1957–2002.

—— *The Poetical Works of S. T. Coleridge*, 2 vols. London, W. Pickering, 1835

Colvin, S. *Landor*. New York, Harper, 1901

Craig, D. M. "Subservient Talents? Robert Southey as a Public Moralist" in Pratt, L. (ed.) *Robert Southey and the Contexts of Romanticism*. Burlington, Ashgate, 2006

Datta, K. S. "Iskandar, Alexander: Oriental Geography and Romantic Poetry" in Niyogi, C. (ed.) *Reorienting Orientalism*. New Delhi, Sage Publications, 2006

Daviau, D. G., ed. *Major Figures of Nineteenth-Century Austrian Literature*. Riverside, Ariadne Press, 1998

Dimock, W. C. "Hemispheric Islam: Continents and Centuries for American Literature", *American Literary History*, vol. 21, no. 1, 2009, pp. 28–52

—— *Through Other Continents: American Literature across Deep Time*. Princeton, Princeton University Press, 2006

Donovan, J. "Epic Experiments: *Queen Mab* and *Laon and Cythna*", in O'Neill, M., Howe, T., and Callaghan, M. (eds) *The Oxford Handbook of Percy Bysshe Shelley*. Oxford, Oxford University Press, 2012

Düntzer, H. *Life of Goethe*, 2 vols. London, Macmillan and Co., 1883

Eichner, H. *Friedrich Schlegel*. New York, Twayne Publishers, 1970

Einboden, J. "The Early American Qur'an: Islamic Scripture and US Canon", *Journal of Qur'anic Studies*, vol. 11, no. 2, 2009, pp. 1–19

—— "Emerson's Exegesis: Transcending Symbols", in Hühn, H. and Vigus, J. (eds) *Symbol and Intuition: Comparative Studies in Kantian and Romantic-Period Aesthetics*. Oxford, Legenda, 2013

—— "The Genesis of *Weltliteratur*: Goethe's *West-östlicher Divan* and Kerygmatic Pluralism", *Literature and Theology*, vol. 19, no. 3, 2005, pp. 238–250

—— *Nineteenth-Century U.S. Literature in Middle Eastern Languages*. Edinburgh, Edinburgh University Press, 2013

—— "Ralph Waldo Emerson, Persian Poetry and the German Critical Tradition". Unpublished PhD thesis, University of Cambridge, 2005

—— "Stoicism or Sufism? Hammer-Purgstall's Persian Meditations", *Middle Eastern Literatures*, vol. 13, no. 1, 2010, pp. 49–68

Elwin, M. *Lord Byron's Wife*. New York, Harcourt, Brace & World, 1963

Emerson, R. W. *The Collected Works of Ralph Waldo Emerson*, 8 vols., Ferguson, A. R. et al. (eds) Cambridge, The Belknap Press of Harvard University Press, 1971–2010

—— *The Journals and Miscellaneous Notebooks of Ralph Waldo Emerson*, 16 vols., Gilman, W. H. et al. (eds) Cambridge, The Belknap Press of Harvard University Press, 1960–1982

—— *The Journals of Ralph Waldo Emerson*, 10 vols., Emerson, E. W. and Forbes, W. E. (eds) Boston, Houghton, Mifflin and Company, 1909–1914

—— *The Later Lectures of Ralph Waldo Emerson, 1843–1871*, 2 vols., Bosco, R. A. and Myerson, J. (eds) Athens, University of Georgia Press, 2001

—— "Persian Poetry", *Atlantic Monthly Magazine*, vol. 1, April, 1858, pp. 724–734

—— "The Phoenix", in *Liberty Bell*, Boston, National Anti-Slavery Bazaar, 1851

—— "Preface", in *The Gulistan or Rose Garden*, trans. F. Gladwin. Boston, Ticknor and Fields, 1865

—— "Saadi", *Dial*, October, 1842, pp. 265–269

Esposito, J. *The Islamic Threat: Myth or Reality*, Oxford, Oxford University Press, 1999

Feltes, N. N. *Modes of Production of Victorian Novels*. Chicago, University of Chicago Press, 1986

Fergus, J. "The Professional Woman Writer", in Copeland, E. and McMaster, J. (eds) *The Cambridge Companion to Jane Austen.* Cambridge, Cambridge University Press, 2011

Ferguson, F. *Solitude and the Sublime: The Romantic Aesthetics of Individuation.* Hoboken, Taylor and Francis, 2013

Fichtner, P. S. *Terror and Toleration: The Habsburg Empire Confronts Islam, 1526–1850.* London, Reaktion Books, 2008

Fisher, B. F. "Poe and the Gothic Tradition", in Hayes, K. (ed.) *The Cambridge Companion to Edgar Allan Poe*, New York, Cambridge University Press, 2002

Forster, J. *Walter Savage Landor: A Biography.* London, Chapman and Hall, 1869

Franklin, C. *Byron.* London, Routledge, 2007

—— *Byron's Heroines.* Oxford, Clarendon Press, 1992

Frederick, C. B. *The German Historicist Tradition*, Oxford, Oxford University Press, 2011

Fulford, T. "Coleridge's Sequel to *Thalaba* and Robert Southey's Prequel to *Christabel*", in Vallins, D., Oishi, K. and Perry, S. (eds) *Coleridge, Romanticism and the Orient: Cultural Negotiations.* London, Bloomsbury Publishing, 2013

Fulford, T., D. Lee and P. J. Kitson. *Literature, Science and Exploration in the Romantic Era: Bodies of Knowledge.* Cambridge, Cambridge University Press, 2004

Fusso, S. "The Romantic Tradition", in Jones, M. V. and Miller, R. F. (eds) *The Cambridge Companion to the Classic Russian Novel*, New York, Cambridge University Press, 1998

Galter, H. D. and Haas, S. (eds) *Joseph von Hammer-Purgstall: Grenzgänger zwischen Orient und Okzident.* Graz, Leykam, 2008

Garcia, H. *Islam and the English Enlightenment, 1670–1840.* Baltimore, Johns Hopkins University Press, 2012

Germana, N. A. "Self-Othering in German Orientalism: The Case of Friedrich Schlegel", *Comparativist*, vol. 34, May, 2010, pp. 80–94

Giles, P. *Transatlantic Insurrections: British Culture and the Formation of American Literature, 1730–1860.* Philadelphia, University of Pennsylvania Press, 2001

Gillies, A. *Herder.* Oxford, Basil Blackwell, 1945

Goethe, J. W. *The Autobiography of Johann Wolfgang von Goethe*, trans. J. Oxenford, 2 vols. Chicago, University of Chicago Press, 1974

—— *Early Letters of Goethe: Facsimile Reprint of the Edward Bell Edition of 1884*, ed. C. E. Schweitzer. Drawer, Camden House, 1993

—— *Gedichte, 1756–1799*, ed. E. Karl. Frankfurt am Main, Deutscher Klassiker Verlag, 1987

—— *Leben Des Benvenuto Cellini, Übersetzungen I*, eds H. Birus and H. Dewitz. Frankfurt am Main, Deutscher Klassiker-Verlag, 1998

—— *West-östlicher Divan*. Stuttgard, Cottaischen Buchhandlung, 1819

—— *Goethes Briefe: Bd. 1. Briefe Der Jahre 1764–1786*, eds K. R. Mandelkow and B. Morawe. Hamburg, Wegner, 1962

—— *Selected Poems*, trans. J. Whaley. London, J. M. Dent, 1998

—— *West-eastern Divan: In Twelve Books*, trans. E. Dowden. London, J. M. Dent, 1914

—— *West-East Divan: The Poems, with "Notes and Essays"*, trans. M. Bidney and P. A. Arnim. Albany, State University of New York Press, 2010

Golz, J. *Goethes Morgenlandfahrten: West-östliche Begegnungen*. Frankfurt am Main, Insel, 1999

Gougeon, L. *Virtue's Hero: Emerson, Antislavery, and Reform*. Athens, University of Georgia Press, 1990

Gray, R. D. *Goethe: A Critical Introduction*. London, Cambridge University Press, 1967

Grosskurth, P. *Byron: The Flawed Angel*. Boston, Houghton Mifflin, 1997

Gürpınar, D. *Ottoman/Turkish Visions of the Nation, 1860–1950*. Basingstoke, Palgrave Macmillan, 2013

Guthrie, J. *Schiller the Dramatist: A Study of Gesture in the Plays*. Rochester, Camden House, 2009

Gwilliam, T. "Cosmetic Poetics: Coloring Faces in the Eighteenth Century", in Kelly, V. and Mücke, D. E. (eds) *Body & Text in the Eighteenth Century*. Stanford, Stanford University Press, 1994

Haddad, E. A. *Orientalist Poetics: The Islamic Middle East in Nineteenth-Century English and French Poetry*. Aldershot, Ashgate, 2002

Ḥāfiẓ, *Der Diwan von Mohammed Schemsed-Din Hafis*, trans. J. Hammer-Purgstall, 2 vols. Stuttgart, In der J.G. Cotta'schen Buchhandlung, 1812–1813

Hammer-Purgstall, J. *"Erinnerungen aus meinem Leben" 1774–1852*. Wien, Hölder-Pichler-Tempsky, 1940

—— *Inschriften des Grabmals der Freiinn Hammer-Purgstall zu Weidling am Bach*. Wien, Druck v. Art. Strauß, 1844

—— *Zeitwarte des Gebetes in Sieben Tageszeiten: Ein Gebetbuch Arabisch und Deutsch*. Wien, Strauß & Sommer, 1844

Hayes, K. J. *The Road to Monticello: The Life and Mind of Thomas Jefferson*. Oxford, Oxford University Press, 2008

Herder, J. G. *Briefe: Achter Band, January 1799–November 1803*, eds W. Dobbek and G. Arnold. Weimar, Hermann Böhlaus Nachfolger, 1984

—— *Briefe: Fünfter Band, September 1783–August 1788*, eds W. Dobbek, and G. Arnold. Weimar, Hermann Böhlaus Nachfolger, 1979

—— *Ideen zur Philosophie der Geschichte der Menschheit*, ed. M. Bollacher. Frankfurt am Main, Deutscher Klassiker Verlag, 1989

—— *Outlines of a Philosophy of the History of Man*, trans. T. Churchill, 2 vols. London, Luke Hansard for J. Johnson, 1800

Hilger, S. M. *Women Write Back: Strategies of Response and the Dynamics of European Literary Culture, 1790–1805*. Amsterdam, Rodopi, 2009

Hobhouse J. C. *A Journey through Albania and other Provinces of Turkey in Europe and Asia, to Constantinople, during the years 1809 and 1810*. Philadelphia, M. Carey, 1817

Hodkinson, J. R. *Women and Writing in the Works of Novalis: Transformation beyond Measure?* Rochester, Camden House, 2007

Hollinger, D. A. *After Cloven Tongues of Fire: Protestant Liberalism in Modern American History*. Princeton, Princeton University Press, 2013

Holmes, R. *Shelley: The Pursuit*. New York, E. P. Dutton, 1975

Irving, W. *The Alhambra: A Series of Tales and Sketches of the Moors and Spaniards*, 2 vols. Philadelphia, Carey and Lea, 1832

—— *Lives of Mahomet and his Successors*. Paris, Baudry's European Library, 1850

—— *Mahomet and his Successors*, eds E. N. Feltskog and H. Pochmann. Madison, University of Wisconsin Press, 1970

Javadi, H. *Persian Literary Influence on English Literature: With Special Reference to the Nineteenth Century*. Costa Mesa, Mazda Publishers, 2005

Jones, B. J. *Washington Irving: An American Original*. New York: Arcade Publishing, 2008

Kahf, M. *Western Representations of the Muslim Woman: From Termagant to Odalisque*. Austin, University of Texas Press, 1999

Kalmar, I. D. *Early Orientalism: Imagined Islam and the Notion of Sublime Power*. London, Routledge, 2012

Keane, P. J. *Coleridge's Submerged Politics: The Ancient Mariner and Robinson Crusoe*. Columbia, University of Missouri Press, 1994

Kidwai, A. R. "'Gorgeous Fabric': Authentic Images of India and the Orient in the Works of British Romantic Women Poets", in Davies, M., Chantler, A., Shaw, P. and Newey, V. (eds) *Literature and Authenticity, 1780–1900: Essays in Honour of Vincent Newey*. Farnham, Ashgate, 2011

—— *Orientalism in Lord Byron's 'Turkish Tales': The Giaour (1813), The Bride of Abydos (1813), The Corsair (1814), and The Siege of Corinth (1816)*. Lewiston, Mellen University Press, 1995

—— "The Outline of Coleridge's and Southey's 'Mohammed'", *Notes and Queries*, vol. 238, no. 40, 1993, pp. 38–39

Köpke, W. "Herder's Views on the Germans and their Future Literature", in Adler, H. and Köpke, W. (eds) *A Companion to the Works of Johann Gottfried Herder*. Rochester, Camden House, 2009

Landor, W. S. *The Complete Works of Walter Savage Landor*, eds T. E. Welby and S. Wheeler. New York, Barnes & Noble, 1969

—— *Gebir*. Oxford, Woodstock Books, 1993

—— *Gebir, Count Julian, and other Poems*. London, E. Moxon, 1831

—— *Gebir, and Count Julian*, London, Cassell, 1887

—— *Imaginary Conversations: Dialogues of Sovereigns and Statesmen*. Boston, Roberts Brothers, 1881

—— *The Poetical Works of Walter Savage Landor*, ed. S. Wheeler. Oxford: Clarendon Press, 1937

Leaman, O., ed. *The Qur'an: An Encyclopedia*. London, Routledge, 2007

Lew, J. W. "The Deceptive Other: Mary Shelley's Critique of Orientalism in *Frankenstein*", *Studies in Romanticism*, vol. 30, 1991, pp. 255–283

Lewes, G. H. *The Life of Goethe*. New York, F. Ungar Publishing Co., 1965

Littlejohns, R. "Collaboration as Ideology: The Theory and Practice of 'Sociability' in German Romanticism", in *Collaboration in the Arts from the Middle Ages to the Present*, in Bigliazzi, S., and Wood, S. (eds) Aldershot, Ashgate, 2006

Lovell, E. J. *Captain Medwin, Friend of Byron and Shelley*. Austin, University of Texas Press, 1962

Ludwig, V. O. "Das Hammer-Purgstall-Grabmal auf dem Weidlinger Friedhof", in Artmann, F. (ed.) *Hammer-Purgstall in Klosterneuburg-Weidling*. Klosterneuburg, Stadtgemeinde Klosterneuburg, 1959

Luedtke, L. S. *Nathaniel Hawthorne and the Romance of the Orient*. Bloomington, Indiana University Press, 1989

Madden, L., ed. *Robert Southey: The Critical Heritage*. London, Routledge and K. Paul, 1972

Mahoney, D. F. *The Critical Fortunes of a Romantic Novel: Novalis's Heinrich Von Ofterdingen*. Columbia, Camden House, 1994

Marchand, S. L. *German Orientalism in the Age of Empire: Religion, Race, and Scholarship*. Washington, German Historical Institute, 2009

Marr, T. *The Cultural Roots of American Islamicism*. Cambridge, Cambridge University Press, 2006

McFarland, T. "Involute and Symbol in the Romantic Imagination", in Bate, W. J., Barth, J. R., and Mahoney, J. L. (eds) *Coleridge, Keats, and the Imagination: Romanticism and Adam's Dream: Essays in Honor of Walter Jackson Bate*. Columbia, University of Missouri Press, 1990

McGann, J. "'My Brain Is Feminine': Byron and the Poetry of Deception", in Rutherford, A. (ed.) *Byron: Augustan and Romantic*. New York, St. Martin's Press, 1990

McLane, M. N. *Romanticism and the Human Sciences: Poetry, Population, and the Discourse of the Species*. Cambridge, Cambridge University Press, 2000

Meagher, S. "Thomas Moore, Ireland, and Islam", in Class, M. and Robinson, T. F. (eds) *Transnational England: Home and Abroad, 1780–1860*. Newcastle, Cambridge Scholars, 2009

Medwin, T. *Conversations of Lord Byron*, ed. E. J. Lovell, Jr. Princeton, Princeton University Press, 1966

—— *The Life of Percy Bysshe Shelley*, 2 vols. London, T.C. Newby, 1847

Menze, E. A. "Herder's Reception and Influence in the U.S.A.: Exploring Transcendentalism", in Gross, S. (ed.) *Herausforderung Herder / Herder as Challenge*. Heidelberg, Synchron, 2010

Mole, T. "*The Bride of Abydos*: The Regime of Visibility and the Possibility of Resistance", in Beatty, B. G., Howe, T., and

Robinson, C. E. (eds) *Liberty and Poetic Licence: New Essays on Byron*. Liverpool, Liverpool University Press, 2008

Mommsen, K. "*Die Bedeutung des Korans für Goethe*", in Reiss, H. S. (ed.) *Goethe und die Tradition*. Frankfurt am Main, Athenäum Verlag, 1972

—— "Goethe and the Arab World", *Bulletin of the Faculty of Arts*, vol. 19, 1965, pp. 77–92

—— *Goethe und der Islam*. Frankfurt am Main, Insel, 2001

—— *Goethe und die Arabische Welt*. Frankfurt am Main, Insel, 1988

—— "*Orient und Okzident sind nicht mehr zu trennen*": *Goethe und die Weltkulturen*. Göttingen, Wallstein, 2012

Monteiro, G. *The Presence of Camões: Influences on the Literature of England, America, and Southern Africa*. Lexington, University Press of Kentucky, 1996

Mostyn, T. *Egypt's Belle Epoque: Cairo and the Age of the Hedonists*. New York, Tauris Parke Paperbacks, 2006

Mulhallen, J. *The Theatre of Shelley*. Cambridge, Open Book Publishers, 2010

Murphy, O. *Jane Austen the Reader: The Artist as Critic*. Basingstoke, Palgrave Macmillan, 2013

Nebes, N. "Orientalistik im Aufbruch. Die Wissenschaft vom Vorderen Orient in Jena zur Goethezeit", in J. Golz (ed.) *Goethes Morgenlandfahrten. West-östliche Begegnungen*. Frankfurt am Main, Insel Verlag, 1999

Nicholls, A. *Goethe's Concept of the Daemonic: After the Ancients*. Rochester, Camden House, 2006

Nitchie, E. *Vergil and the English Poets*. New York, Columbia University Press, 1919

Novalis. *Heinrich von Ofterdingen, Schriften*, ed. P. Kluckhohn, R. Samuel, G. Schulz, and H. Ritter. Stuttgart, W. Kohlhammer Verlag, 1960

—— *Henry of Ofterdingen: A Novel*, trans. Palmer Hilty. Prospect Heights, Waveland Press, 1992

—— *Henry of Ofterdingen: A Romance*. Cambridge, J. Owen, 1842

Ober, W. U. "'Mohammed': The Outline of a Proposed Poem by Coleridge and Southey", *Notes and Queries*, vol. 5, 1958, p. 448

O'Brien, W. A. *Novalis, Signs of Revolution*. Durham, Duke University Press, 1995

Perry, S. "Romanticism: The Brief History of a Concept", in Wu, D. (ed.) *A Companion to Romanticism*. Oxford, Blackwell Publishers, 1998

Poe, E. A. *Collected Works of Edgar Allan Poe*, ed. T. O. Mabbott, 3 vols. Cambridge, Belknap Press of Harvard University Press, 1969–1978

—— *The Complete Works of Edgar Allan Poe*, ed. J. A. Harrison, 17 vols. New York, AMS Press, 1965

—— "Marginalia", *United States Magazine and Democratic Review*, vol. 15, 1844, pp. 580–594

Quinn, A. H. *Edgar Allan Poe: A Critical Biography*. Baltimore, Johns Hopkins University Press, 1998

Quinn, F. *The Sum of All Heresies: The Image of Islam in Western Thought*. Oxford, Oxford University Press, 2008

Rawes, A. "Byron's Confessional Pilgrimage", in Hopps, G. and Stabler, J. (eds) *Romanticism and Religion from William Cowper to Wallace Stevens*. Aldershot, Ashgate, 2006

Riasanovsky, N. V. *The Emergence of Romanticism*. New York, Oxford University Press, 1992

Richards, D. B. *Goethe's Search for the Muse: Translation and Creativity*. Amsterdam, John Benjamins Publishing Company, 1979

Richards, R. J. *The Tragic Sense of Life: Ernst Haeckel and the Struggle over Evolutionary Thought*. Chicago, University of Chicago Press, 2008

Ridgeon, L. *Sufi Castigator: Ahmad Kasravi and the Iranian Mystical Tradition*. London, Routledge, 2006

Robinson, B. S. *Islam and Early Modern English Literature: The Politics of Romance from Spenser to Milton*. New York, Palgrave Macmillan, 2007

Schiller, C. *Briefe von Schillers Gattin an einem Vertrauten Freund*. Leipzig, F.A. Brockhaus, 1856

Schiller, F. *The Poems of Schiller*, trans. E. P. Arnold-Forster. New York, H. Holt, 1902

Schiller, F. and Goethe, J. W. *Correspondence between Schiller and Goethe from 1794 to 1805*, trans. L. D. Schmitz. London, Bell, 1890

Schimmel, A. *A Two-Colored Brocade: The Imagery of Persian Poetry*. UNC Press Books, 1992

Schlegel, F. *Friedrich Schlegel's Lucinde and the Fragments*, trans. P. Firchow. Minneapolis, University of Minnesota Press, 1971

Schueller, M. J. *U.S. Orientalisms: Race, Nation, and Gender in Literature, 1790–1890*. Ann Arbor, University of Michigan Press, 1998

Seibt, G. *Goethe und Napoleon: Eine Historische Begegnung*. München, C. H. Beck, 2008

Seymour, M. *Mary Shelley*. New York, Grove Press, 2000

Sharafuddin, M. *Islam and Romantic Orientalism: Literary Encounters with the Orient*. London, Tauris, 1994

Shelley, M. *Frankenstein; or the Modern Prometheus*, ed. M. K. Joseph. London, Oxford University Press, 1969

—— *Frankenstein, or the Modern Prometheus: The 1818 Text*, ed. J. Rieger. Chicago, University of Chicago Press, 1982

—— *The Journals of Mary Shelley, 1814–1844*, ed. P. R. Feldman and D. Scott-Kilvert. Oxford, University Press, 1987

—— *The Letters of Mary Wollstonecraft Shelley*, ed. B. T. Bennett, 3 vols. Baltimore, Johns Hopkins University Press, 1980–1988

Shelley, P. B. *The Complete Poetry of Percy Bysshe Shelley*, ed. D. H. Reiman, N. Fraistat and N. Crook, 3 vols. Baltimore, Johns Hopkins University Press, 2000–2012

—— *The Complete Works of Percy Bysshe Shelley*, ed. R. Ingpen and W. E. Peck, 10 vols. New York, Gordian Press, 1965

—— *The Faust Draft Notebook: A Facsimile of Bodleian Ms. Shelley Adds. E. 18*, ed. N. Crook and T. Webb. New York, Garland Pub, 1997

—— *The Letters of Percy Bysshe Shelley*, ed. F. L. Jones, 2 vols. Oxford, Clarendon Press, 1964

Silverman, K. *Edgar A. Poe: Mournful and Never-Ending Remembrance*. New York, HarperCollins Publishers, 1991

Singley, C. J., ed. *A Historical Guide to Edith Wharton*. Oxford, Oxford University Press, 2003

Small, C. *Mary Shelley's Frankenstein: Tracing the Myth*. Pittsburgh, University of Pittsburgh Press, 1973

Smith, J. I. and Haddad, Y. Y. *The Islamic Understanding of Death and Resurrection*. Albany, State University of New York Press, 1981

Solbrig, I. H. *Hammer-Purgstall und Goethe: "Dem Zaubermeister Das Werkzeug"*. Bern, Herbert Lang, 1973

—— "The Theater, Theory and Politics, Voltaire's *Le Fanatisme ou Mahomet le Prophete* and Goethe's *Mahomet* Adaptation", *Michigan Germanic Studies*, vol. 16, 1990, pp. 21–43

Southey, R. *The Collected Letters of Robert Southey*, eds. L. Pratt, T. Fulford, and I. Packer, 8 vols. Romantic Circles Online Edition. www.rc.umd.edu/editions/southey_letters

—— *The Destroyer; or, the Sorcerers of the Domdaniel*. H. Hetherington, London, 1842

—— *The Life and Correspondence of Robert Southey*, 6 vols. London, Longman, Brown, Green & Longmans, 1850

—— *Poetical Works, 1793–1810*, eds. L. Pratt and T. Fulton, 5 vols. London, Pickering & Chatto, 2004

—— *The Poetical Works of Robert Southey*. New York, D. Appleton, 1839

—— "Review of *Gebir*", *Critical Review*, vol. 27, 1799, pp. 29–39

—— *Selections from the Letters of Robert Southey*, ed. J. W. Warter, 4 vols. London, Longman, Brown, Green, and Longmans, 1856

Speck, W. A. *Robert Southey: Entire Man of Letters*. New Haven, Yale University Press, 2006

Spencer, V. *Herder's Political Thought: A Study of Language, Culture, and Community*. Toronto, Toronto University Press, 2012

Stahuljak, Z. *Pornographic Archaeology: Medicine, Medievalism, and the Invention of the French Nation*. Philadelphia, University of Pennsylvania Press, 2013

Straight, J. "Women, Religion, and Insanity in Mary Lamb's 'Margaret Green: or, The Young Mahometan'", *European Romantic Review*, vol. 16, no. 4, 2005, pp. 417–438

Strathman, C. A. *Romantic Poetry and the Fragmentary Imperative: Schlegel, Byron, Joyce, Blanchot*. Albany, State University of New York Press, 2006

Super, R. H. *Walter Savage Landor, a Biography*. New York, New York University Press, 1954

Swanwick, A. and Frothingham, E. (eds) *Johann Wolfgang Von Goethe: Faust, Part I, Egmont, Hermann and Dorothea; Christopher Marlowe: Doctor Faustus*. New York, P. F. Collier & Son, 1909

Teo, H. *Desert Passions: Orientalism and Romance Novels*. Austin, University of Texas Press, 2012

Unseld, S. *Goethe and His Publishers*. Chicago, University of Chicago Press, 1996

Varisco, D. M. *Reading Orientalism: Said and the Unsaid*. Seattle, University of Washington Press, 2007

Wendling, R. C. *Coleridge's Progress to Christianity: Experience and*

Authority in Religious Faith. Lewisburg, Bucknell University Press, 1995

White, N. I. *Shelley*, 2 vols. New York, Octagon Books, 1972

Whitehead, A. "'A wise tale of the Mahometans': Blake and Islam, 1819–26", in Mee, J. and Haggarty, S. (eds) *Blake and Conflict*. Basingstoke, Palgrave Macmillan, 2008

Williams, S. T. "The Sources of Landor's *Gebir*", *Modern Language Notes*, vol. 36, no. 5, 1921, p. 315

Yohannan, J. D. "Emerson's Translations of Persian Poetry from German Sources", *American Literature*, vol. 14, no. 4, 1943, pp. 407–420

—— "The Influence of Persian Poetry upon Emerson's Work", *American Literature*, vol. 15, no. 1, 1943, pp. 25–41

Zapf, H. *Alphabet Stories: A Chronicle of Technical Developments*. Rochester, RIT Cary Graphic Arts Press, 2007

Zonana, J. "'They Will Prove the Truth of My Tale': Safie's Letters as the Feminist Core of Mary Shelley's *Frankenstein*", *Journal of Narrative Technique*, vol. 21, no. 2, 1991, pp. 170–184

Zwarg, C. *Feminist Conversations: Fuller, Emerson, and the Play of Reading*. Ithaca, Cornell University Press, 1995

Index